ASSOCIATE REFORMED PRESBYTERIAN

DEATH AND MARRIAGE NOTICES

VOLUME II
1866–1888

COMPILED
BY

Lowry Ware

HERITAGE BOOKS
2022

HERITAGE BOOKS
AN IMPRINT OF HERITAGE BOOKS, INC.

Books, CDs, and more—Worldwide

For our listing of thousands of titles see our website
at
www.HeritageBooks.com

Published 2022 by
HERITAGE BOOKS, INC.
Publishing Division
5810 Ruatan Street
Berwyn Heights, Md. 20740

Library of Congress Catalog Card Number: 93-83567

Heritage Books by Lowry Ware:

Associate Reformed Presbyterian Death and Marriage Notices from The Christian Magazine
of the South, The Erskine Miscellany, *and* The Due West Telescope, *1843–1863*

Associate Reformed Presbyterian Death and Marriage Notices, Volume II: 1866–1888

Associate Reformed Presbyterian Death and Marriage Notices, Volume IV, 1897–1902

Chapters in the History of Abbeville County: The "Banner County" of South Carolina

Old Abbeville: Scenes of the Past of a Town Where Old Time Things Are Not Forgotten

International Standard Book Number
Paperbound: 978-0-7884-1947-8

INTRODUCTION

This second volume of notices compiled by Lowry Ware, Ph.D., is a most welcome addition to the growing bibliography of such newspaper notices. On page 1 area two lists of members of Cedar Spring and Long Canes Associate Reformed Presbyterian churches (Abbeville County, South Carolina) who died during the difficult War period. During this period the publication of the newspaper was suspended, and the church records have not survived, either. Similar lists from other areas are included as they occurred in the newspaper. Therefore, there are notices from an earlier period than the title would indicate. The first four pages are from undated clippings in the scrapbook of Rev. S. A. Agnew, housed in the McCain Library, Erskine College, Due West, South Carolina.

The remainder of this volume is compiled from notices which appeared in the *Associate Reformed Presbyterian*, from the beginning of its publication in 1867 through the end of 1888. Only a few issues have survived for the period between 1878 and 1884. These newspapers are available on microfilm at the McCain Library, Erskine College. There are notices are for people who lived in Virginia, North Carolina, South Carolina, Georgia, Tennessee, Arkansas, Alabama, Mississippi, Illinois, Missouri, and Texas. The death notices are quite important for this period, not only because of the details of the lives of the individuals including the places of birth and former residences, but because during the difficult years of reconstruction, many persons could not afford tombstones or erected only wooden markers which have not survived. Marriage notices are especially important for South Carolina, where marriage licenses were not required until 1911.

Brent H. Holcomb
January 14, 1998

H. T. Sloan, "The Roll of Honor and the Ravages of Death in Cedar Spring and Long Cane Church, A. R. Presbyterian, from the Commencement of the late War . . . .," *Abbeville Press*, July 6, 1866. Reprinted in the *Associate Reformed Presbyterian*, January 7, 1867.

On the roll of our church book we find the names of twenty-two members who were either slain in battle or died of disease in the service of their country, and nineteen others who belonged to the families of church members -- all of whom were in the pride and glory of manhood, and were looked to as the future hope of the church.

Church Members who were either killed or died in war

Hamilton Young, Jas. C. M'Bryde, Robert S. M'Clinton, Abner Young, John Bradley, Jr., John McQuerns, Jas. M. Purdy, Robert Lewis Drennan, Wm. Gibson (Elder)**, Jas. A. Wilson, George Davis, Jas. D. Malone, John A. Weed, Lt. J. T. Jordan, John C. Martin, Jas. H. Harris, John Bicket, Robert D. Drennan, Archibald Boyd** (Deacon)**, Thomas Creswell, Wm. T. Bearden, Nathaniel Napper.**

Deaths in Families of the Church

Thos. Jordan, Jas. Kennedy, Samuel P. M'Gaw, Thos. C. Chiles, Elias Gibson, J. F. Martin, Wm. Bradley, Jr., Henry Gray, Thos. C. Bradley, Thos. Robinson, Thos. Fell, Robert M'Clain, John Adamson, John Goodwin, John Neal, Wm. Kennedy, John B. Laird, Mr. Walker, Wm. Crawford. Three Ruling Elders, *viz.*, **John Bradley, Sr.**, Dr. **Rob't. Devlin** and **Wm. Gibson,** also died during the same period, the last named immediately after entering the service of his county. Two Deacons, *viz.*, **Wm. Butler** and **Archibald Boyd** ... [latter] died in the service of his country, although permitted to reach home, and was followed by the partner of his bosom in two brief weeks to the tomb, leaving their orphan offspring. . . . .

During the same period, we lost. . . . . **Mrs. Lindsay,** aged 65; **Mrs. Kennedy,** aged 52; **Mrs. Martin** in her 79th year; **Mrs. Jordan** in her 55th year; **Mrs. M'Cartney,** aged 63; **Mrs. Wadkins,** aged 64; and **Mrs. Jordan,** aged 77, together with a blooming damsel, Miss **Jenny Lites** on her graduation day and **Mrs. Creswell** in middle life.

Nor are the ravages of death yet complete. The roll of honored names is still unfolding -- the subsequent fruits, perhaps of cruel war. In October last, **Thomas Chiles,** a worthy, upright citizen of 73 years . . . . On the 12th of February last, **Archibald Bradley** departed this life, aged 74 years . . . . On the 7th of May last, **Isaac Kennedy,** Esq. . . . 60 years.

Rev. S. A. Agnew's Scrapbook, McCain Library, Erskine College which contains undated clippings, the first two death notices were likely from *The Due West Telescope,* the rest were from the *Associate Reformed Presbyterian.*

Departed this life, December 24th, 1855, in the sixty first year of her age, Mrs. **Mary Hunter,** wife of Matthew Hunter and daughter of the late Chartiers Nichols of Laurens District, S. C. . . . [member of] A. R. church at Head Spring, Laurens District . . . . About three years ago, she with her husband and family removed to Tippah County, Miss. . . . [and joined] the church at Bethany.

Died on Monday, February 25th, [1856] at the residence of John T. Pressly, Alleghany, Pa., **Jane Patterson Pressly**, in the 87th year of her age. . . . native of County Down, Ireland, and emigrated to this country when two years old with her father Samuel Patterson who settled in Abbeville, S. C. Her father was a ruling elder. . . . [died] leaving behind him four sons and four daughters. . . . The deceased was the last survivor of her father's family. She was the mother of nine children; two of whom died in their youth. Her oldest son, Dr. Samuel Pressly, died some fifteen years hence. . . Of her sons, two are physicians and ruling elders, two are ministers, and one is a merchant and a ruling elder. Her oldest daughter is the widow of Dr. George R. Brown, and the youngest daughter is the widow of Rev. Joseph Lowry.

Died on Wednesday, April 15th, 1868, at the residence of James Bryson in Lee County, Miss., Mrs. **Catherine Bryson**, a member of the Associate Reformed church at Bethany. Mrs. Bryson was a native of Laurens District, S. C., and a daughter of Mr. Chartiers Nichols and was born in 1791. In early life she identified herself with the church at Head Spring, Laurens District, S. C. In 1831, she was married to William Bryson, in 1855 she removed to Mississippi and connected herself with the church at Bethany. . . . seventy seven years old.

Died in Pontotoc Co., Miss., July 14, 1869, **John Andrew Carlile**, son of James F. and Martha J. Carlile, aged two years and nine months.

Died in Lee County, Miss., August 24th, 1869, **John Cooper Morrow** in the 61st year of his age. . . . was born in Abbeville District, S. C., November 1, 1808 and was reared in the bounds of the Cedar Springs and Long Cane congregation. He emigrated to Lowndes County, Miss. about 1834. Here he lived, excepting two years spent in Holmes County, till 1850, when he removed to Pontotoc County (now Lee). . . [more than a year ago joined] Bethany church. . . . leaves a wife and six children, five of them daughters.

Died in Lee County, Miss., September 23d, 1869, **Argle Rhett Bryson**, youngest child of Samuel and Martha Bryson, aged three years, three months and twenty days.

Died at the residence of his grandfather, Dr. E. Agnew, in Tippah County, Miss., on Friday, November 5th, 1869, **Enoch David Agnew**, eldest son of Rev. S. A. Agnew, aged 4 years, 8 months and 27 days.

Died June 15th, 1870, in Pontotoc County, Miss. at the residence of John R. Hill, Miss **Sarah S. Buchanan** in the 52nd year of her age. . . . native of Bedford County, Tenn. Having resided in Tuscaloosa, Ala. several years, she came to Pontotoc County several years ago. . . member of church at Hopewell.

Died in Pontotoc County, Miss., Friday, June 17th, 1870, **Marietta**

2

Haynie, daughter of James R. and Rebecca F. Haynie, aged 3 years, 6 months and 21 days.

Died near Poplar Springs, Pontotoc County, Miss. on Friday, August 12th, 1870, Mrs. **Nancy Chapman**, wife of Samuel Chapman, in the 64th year of her age. . . . daughter of James McNeil and native of Newberry District, S. C. where she was born March 13, 1807. Early in life she joined the Associate Reformed church at Cannon's Creek. In 1853, she with her husband, emigrated to Mississippi and settled in Pontotoc County. Here she united with Hopewell church . . . left husband and five children.

Died at his residence in Union County, Miss. at 15 minutes after 2 o'clock on the morning of Thursday, March 2d, 1871, Dr. **Enoch Agnew**, in the 63d year of his age. . . . eldest son of Samuel and Melinda (Dodson) Agnew, and was born in Abbeville District, S. C., October 30th, 1808. . . . graduated from the Medical College of South Carolina in the spring of 1830. . . [practiced in his native community]. About 1831, he united with the church at Due West, then under the pastoral care of his brother-in-law, Rev. E. E. Pressly. On the 22d of November, 1832, he was united in marriage with Miss Letitia S. Todd, daughter of Andrew Todd of Laurens. In the fall of 1839, he removed to Due West Corner . . . and in conjunction with the practice of his profession, kept the boarding house which had been erected to accomodate the pupils of Clark and Erskine Seminary. After two years, he removed to a residence he had erected in Due West. He gave up the practice of medicine about 1845 . . .[and] engaged in mercantile business. . . . In 1852, he removed from Due West to Tippah [now Union] County, Miss. Here he settled in the bounds of Bethany church [and the following year was chosen a ruling elder].

Died in Union County, Miss. on Monday, May 15th, 1871, Mrs. **Lany Ann Holland**, wife of H. L. Holland, Esq. in the 44th year of her age. . . . daughter of Mr. A. C. Hawthorn of Due West, S. C. and born in Abbeville District, S. C., January 4th, 1828. In early life she became a member of the church at Due West. On the 8th of October, 1850, she was united in marriage with H. L. Holland and resided in Due West until December, 1856, when he removed to Mississippi. . . .[member of Bethany church] leaves a husband and six children.

Died in Union County, Miss., May 19th, 1871, Mrs. **Elizabeth Caldwell**, in the 80th year of her age. . . . native of Newberry District, S. C., and was a daughter of John and Nancy Caldwell. She was born August 21st, 1791 - - was married to Dickson Caldwell, October 17th, 1845. In 1849, she lost her husband by death. In December, 1852, she removed to Pontotoc (now Union) County, Miss. and united with Hopewell church by a certificate from Head Springs, Newberry, S. C.

Died in Union County, Miss., July 25th, 1871, **Samuel Josephus Fife**, aged 37 years, 7 months and 29 days. . . . son of Dr. James Fife and was born in Wilcox Co., Ala., November 26, 1833. He grew up in Wilcox

3

and emigrated to Tippah County, Miss. in 1852. . . . [member of Ebenezer church] in 1865 he was married to Miss Sarah A. Randolph. In 1869, he removed to the bounds of Hopewell church.

Died in Union County, Miss. on Tuesday morning, August 29, 1871, **John Lindsay Martin**, youngest son of John and Sarah E. Martin, in the 15th year of his age.

Died in Union County, Miss., October 20th, 1871, **Harvey Martin Haddon**, in the 19th year of his age. . . . son of the late John Haddon, born in Abbeville County, S. C., October 27th, 1852. His father moved to Mississippi in 1857.

Died in Union County, Miss. on Friday, March 1st, 1872, **Samuel Cornelius Galloway** in the 25th year of his age. . . . son of A. M. Galloway, was born in Lincoln Co., Tennessee, September 17th, 1847. His father moved to Miss. when Cornelius was about eight.

Married at the residence of the bride's mother on Wednesday, July 26th, 1869 by Rev. S. A. Agnew, assisted by Rev. D. A. Todd, **James L. Young**, Esq. and Miss **Jennie F. Thompson,** all of Lee County, Miss.

- - - December 8th, 1870 by Rev. S. A. Agnew, Mr. **Samuel W. Hawkins** of Baldwin and Miss **Willie E. Beal** of Guntown, Miss.

- - - December 15th, 1870 by Rev. S. A. Agnew, Mr. **Asbury Billingsley** and Miss **M. P. Gordon**. All of Union County, Miss.

- - - December 22d, 1870 by Rev. S. A. Agnew, Mr. **John W. Williams** of Lee County and **Miss N. P. Morrow** of Union County, Miss.

- - - January 10th, 1871 by Rev. S. A. Agnew, Capt. **Rufus Y. King** of Lexington, Texas and **Miss M. Clifford Whitten**, daughter of C. T. Whitten, Esq. of Guntown, Miss.

- - - January 19th, 1871 by the same, **T. Jefferson Davis** and Miss **Edney D. Martin**. All of Union County, Miss.

- - - August 24th, 1871 by Rev. S. A. Agnew, Mr. **E. W. Downs** and Miss **Angerona Haskins**, all of Union County, Miss.

- - - September 7th, 1871 at the residence of the bride's mother by Rev. S. A. Agnew, Mr. **R. A. Simpson** of Pendleton, S. C. and Miss **Maggie J. Agnew**, daughter of the late Dr. E. Agnew of Union County, Miss.

- - - March 6th, 1872 by Rev. S. A. Agnew, Mr. **W. Jasper Shirley** and Miss **J. A. A. Gambrell**. All of Union County, Miss.

January 14, 1867

Married on Tuesday evening, the 8th Jan. inst., at the residence of Prof. Young in Due West by Rev. R. C. Grier, D. D., Rev. **James L. Young** of Mississippi and Mrs. **Jane Pressly**.

- - - by Rev. J. I. Bonner on Thursday evening, the 20th December, ult., **Dr. _____ Anglin** of Banks Co., Ga. and Miss **Sallie Roberts**, daughter of Col. T. J. Roberts of Anderson District, S. C.

January 28, 1867

Died at his residence in Drew County, Arkansas, of pneumonia, on the 1st of December, 1866, Mr. **John W. McKinstry** in the 55th year of his age. . . . [he] was born in Chester District, S. C., where at an early age he connected himself with the Associate Reformed Presbyterian church . . . . In the year 1850 he removed with his family to West Tennessee, where in 1858 he was called upon to mourn the loss of his companion. He then removed to Arkansas and returning to South Carolina on a visit in 1859 married Miss Sarah Strong who now, with the children of the first marriage, mourns his loss. He was elected to the office of ruling elder.

Died at Due West, January 26th, 1867, **Mattie Elizabeth**, daughter of E. S. and E. P. **Kennedy**, aged 6 years and 7 months.

Married by Rev. J. I. Bonner on Thursday, the 17th January, Mr. **William McAdams** and Miss **Elmina Tribble**, all of Abbeville, S. C.

- - - on Thursday the 24th January by Rev. J. I. Bonner, Mr. **John T. Townes** and Miss **Julia L.**, daughter of Col. T. J. **Roberts**, both of Anderson District, S. C.

- - - on Wednesday, 30th January by Rev. W. E. Walters, Capt. **James Pratt** of Abbeville District and Miss **Susie Sharpton** of Edgefield District.

- - - by Rev. Thos. G. Herbert on the evening of the 24th January, 1867, Mr. **C. G. Waller** to Miss **Emma C. Coleman**, daughter of Mr. Thomas L. Coleman, all of Greenwood, S. C.

February 23, 1867

Letter from North Carolina.

Pisgah, Gaston Co., N. C.

Mr. Editor:

The wheels of time roll smoothly on, but they leave much which the present generation will not soon forget. Our hearts sicken when we look back over the last six years, and recount the number of fathers and mothers and brothers and sisters of Pisgah (a branch of the Rev. E. E. Boyce's charge) who have gone to the house prepared for all the living. Forty members, and baptized members have died and been slain since 1861. These are their names: *viz.*, **Joseph Blackwood, Joseph W. Servis, Thosas O. Servis, A. Robinson MAy, John G. Thomas, Sidney White, Larkin White, Thos. A. Wilson, John Wilson, Alexander Weer, James Carson, John G. Whitesides, Samuel Whitesides, Robert Whitesides, Wm. Whitesides, Caleb Whitesides, Robert Grier Whitesides, Major Whitesides, Thomas O. Crawford, William Falls, Franklin Quinn, William Crawford, Thomas Ferguson, Sen., Thomas Ferguson, jr., Thomas W. Ferguson, J. Harvey Hannah, William M. Ferguson, S. William Love, John A. Love, C. Anderson Love, Joseph W. Blackwood, E. W. Adams, William Adams, Samuel F. Pearson, James J. Pearson, F. Marion Beattie, Arthur P. Neelle, Joseph Morrow, William Gamble, Franklin Gamble, Nancy Oates, Mary P. Ferguson, Rebecca Falls, Martha Service, Jane Service, Martha Antony, Margaret Carson.**

Some of these held places of honor and trust, but I forbear annexing any wordy marks to their names. Two of this number were Ruling Elders, Alexander Weer and William Crawford, and S. William Love was an Elder elect, but never got home to be ordained. . . . Thomas Ferguson was about seventy three years of age, William Whitesides about seventy, and several about, or over fifty. Margaret Carson was seventy six, Martha Service and Rebecca Falls about sixty or seventy.

J. B. C. [John B. Carson]

Married, by Rev. R. W. Brice on the 8th November last, **Charles S. Brice**, Esq. and Miss **Kate**, daughter of the late Dr. John B. **Gaston**, all of Chester, S. C.

March 2, 1867

Married by Rev. R. W. Brice on the 22d November last, Mr. **Thomas Torbit** and Mrs. **Jane H. Flenniken**, all of Chrster District, S. C.

- - - by Rev. R. W. Brice on the 9th of October last, Rev. **John Hunter** of Mecklenburg, N. C. and Miss **Mary Ann**, daughter of Mr. Thomas **McDill** of Chester District, S. C.

- - - by the same, on the 18th December last, Mr. **R. R. Peoples** of Mecklenburg, N. C. and Miss **Agnes A.**, daughter of Col. James **McDill** of Chester, S. C.

March 9, 1867

Married February 19th by Rev. H. T. Sloan, Mr. **James L. Morrow** and Miss **Cornelia Wilson**, daughter of Mr. John and Mary Wilson, all of Abbeville, S. C.

March 16, 1867

Died, September 11th, 1866, in Monmouth, Ill., Mr. **Reuben C. Weede**, in the 80th year of his age.

- - - February 3d, 1867, near Elvaston, Hancock Co., Ill., Mrs. **Mary Ann Mayne**, about 53 years of age.

Mr. Weede was born in Abbeville Dist., S. C., November, 1786; was married about the age of twenty five; moved to Preble Co., Ohio where he was a ,member of Hopewell about twenty years; was a resident of the State of Indiana and member of the A. R. Church of Shiloh ten or twelve years; and at the time of his death was a member of the U. P. Church of Harmony, Smithville, Peoria Co., Ill. with which he had been connected most of the time of his residence in Illinois. . . . Having, after a long visit to his friends in the neighborhood of Monmouth, left the house of his son-in-law, Mr. John Wylie, with a view of returning to Smithville, he was suddenly prostrated in the house of his relative, Mr. John D. Smith of Monmouth.

At the time of his death, one son, Rev . N. C. Weede, and five daughters survived. But since that time, his daughter, Mary Ann, widow of the late Rev. Hugh Mayne, was called to follow him. [She leaves two sons, James and Reuben.]

March 23, 1867

Samuel Blain Marion, the fourth son of John A. and Margaret J. Marion, was born February 12th, 1851, and died April 30th, 1866, aged fifteen years, two months and eighteen days. His disease was measles complicated with pneumonia.

Died near Relfs Bluff, Arkansas, January __, 1867, **E. G. Cameron**, a professed christian, an humble disciple, a loving husband and dutiful son.

Married on the 19th February by Rev. R. W. Brice at the residence of Mr. John F. B. Bigham in Chester District, S. C., Mr. **W. W. Beattie** of Gaston Co., N. C. and Miss **Elizabeth Bell**.

- - - by the Rev. R. W. Brice on the 7th of March, Me. **John D. Boyd** and Miss **Mary McKeown**, all of Chester, S. C.

April 13, 1867

Departed this life in Fulton Co., Arkansus on the 21st day of February, 1867, **Frances C. Nisbett**, daughter of James H. and Elizabeth Cooper and wife of Joseph C. Nisbett, aged 22 years, 11 months and 3 days. Member of A. R. Church at Starkville, Miss. . . . leaves husband and two small children.

<u>May 4, 1867</u>

Married by Rev. J. I. Bonner on Thursday evening, 25th April, Mr. **James Botts** and Miss **Margaret Bell**, daughter of Mr. Frederick Bell, all of Abbeville District, S. C.

<u>May 11, 1867</u>

Married at the residence of the bride's father on Tuesday evening, April 22d, 1867 by Rev. A. Rice, Rev. **William E. Walters**, Editor of the *South Carolina Baptist* and Miss **Anna M. Milford**, eldest daughter of Dr. W. J. Milford--all of Anderson District.

<u>May 18, 1867</u>

Died March 27th, 1867, after a long and painful illness, Mr. **John Isaac Crawford**, son of Mr. Robert Crawford, in the 26th year of his age. His disease was a pulmonary affection, occasioned, perhaps by a wound and exposure in the late war; for he was a soldier during the entire four years of that dreadful conflict [H. T. Sloan].

Died at his residence in Newberry District on Sabbath, the 12th inst., Mr. **Micajah Harris** in the 70th year of his age. . . . consistent member of the Associate Reformed church at Cannon's Creek, where for twenty years, during middle life, he served the congregation as Precentor. He lived 70 years on the same farm, and was known and respected in the community.

Departed this life near Due West, April 29th, Mrs. **Mary Austin** after only a few hours of illness. She was for many years a member of the A. R. church at Due West. . . . The deceased had almost reached her four score years. . . . She leaves an only son and daughter.

Married on Wednesday evening, 27th February by Rev. S. A. Agnew, Capt. **John G. Mahon** and Miss **Laura L.** at the residence of the bride's father, Rev. J. L. **Young**, all of Lee County, Miss.

- - - by Rev. H. T. Sloan, Mr. **Robert Ferrin** and Miss **Jane Malone**, March 19th, 1867.

<u>July 5, 1867</u>

Died in York District, S. C., on the 8th of May --Mrs. **Elizabeth McElwee**, wife of J. N. McElwee. The deceased was somewhat up in years, but in the midst of her activity and usefulness, having raised seven children, all of whom she lived to see fully grown, all of whom precededher to the grave, except one son. . . . was a daughter of Esquire Wm. McGill, at King's Creek.

Died on the 26th of April, 1867, Mrs. **Nancy Wilson**, consort of David Wilson, deceased. . . was a native of Ireland, County Antrim whence in 1803, or about that time, she, with her husband and three children, emigrated to South Carolina and settled in Fairfield District. In 1819, they removed to Missouri. There, after two years, her husband died, leaving a widow and ten children. . . . Three daughters preceded her to the grave. Two daughters and five sons survive. She attained the great age of fourscore and fourteen years. In Ireland, she became a member of the Presbyterian church under the care of Rev. Matthew Elder. In South Carolina, she became a parishioner of Rev. James Rogers. At the organization of the A. R. congregation in Lincoln Co., Missouri, she identified herslef with it.

Died, April 11th, 1867 in York District, S. C., of consumption, Mrs. **A. Louisa Harris**, wife of James Harris, in the 35th year of her age. . . . for fifteen years member of A. R. Church of Lower Steel Creek, York Dist.

Also, on the 11th of April after a short illness little **James H. Harris**, aged one year and four months.

Married, June 5th in Mecklenburg Co., N. C. by Rev. J. C. Chalmers, Capt. **John R. Erwin** to Miss **Jennie E. Grier**, daughter of Maj. Zenas A. Grier.

August 9, 1867

Died in Bedford Co., Va., on the night of the 23d of June, Mrs. **Eliza F. Ewing**, in the 41st year of her age. . . . a native of Washington Co., Pa. and was a daughter of the late Samuel Patterson. When her father removed to Virginia in 1848, she came with him, and was subsequently married to Charles H. Ewing of Bedford Co. who . . . . [died] in 1855. [She is] survived by two little boys.

Died of pneumonia at her residence in Chester District, S. C. on the 22d of January, 1867, Mrs. **Elizabeth Westbrooks**, wifow of the late William Westbrooks, in the 59th year of her age. . . a woman of great energy--had raised a large, industrious and respectable family, nearly all of whom she had lived to see settled in life and members of the church. She had been a member of the church at Union above twenty five years.

Died in Mecklenburg, N. C., July 13th, 1867 of chronic inflammation of the stomach, Maj. **Zenas A. Grier**, aged 61 years . . . [member] Little Steel Creek . . . . left an affectionate widow, two daughters, three sons-- his two oldest sons having fallen in battle in defence of Southern independence.

Died in Mecklenburg, N. C., 28th of June, **Maggie**, infant daughter of Wm. and Nancy **Tolman**, aged one year, two months and seven days.

Died of congestive fever, July 19th, 1867, little **Sallie Steel**, daugther of Wm. P. and Margaret **Kennedy**.

Died in Portersville, Tenn. on the 21st of April last, **Robert Hill**, Esq. in the 77th year of his age. . . . native of Abbeville District, S. C., but since 1843 has been a wealthy and influential citizen of Tipton Co., Tenn. and a member of the Associate Reformed Church at Salem.

Married, by Rev. W. M. Grier at Oak Hill, Wilcox Co., Ala., Mr. **John T. Dale** and Miss **Evelyn Jones**.

- - - by Rev. J. H. Peoples, July 25th, Mr. **Edward F. Henderson** and Miss **Euphemia F. Fleming**, all of Maury Co., Tenn.

August 23, 1867

Died on the 28th aof August in Newberry, S. C., Miss **Carrie Spence** of bilious fever, in the 23d year of her age. . . . She leaves parents, brother and a little band of children whe was engaged in teaching to mourn her loss.

Died at the residence of her father in Maury Co., Tenn. on February 14th, 1867, Miss **Manerva McCain**. . . . cut down in early life by consumption.

August 30, 1867

Married on the 13th instant, by Rev. David Pressly, Mr. **Jackson Hatfield** to Miss **Susan Russel**, all of Oktibbeha Co., Miss.

Brother Bonner:
During the war and the suspension of the paper, the good passed away without the knowledge of friends. I send you a brief notice of the departure of some who "died in faith," and are now, we trust, in the "better country." H. [W. R. Hemphill]
Mr. **Robert Craig**, born May 19th, 1790; died of cancer, October 14th, 1863. Long a member of the church at Prosperity, Ala. . . .
Mrs. **Martha A. Craig**, wife of the above, born June 12th, 1790; died of consumption, March 15th, 1857. . . .
Mr. **N. H. Craig**, son of Robert Craig, born August 8th, 1828; died of typhoid fever, July 20th, 1865. In the war more than a years. . . .
Mrs. **Martha A. Hodges**, daughter of Robert Craig, born may 1st, 1831; died of typhoid fever, November 28th, 1865. . . .
Robert M. Hodges, son of J. C. and M. A. Hodges, died August 23d, 1863, in the fifth year of his age.
Mary E. Hodges, daughter of J. C. and M. A. Hodges, an infant in her third month, died August 18th, 1863. Both children died of whooping cough.
Mr. **Robert Craig Chestnut**, son of John and Elizabeth Chestnut. Born December 12th, 1941 [1841]; died October 29th, 1861 in Richmond, Va. in a hospital.

September 6, 1867

Died after a short illness on Tuesday, the 7th of August, 1867, in the 8th year of his age, **Claude Ross**, second and youngest son of Rev. J. A. and M. C. **Dickson**.

September 13, 1867

Died at Wacahoota, Florida of congestion of the brain on the evening of the 16th of August, 1867, **George Baxter Hunter**, son of Dr. George B. Hunter, deceased, and Mrs. Sallie Hunter and grandson of Mr. and Mrs. John Fleming, aged three years and ten months.

Married on the 20th of August by Rev. D. F. Haddon, Dr. **Thomas Wright** of Spartanburg and Miss **Elizabeth Bryson** of Laurens.

October 18, 1867

Married on Thursday, the 3d October, inst. by Rev. J. I. Bonner, Dr. **D. Holloway** of Edgefield District and Miss **Lizzie Cowan**, a graduate of the Due West Female College of the Class of 1866 and a daughter of Capt. John Cowan of Due West.

- - - on Thursday, the 10th of October, inst. in Newberry District by Rev. J. I. Bonner, Mr. **W. Caldwell McMorries** and Miss **Rosa A. Renwick**, a graduate of the Due West Female College of the Class of 1866 and a daughter of Col. Jno. S. Renwick.

- - - on Thursday, the 10th of October, inst., in Edgefield District, S. C. by Rev. J. O. Lindsay, Mr. **Len Lyon** and Miss **Lizzie R. Jennings**, a graduate of the Due West Female College and a daughter of Dr. J. H. Jennings.

November 1, 1867

Died on the 10th inst., after an illness of some two weeks, **Florence L. Cunningham**, wife of Dr. Jno. Cunningham and daughter of Jno. T. Miller. She had just entered her 23d year.

Franklin G. Lewis, after a protracted illness, departed this life on the 2d May, 1867, leaving a lonely widow [O. B.--Louisville, Ga.].

Departed this life on the 26th inst., **Anna M. Trimble**, daughter of J. L. and L. A. Trimble, aged 14 years [O. B. --Louisville, Ga.].

Married on the night of the 15th October on Little River, Fairfield District by Dr. Boyce, Mr. **A. Hamilton** of Jackson's Creek to Miss **Mattie Bell**.

- - - by the same at the same time and place, Mr. **Henry Brice** to Miss **Mary Douglas**, all of Fairfield.

- - - near Anderson, C. H., S. C. on the 8th October, inst., by Rev. Mr. Beverly, Mr. **J. H. Clark** and Miss **Annie M. Burriss**, a graduate of the Due West Female College of the Class of 1865 and a daughter of Milford Burriss, Esq.

- - - by the same at the same time and place, Mr. **T. M. Cater** and Miss **S. Lizzie Burriss**, a graduate of the Due West Female College of the Class of 1866 and a daughter of Milford Burriss, Esq.

- - - August 8th, 1867 by Rev. S. A. Agnew, Mr. **Robert Gambrell** to Miss **Mary E. Bryson**, all of Lee County, Miss.

- - - October 10th, 1867 by Rev. S. A. Agnew, Mr. **William J. Caldwell** of Pontotoc Co. to Miss **Esther Spence** of Lee Co., Miss.

- - -October 9th, 1867 by Rev. S. A. Agnew, Mr. **John B. Galloway** and Miss **Mollie McGee**, all of Lee County, Miss.

November 8, 1867

Married on the 3d of October by Rev. R. L. Grier, Mr. **S. A. Baker** and Miss **M. A. Harold**, all of Obion County, Tenn.

- - - in Laurens District by Rev. J. I. Bonner on Tuesday, the 22d October, Mr. **John H. Allen** of Due West and Miss **Lizzie Johnson**.

- - - near Due West on Thursday the 31st October by Rev. J. I. Bonner, Mr. **Alfred Sheriff** of Pickens District and Miss **Jane Drake**.

- - - at the residence of Mr. Robert Banks near Portersville, Tenn. at 2 p m., October 24th by Rev. D. H. Cummins, Mr. **David Moffit** of Bloomington, Indiana and Miss **Martha L. Strong** of Portersville, Tenn.

November 22, 1867

Died in Laurens District, S. C. September 2d, 1867, Mrs. **Martha Sloan**, relict of Robert Sloan in the 72nd year of her age. From her youth she had been a member of the Associate Reformed church of Providence.

Died in Laurens District, S. C., February 11th, 1867, Mrs. **Anna Bryson**, wife of John Bryson in the 73d year of her age, leaving a large family to mourn her departure.

Mrs. **Jane H. McCrady**, wife of Robert McCrady . . . died on the evening of 23d of August in the 65th year of her age. .. . . [member of] Head Spring, Laurens District.

Married on the 20th October at Orrville, Ala. by Rev. J. A. Lowry, Mr. **Emmet Craig** and Miss **Millie Kitrer** (?).

- - - on the 5th inst. by Rev. J. A. Lowry, Mr. **Rufus Moore** to Miss **Lou Spears**, all of Dallas County, Ala.

- - - by the same on the 11th inst. at the residence of Judge Cooper, Mr. **James Craig** of Dallas to Miss **Lizzie H. Cooper** of Wilcox County, Ala.

December 6th, 1867

Died on the 13th of October in Obion County, Tenn., Mrs. **Jane Brown**, in the 73d year of her age. . . . . born in Chester District, S. C. and lived many years in connection with the Associate Reformed church at Hopewell. In 1840, whe moved with her husband and identified themselves with the church at Troy. She survived her husband 17 years.

Married on the 7th ult. in Newberry District by Rev. J. C. Boyd, Mr. **John C. Wilson** and Miss **Emma Moffatt**.

- - - on the 14th ult. in Newberry District by Rev. J. C. Boyd, Mr. **Wesley Sligh** and Miss **Hattie Reid**.

- - - on the evening of the 27th inst. at the residence of the bride's mother by Rev. J. R. Riley, Col. **B. W. Ball** to Miss **Eliza**, daughter of the Judge W. D. **Watts** and Mrs. S. S. Watts, all of Laurensville, S. C.

- - - on Thursday evening, 38th ultimo. at the residence of the bride's father in Anderson, S. C. by Rev. J. Scott Murray, Mr. **Geo. W. Miller** of Abbeville, S. C. to Miss **Emelia L. Reid**, daughter of J. P. Reid, Esq. of the former place.

December 13, 1867

Obituaries of an Elder's Family

Jane C. Weir, a worthy member of the A. R. church, Nebo, Tenn., August 8th, 1859.

John McClerkin Weir, father of J. Catherine, of McMinn Co., and elder of Nebo church, died August 8th, 1861.

Patrick B. Weir, son of the former and member of the same church, died January 3d, 1864. Death supposed to be occasioned not by ordinary sickness, but troubles of existing war.

Joseph McMinn, son-in-law of the late J. M. W., died September 26, 1866.

Annie Belle McMinn, July 31st, 1866, near 5 months old.

Anna Weir, consort of J. Mc. and mother of Catherine and Brown, died August 8th, 1867.

Thus T. J. Weir, youngest son, and Civilla McMinn, youngest daughter, with Margaret and Isabella, are left on the ancient and lovely homestead, to mourn the loss of father and mother, sister and brother, husband and infant daughter with their distant brother and family, John H. Weir, Fort Smith, Sebastin Co., Arkansas [Rev. T. Turner].

Died on the 16th of November in Burke Co., Ga., Miss **Laura C. L.,** daughter of J. B. and C. M. P. **Netherland,** of pneumonia, aged 27 years and one month . . . [member of] A. R. church of Bethel.

Died in Pontotoc Co., Miss, November 1, 1867, Mr. **John Pressly Caldwell** in the 40th year of his age. . . . son of John Caldwell and was born in Anderson District, S. C., January 14, 1828. He connected himself with the A. R. church at Shiloh in 1846, removed to Pontotoc, Miss. in 1850, and was one of the number of those who united in the organization of Hopewell church in 1851. . . .He leaves a wife and four little children--all girls.

Died in Mecklenburg Co., N. C. on the 15th October, Mrs. **Agnes Peoples,** wife of Richard R. Peoples, Jr., in the 27th year of her age. She was the daughter of Col. James McDill of Chester District, S. C. . . . After her marriage, about a year ago, she removed with her husband to Mecklenburg Co., N. C., and became a very welcome inmate of the family of her father-in-law, Mr. R. Peoples. . . . She left a sorrow stricken husband and helpless infant.

Married at the residence of the bride's mother in Due West, Thursday night at 12 o'clock, December 5th by Rev. J. I. Bonner, Mr. **W. E. Henderson** of Laurens and Miss **Mattie A. Drennan.**

Married on the 8th of November in Portersville, Tenn. by Rev. J. H. Strong, Mr. **J. J. Weaver** to Miss **M. C. Elmore.**

---- by the same on the evening of the 26th of November, Mr. **T. J. Franklin** to Miss **M. A. McCain** of Tipton County, Tenn.

- - - at the home of the bride's father, 1st November, 1867, by Rev. T. J. Bonner, **J. C. Dunn** and Miss **Abellah McCrory,** all of Freestone County, Texas.

January 3, 1868

Married in Newberry District, December 12th, by Rev. J. C. Boyd, Mr. **Luther Long** and Miss **Jane Martin.**

- - - at the residence of the bride's mother in Edgefield District, Thursday evening, December 19th by Rev. J. L. Hemphill, Mr. **Samuel Pressly** of Due West, Abbeville District, and Miss **Nannie Holloway.**

January 10, 1868

Died in Cabarrus Co., N. C., November 9th, 1867, Mrs. **Mary Jane Wallace** in the 26th year of her age. . . . member of the Associate Reformed Presbyterian church at Coddle Creek.

January 17, 1868

Married, December 11, 1867 by Rev. S. A. Agnew, Mr. **Thomas W. Houston** of Tippah Co. to Mrs. **Margaret E. Watt,** daughter of Samuel Bryson of Lee County, Miss.

- - - December 12, 1867 by Rev. S. A. Agnew, Mr. **John H. Darter** of Tarrant Co., Texas to Miss **Abbie E. Gambrell** of Lee County, Miss.

- - - December 19, 1867 by Rev. S. A. Agnew, Mr. **L. A. Richey** of Guntown to Miss **Mary M.,** daughter of Dr. E. **Agnew**, of Tippah Co., Miss.

- - - on the 19th December, 1867 by Rev. R. W. Brice, Mr. **Charles Bell** and Miss **Rachel,** only daughter of Thomas G. **Bigham.** all of Chester District, S. C.

January 24, 1868

Annie, the eldest daughter of Col. R. A. **Fair.** . . . [died] on the 14th of December, 1867 at the early age of eighteen.

Died at the residence of William McKinstry in Drew County, Arkansas, on the 15th of April, 1867, Mrs. **Sallie McKinstry.** She was about forty six years of age. She only survived her lamented husband J. W. McKinstry about six months.

Also, on the 24th October, 1867 at the residence of his daughter, Mrs. Sarah Dickson, died, **Andrew McQuiston** at the advanced age of 77 years.. . . . for some thirty five years an elder of the Associate Reformed church. He was elected and ordained an elder in Hopewell, Chester District, S. C. In the fall of 1837, he removed to Tipton County, Tenn. where he continued to exercise his office in Salem and Bloomington congregations until the fall of 1865, when he broke up house keeping and came to Arkansas.

Married in Anderson District, January 9th by Rev. W. L. Pressly, Mr. **James Stevenson** and Miss **Catherine Ranson.**

January 31, 1868

[Killed by falling log] January 15, 1868, **John Haddon**, in his fifty first year. . . .the son of John Haddon, was born in the vicinity of Due West, Abbeville Dist., S. C., October 29, 1817. He married Miss Elizabeth Martin, daughter of James Martin, Due West, January 12, 1843. . . .[joined church in Due West in 1845], removed from South Carolina in 1857, and settled in Tippah Co., Miss. in the bounds of Bethany congregation. . . elected elder in 1860. . . . leaves wife and seven children.

Married, on the 9th of February, 1868, by Dr. Boyce, **Dr. Madden** of Winnsboro to Miss **Mattie Brice**, daughter of Wm. Brice, Esquire.

- - - Dec. 26th, 1867, by Rev. J. C. Chalmers, Mr. **E. J. Garrison**and Miss **Catherine Youngblood**, both of Mecklenburg Co., N. C.

- - - Jan. 9th, 1868, by the same, Mr. **W. S. McClelland** of Charlotte, N. C. and **Miss M. F. Stewart** of York District, S. C.

- - - by the Rev. J. A. Lowry on the 12th of December, 1867, at the residence of Samuel Chesnut, Esq., Mr. **J. W. Hansucker** to Miss **Lizzie Chesnut**.

- - - by the same on the 8th inst., Mr. **Robert Craig** to Miss **Lizzie McCraw**, all of Dallas Co., Ala.

February 14, 1868

Lillie Lockridge of Sharpsburg, Kentucky . . . . [died] on Saturday, the 18th of January.

Died in Lebanon church, Wilcox Co., Ala. on the evening of the 16th of January, **A. M. Cook** in the 56th year of his age.

Jas. Sloan . . . . [died] on the morning of the 15th, January, in the 72nd year of his age. . . . It was his lot to see all his children allied to the cause which he had espoused--members of the church of his heart. Two of them, Revs. A. S. and H. T. Sloan . . . . nearly forty years he was a ruling elder in Cannon's Creek. . . Nearly the last act of his life was subscribing to the sustenation fund of Erskine College.

Died on the 11th of January, 1868, **Sarah Elizabeth Dickson** in the 15th year of her age. . . . the daughter of the late Samuel Dickson who was killed by the Yankees near his own house.

Married, November 12th, 1867, by Rev. David Pressly at the residence of Mrs. W. M. Bell, Mr. **Wm. B. McKell** to Miss **Davie Rushing**, all of Oktibbeha Co., Miss.

- - - also by the same on the 21st of November, 1867 at the residence of Mrs. Burrell Taylor, Mr. **Daniel Deanes** to Miss **Jennie Logue**, all of Oktibbeha Co., Miss.

-- - - also by the same on the 16th of November, 1867 at the residence of the bride's father, Mr. **John A. Buntin** to Miss **Emma Love**, all of Oktibbeha Co., Miss.

- - - also by the same on the 7th January, 1868 at the residence of Mrs. John Scott, Mr. **G. F. Hillhouse** to Miss **Martha D. Worrell**, all of Oktibbeha Co, Miss.

- - - also by the same on the 9th of January, 1868 at the residence of Mr. B. F. Bell, Mr. **Thos. W. Ware** to Miss **Annie E. Williams**, all of Oktibbhea Co., Miss.

- - - at the residence of the bride's father, 26th December, 1867, by Rev. Dr. Martin, **Silas Hemphill Cooper** and Miss **Eliza H. Gault**, all of Fulton Co., Ark.

- - - on the evening of the 29th of January by Rev. J. H. Strong, Mr. **John Baird** to Miss **Eliza Miller**, all of Tipton Co., Tenn.

- - - at the same time and place by the same, Mr. **John Poole** to Miss **Jane Miller**.

- - - on the morning of the 30th by the same, Mr. **Wm. Ellison** to Miss **Ann Jane Dunlap**, all of Tipton Co., Tenn.

- - - on the evening of the 30th by the same, Mr. **A. J. Wright** of Drew Co., Ark. to **Miss E. A. McQuiston** of Tipton Co., Tenn.

February 21, 1868

Died in York District, S. C., October 13th, 1867, Mrs. **Martha**, consort of Wm. **McGill**, Sr. in the 74th year of her age . . . [joined] Bethany . . . . leaves a husband in the 93d year of his age and nine children.

Died on February 1st, **John Moffett** in his 69th year . . . . born in Chester District, S. C. . . . . was elected a ruling elder in Hopewell congregation. He removed to Monroe County, Indiana in 1838, was there elected as elder in Union congregation, Rev. Wm. Turner, pastor.

Died in Anderson District, S. C., November 4th, 1867, Mrs. **Rachel Moorehead**, relict of the late Alex Moorehead, Esq. in the 74th year of her age. The deceased was a member of the Associate Reformed church at Concord.

Died in Iredell County, N. C., November 27th, 1864, Mr. **John H.**

17

Cavin in the 69th year of his age. Mr. Cavin was for 28 years a ruling elder of the Associate Reformed church at New Perth.

Mr. **James C. Cavin**, a son, died May 19th, 1863, in the 27th year of his age. He was a member of the same church.

Married by the Rev. J. Patrick on the 21st inst., Mr. **Franklin C. Falls** and Miss **Margaret A. Dickey**, all of Pope County, Ark.

- - - on the evening of the 30th January, 1868 at Wacahoota, Florida, by the Rev. W. J. McCormick, Mr. **Wm. T. Winecoff** to Mrs. **Sallie F. Hunter**, daughter of Mr. John Fleming, all of Wacahoota, Fla.

- - - in Chester District on 31st of January, 1868 by Rev. R. W. Brice, Mr. **James W. Aiken** and Miss **Sarah**, daughter of Mr. John **Boyd**.

February 28, 1868

Married on the 9th of January, 1868, by the Rev. R. L. Grier, Mr. **D. B. Marshall** to Miss **M. M. McGaw**, all of Obion County, Tenn.

- - - on February 4th by Rev. Jas. H. Peoples, Mr. **S. J. Crawford** to Miss **E. D. Lusk**, all of Maury County, Tenn.

- - - on the 13th inst. by Rev. H. T. Sloan, Mr. **William P. Devlin** and Miss **Lilas J. Purdy**, all of Cedar Spring, Abbeville, S. C.

March 13, 1868

Died in Iredell Co., N. C., January 12th, 1868, Mrs. **Sarah Cavin** in the 74th year of her life . . . a consistent and devoted member of the A. R. Presbyterian church at New Perth, and was the worthy companion of Mr. John Cavin . . . . a worthy son, with his two sisters and their aged aunt, now constitute the household.

Died at Opelousa, La. on the 24th October, 1867, **Thomas C. Gray**, second son of the Dr. R. F. and Francis C. Gray, in the 25th year of his age. He was born in Winton, Miss., but moved with his parents to La. when he was quite young. He came to S. C. in the early part of 1857 for the purpose of completing his education. After studying first under Professor J. P. Kennedy, and then under Mr. Adophin, both teachers of fine abilities, he entered the S. C. College in the fall of '58. . . . Early in the year 1861, he entered the service of S. C. as a private in the Company of College Cadets . . . . [later] enlisted in Company C, 7th S. C. Vol. [served through the war]. . . . At the close of the year 1866, he returned to La. . . . [and] commenced the study of medicine.

Married, February 6th, in Newberry District by Rev. J. C. Boyd, Mr. **Henry Boozer** and Miss **Emma Brooks**.

- - - also, February 27th by the same, Mr. **J. A. Crotwell** and Miss **Sallie Cannon**.

March 20, 1868

Married on Tuesday, 12th Feb., at the residence of the bride's mother in Chester Dist., S. C. by Rev. R. W. Brice, Lieut **Edward Shannon** to Miss **Nannie Barber**, the only daughter of Mrs. Ellen Barber.

April 3, 1868

Departed this life on the 29th of August, 1867 in the vicinity of Starkville, Mr. **James McKell** in the 53rd year of his age. . . . . He was a worthy member of the A. R. church, Starkville [Miss.]. . . . He has left a widow with three sons and five daughters.

Also, departed this life near Starkville, Miss. on the 28th of October, 1867, Mr. **William Brown**, aged 66 years, 5 months and 13 days. . . . was born in Monahan County, Ireland. At the age of fifteen, he came to the United States and located in Fairfield District, S. C. He was a nephew of the late Rev. James Rogers of the same district and State. In early life he joined the A. R. Church, then under the pastoral care of his uncle. About thirty years ago, he removed to Oktibbeha County, Miss. and became identified with the Associate Reformed Church in Starkville soon after its organization. . . . [left] a widow, an only son, and three daughters.

Married on the 5th inst. by Rev. E. L. Patton, Lieut. **James M. Truitt** and Miss **Sallie Goodwin**, all of Abbeville District.

- - - February 18th in Fairfield District by the Rev. James Boyce, D. D., Mr. **James McMeekin** to Miss **Sallie E. Douglas**.

- - - by Rev. David Pressly at the residence of the bride's father on the 20th of February, Mr. **John Erwin** to Miss **Bettie Steele**, all of Oktibbeha Co., Miss.

- - - also, on the 27th of February at the residence of the bride's mother by Rev. David Pressly, Mr. **W. S. Broughton** to Miss **M. L. Reese**, all of Oktibbeha Co., Miss.

April 10, 1868

Died on the 4th of February last, little **Johnnie**, son of R. C. and M. E. **Simonton** in the 7th year of his age.

Died of pneumonia in Tipton Co., Tenn on the 12th of October last, Mr. **Samuel Adams** at the advanced age of 86 years. . . . born in County Antrim, Ireland . . . emigrated to South Carolina about 42 years ago, and subsequently to Tenn. . . . . member of A. R. church at Salem [Tenn.].

Also, on the 18th of October of the same disease, Mrs. **Rosanah Linn**, eldest daughter of the above. She left home to see her father die -- while waiting on him she herself fell sick and soon followed.

April 17, 1868

Died of pneumonia in Obion County, Tenn. on the 3d of March, Miss **Jane McDonald** in the 48th year of her age. . . . born in Chester District, S. C., and raised in the congregation of Hopewell. . . for years has belonged to the Associate Reformed church at Troy.

Married by Rev. J. A. Lowry on the 7th inst., Mr. **W. A. Brantly** to Miss **Mattie F. Bell**, all of Dallas County, Ala.

- - - on the evening of the 18th February by Rev. R. L. Grier at the residence of the bride's father, Mr. **Samuel Curry** to **Miss Rispie Young**, all of Obion Co., Tenn.

Died of consumption at her residence in Due West on Monday morning the 20th of April, inst., **Mrs. P. A. Lindsay**, relict of the late James Lindsay, in the 66th year of her age.

Died in DeKalb County, Ga., February 27th, 1868, Mrs. **Ann Miller**, in the 71st year of her age, of cancer on her face. . . . was born in County Antrim, Ireland in 1796, emigrated to America with her parents, John and Margaret Wilson, in 1801. The ship in which she and her parents sailed was partially wrecked out at sea and was driven into the cove or harbor at Cork, where two of her sisters died of small pox. After the repair of the vessel, with a favoring Providence, she and her parents landed at Charleston in May, 1801, and settled in Lancaster District in the Waxhaw settlement under the pastoral care of Rev. Dickson, then removed with her mother and stepfather, J. Harmon, until after the War of 1812. In 1815, she and Mr. Robert Miller were united in the bonds of marriage, shortly afterwards connected themselves with the Presbyterian church at Catholic, then under the pastoral care of Rev. Robert McCullough. In 1825 she with her husband removed to Newton Co., Ga., and were among the founders of the Associate Reformed church, called Hopewell, near the Snapping Shoals on South River. In 1852, after the death of her husband, she removed with her children, seven sons, up into DeKalb Co., Ga., and connected with Prosperity church by letter, in which church she remained a worthy member.

May 1, 1868

Died after protracted illness in Bolivar County, Miss. on the 10th of March, 1868, **Hugh Mitchel Simpson**, son of Thomas and Drusilla B. Simpson, aged about 29 years. . . . born in York, S. C., emigrated to Madison Co., Miss. with his parents in the autumn of 1845. He was married in 1859 to the daughter of Thomas Mealy of Holmes Co., Miss. She and three children are left . . . in 1860, he settled in Bolivar Co. - - took up arms in the South's Cause in an early period - - remained in the service till the close of the war. His health began to decline toward the close of the war.

May 8, 1868

Died on the morning of the 8th of January, 1868, Mrs. **Elizabeth Anthony**, consort of James C. Anthony, whom with three children she left to mourn her loss . . . born 6th of September, 1835.

Died in York District, S. C., Mrs. **Martha H. Pursley**, wife of William Pursley, March 17, 1868. . . . She was a member of the Associate Reformed church at Bethany.

Married on the morning of the 16th of April by Rev. Horatio Thompson, D. D., at the home of the bride's father, assisted by Rev. Robert Taylor, Mr. **Samuel Givens Thompson** to Miss **Sallie F. Adams**, daughter of Joseph Adams, Esq.

June 12, 1868

Departed this life at his residence in Starkville, Miss. on the 29th of February, 1868, Dr. **C. P. Montgomery**, aged nearly 54 years. He was the oldest surviving son of Hon. David and Martha Montgomery. He was a native of Fairfield District, S. C. About thirty years ago, he removed to the opening West and permanently located in Oktibbeha County, Miss. . .[His life was devoted] to the medical professison. . . . remarkably successful in the treatment of disease . . . he then engaged for a few years in merchandizing. . . the last years of his life were occupied in the improvement of stock, and the development of the agricultural resources of the country.

June 12, 1868

Married by Rev. H. Quigg on the 14th November, 1867, Mr. **J. W. Adair** to Miss **L. J. McClelland**, daughter of John McClelland, Esq. of Henry Co., Ga.

- - - by the same on the 19th of December, 1867, Mr. **P. W. Turner** to Miss **F. W. C. Stewart**, daughter of Mrs. Margaret Stewart and grand-daughter of John McClelland, all of Henry Co., Ga.

June 19, 1868

Died at her father's residence in Donaldsville on Wednesday night the 10th of June, inst., Miss **Mary Jane Donnald**, familiarly called "Chappie," daughter of Col. Samuel Donnald in the 84th year of her age. The deceased was born blind, could only distinguish light from darkness. . . . member of Greenville Presbyterian Church.

Departed this life, May 17th, 1868, Mr. **T. O. Creswell** in the 40th year of his age, leaving a wife and two children. . . . Thus another head of a family has been taken from his place in Old Long Cane.

June 26, 1868

Married on the 18th inst. by Rev. J. I. Bonner at the residence of the bride's father, Dr. **H. I. Epting** of Williamston, S. C. and Mrs. **Mary Jane Knox**, daughter of William Hill, Esq. of Abbeville, S. C.

July 10, 1868

Married on the 16th ulti. by Rev. E. L. Patton at the residence of the bride's father, Mr. **J. A. Wideman** of Abbeville District and Miss **Georgiana Wells**, daughter of C. Wells, Edgefield District.

July 24, 1868

Died on Saturday, April 4th, 1868 near Ellistown, Lee Co., Miss., **Nehemiah Johnson**, in the eighty fifth year of his age. . . .born in Iredell Co., N. C., January 1, 1784, and in his youth joined one of the Associate Reformed churches of that country, but I [Rev. S. A. Agnew] am not able to state which one. He loved to talk of those olden times and sainted ministers. The son with whom he was living at the time of his death is named William Blackstocks in honor of one of the fathers of the Associate Reformed church. Mr. Johnson was married to Ann Templeton, September 26, 1809. In the fall of 1810, he left N. C. and removed to what was then called Mississippi Territory, and settled within nine miles of the present site of Huntsville, Ala. During his residence there he served as a soldier for three months in the Indian War of 1812. In the year 1817, he moved south of the Tennessee River into Lawrence County, Ala. Here in 1820, he joined the Methodist church, and here, too, on October 2d, 1834, his wife died. Like her husband, she was reared and had become a member of the Associate Reformed church in North Carolina. In 1835, he moved to Fayette County, Ala where he remained until 1841, when he went to Greene County, Ala. In 1850, he came to Pontotoc Co., Miss., and became a member of the Hebron Presbyterian church. In 1860, he came within the bounds of Hopewell and was rejoiced to find an ecclesiastical organization similar to the one in which he had been reared long years ago. The Psalms sounded sweetly in his ears, and he seemed to be greatly delighted with the services of the sanctuary. He united with the church and his walk and conversation were such as becometh the Gospel. For several years after leaving N. C., Mr. Johnson refused to join any church, because none of those to which he had access accorded with his views. "Finding," to use his own language, "that living out of the church was not favorable to a religious life," he pursued a different policy and first connected himself with the Methodist church and subsequently with the Presbyterians.

Died in Marshall County, Miss. on the 14th of October, 1867, Mrs.

Sarah Therrell, aged 66 years, 8 months and 14 days. . . . the daughter of Robert Hall of Orange County, N. C. . . . first married to Mr. Alfred Carrington, with whom she removed in 1831 to western Tennessee, and thence in 1833 to the neighborhood where she [died] . . . . [Following the death of her husband] she was some time afterward married to Mr. Wm. Therrell. Soon after this event she connected herself with the Associate Reformed church at Mt. Carmel . . . .[She leaves] an aged husband, three children.

Died in Bedford County, Tenn., **Bennie L.**, only child of Maggie J. and R. N. **Carmical**, aged one year, two months and nineteen days. His parents living at the house of his grandfather [Rev. A. McElroy].

August 7, 1868

Died in Tippah Co., Miss., on the 16th of October, 1867, Mr. **A. R. Johnson**, aged 58 years, 10 months and 8 days. . . . native of Abbeville District, S. C. He was a son of Henry Johnson, who lived a few miles below Due West on Little River. He was a pioneer to this section, coming here some time before the Indians left the country. Soon after the organization of Ebenezer church (the A. R. P.) he identified himself with it. . . a short time before his death, he was called by his brethren to the office of Deacon. . . . He leaves a wife and ten children.

Also, on the 16th of December, 1867, Mrs. **Eliza Johnson** in her fifty fourth year. Thus were these children in twelve months deprived of both father and mother. . . Mrs. Johnson was the daughter of Mr. Benjamin and Margaret Gassaway of Anderson District, S. C.

Died in Tippah County, Miss. on the 28th day of January, 1868, Mrs. **Sarah R. McBryde** in the 73d year of her age. "Aunt Sallie," as she was familarly called. . . was a native of Cedar Springs, Abbeville District, and was a daughter of Robert and grand-daughter of Dr. Timothy Russel, who came to this country as a Surgeon of the British army during the Revolutionary War, but who after his arrival, espoused the cause of the colonies and devoted himself to their interest. She has left an aged husband, Major Robert McBryde.

Died near Due West on 1st August, Mr. **John Johnson**, (familiarly known as "Uncle Peter"), nearly or quite eighty years old. He was a native of Ireland. . . . [lived from] the diligent use of the needle. He had been for the last ten or twelve years an orderly member of the church at Due West.

August 21, 1868

Died at the home of his parents, March 30, 1864, **Charles J. Boyd.**

Died in the same hospital near Atlanta, Ga., April 27, 1864, **Edward M. Boyd.**

Died in Laquena Co., Miss., October 16, 1867, **A. P. Boyd**.

Died on the 13th of July at her home in Rienzi, Miss., after a short illness, Mrs. **Catherine Henry**, wife of Capt. D. T. **Beall**, and daughter of Mr. Ames McElwee of York, S. C. in the 29th year of her age. . . . connected herself with the Associate Reformed church in Yorkville when she was about sixteen years old. For many years her home has been in Mississippi.

Married on the 16th of July at the residence of Mr. Samuel Brice by Rev. J. A. Lowry, Mr. **W. A. Cochran** of Dallas Co., Ala. to Mrs. **Mollie Chisolm**, late of Fairfield District, S. C.

September 11, 1868

Died , near Branchville, Drew Co., Arkansas, in the 68th year of her age, Mrs. **Jane Gains**, wife of Jesse Gains.

Died near Relfe's Bluff, Drew Co., Arkansas, in the 30th year of his age, **Charles Boyd, Sr.**, a brother of Mrs. Gains. . . . The deceased came to this country from Chester Dist., S. C. about twelve years ago. They both took part in the organization of Mt. Zion congregation. . . . About three years ago, Mr. Boyd was elected and ordained an elder.

Died of congestive chill, August 21st, 1868, **Horatio Thompson Bradley**, only son of Mrs. Mary Bradley, in the eighth year of his age. . . . [survived by] mother and three sisters.

Died about mid-day on Sabbath, August 30th, 1868, Mrs. **Margaret Wardlaw** in the 89th year of her age. The deceased had been twice married and left two families of children--the first is in the far West, and the other, consisting of one son and two daughters, were about her in her last sickness and followed her to her last resting place in that venerable city of the dead-- Cedar Spring graveyard.

Old **Mrs. Findley**, familiarly known as "Old Ganny Findley," departed this life . . . June 20th, 1868, aged about 92 years. she was born, lived and died not far from the same place.

Departed this life at the residence of her mother near Starkville, Miss. on the 24th of July, Mrs. **Nannie E. Agnew**, aged 26 years, 9 months and 17 days. . . . born in Oktibbeha County, Miss. . . . She leaves a husband and two infant sons , a pious mother, brothers and sisters.

September 18, 1868

Died at his residence near Honea Path on the 6th of September, 1868, Dr. **A. Branyon**, born March 2d, 1814, in the 55th year of his age. While an infant, he had the paralysis, which caused him to be a cripple in his left arm and leg during life, and rendered him unable to engage in any active business; but being of industrious and energetic habits, although of poor parentage, he acquired while young a good English education, and employed himself in teaching school, and gave general satisfaction to his patrons. In the year 1843, he was severely afflicted and had to spend a large portion of his hard earned money. Being again restored, he entered with new vigor upon his former pursuit. Accumulating more money, he commenced the study of medicine and entered the Medical College at Macon, Ga.; after graduating, commenced the practice of his profession. In the year 1847, he connected himself with the A. R. P. church in Due West, and remained a consistent member until his death.

September 25, 1868

Departed this life August 31st, **David P. Lowry** in the forty fourth year of his age [Louisville, Ga.].

October 23, 1868

Little **Allen Boyd**, son of the late Archibald Boyd of Long Cane, died of congestive chill, on Sabbath morning, September 27th, 1868 in the tenth year of his age. . . . one of a large family of brothers and sisters, who were deprived of both of their parents within a few weeks, three years ago. The little boy found a good home in the house of Mr. Weed.

Jonathan Belton Adamson, son of Mrs. Matha Adamson, died of congestive fever, after a few days of sickness, October 11th, 1868, in the seventeenth year of his age.

Married by Rev. W. T. Walters on Thursday, the 15th October inst., Mr. **T. L. Hadden** and Miss **Lizzie**, daughter of J. B. **Kay**, both of Abbeville, S. C.

- - - in Due West, S. C. on Thursday evening, October 15, 1868 by Rev. J. I. Bonner, Mr. **Samuel Agnew** of Honea Path, S. C. and Miss **Rebecca J. Drennan**, a graduate of the Due West Female College.

October 30, 1868

It becomes our painful duty to record another death among the youth of Long Cane. . . Miss **Jane Wideman**, daughter of Esq. Adam and Mrs. Eliza Wideman, aged 18 years. . . . Tuesday night about 8 o'clock, October 20th, 1868. . . [She] was a graduate of Due West Female College Class of 1866.

Died at the residence of her father, Robert Mills, in Chester District, S. C., on the 27th of September last, Miss **Jinnie B. Mills**, being a few days over forty seven years old. She was a member of the Associate Reformed church of Hopewell.

Married on the 20th inst. by Rev. H. T. Sloan, Mr. **W. W. Purdy** to Miss **Kitty Devlin**, daughter of J. J. Devlin - - all of Cedar Spring.

November 20, 1868

Married by Rev. J. I. Bonner on Thursday the 29th October, Mr. **A. R. Ellis** and Miss **Jane Dunn**.

January 14, 1869

Mrs. **Cecelia Fowler**, the beloved wife of Mr. James W. Fowler of Abbeville C. H., S. C. and daughter of Dr. A. W. and Mrs. Frances Chalmers of Newberry C. H., fell asleep in Jesus on the 25th of December, 1868 in the 27th year of her age.

Died on the 2nd of November, Mrs. **M. Ellen White**, wife of John White and grand daughter of John and Mary Johnson . . . was thirty years old and had been married only three years. . . . [member] Prosperity congregation.

Died of pneumonia at his home in Dallas Co., ala on the 6th of November, Mr. **Samuel Stewart** in the 69th year of his age. . . . born in Abbeville District, S. C., emigrated to Alabama about the year 1832 where he has lived ever since . . . leaves a wife and five children.

Died on the 11th May, 1868 of congrestion, Mrs. **Nancy Jane McQuiston**, aged 38 years, 2 months and 1 day. The deceased was the daughter of Hance and Elizabeth Wylie.

Married, December 24th, 1868, by Rev. H. T. Sloan at the house of Mr. A. B. Kennedy, Mr. **R. H. McCaslan** and Miss **Rebecca**, youngest daughter of Mrs. Sarah **Kennedy**, all of Long Cane, Abbeville Dist., S. C.

- - - January 7th, 1869, by Rev. H. T. Sloan, Mr. **Wm. Scanland** of Dublin, Ireland and Mrs. **Virginia Caroline Wilson** of Abbeville, S. C.

- - - On the 22d ult. at Jalapa, S. C. by Rev. J. K. Mendenhall, **W. R. Spearman**, Esq. and **Mattie C.**, daughter of Dr. R. P. **Clark**.

March 25, 1869

Departed this life on Jackson Creek, Fairfield, S. C. on Friday night, the 5th of March in the 22d year of her age, Mrs. **Mattie M. Hamilton**, formerly Bell, daugher of Edward and Martha Bell. . . [member] New Hope. . . until after her marriage, when her membership was transferred to Jackson's Creek congregation, near to which her husband, Mr. Hamilton, lived and where he was a member. . . married about sixteen months.

W. Weldon Thompson was born June 17th, 1832 and died February 13th, 1869. . . In 1855, he connected himself with the A. R. church at Hopewell, Newton Co., Ga.

Departed this life in Oktibbeha Co., Miss., on the 11th of October, 1868, Miss **Margaret Aroline Elliott**, the third daughter of Mr. J. A. Elliott, aged 13 years and 10 months. . . A father, mother, two brothers and three sisters [survive].

Departed this life on the 13th of February, of inflammation and ultimate mortification, resulting from neglected hernia, **Dr. Henry C. Castles**, in the 49th year of his age. . . . among the earlier graduates of Erskine College. Soon after graduation, he studied medicine and began its practice in Fairfield, his native district. About this time he married Miss Sarah Watt, daughter of James and Margaret Watt, of said district, who is now left with eight small children, to mourn his death. Soon after his marriage, Dr. Castles removed to Chester District, near to Catholic Church, of which he was elected a ruling elder. Sometime before the war, in order to be near his brother, Rev. J. R. Castles, then pastor of Smyrna, York District, he removed into the bounds of said congregation, to which he transferred his church membership, and was received as ruling elder.

Departed this life in Pickens Co., Ala., on the 29th of October, 1868, Mrs. **Sallie S. Gibson**, wife of Mr. John Gibson, aged 29 years. . . . second daughter of the late William Brown of Oktibehha Co., Miss. . . member of Associate Reformed Presbyterian in Starkville, Miss. . . . [married for two years]. An affectionate husband, an infant son, two loving sisters and an only brother [survive].

Married , March 18th, 1869, at the residence of Mrs. Lou Richey, by Rev. W. F. Pearson, Mr **John L. McLecklin** of Anderson, S. C. and Miss **F. Ann Richey** of Abbeville, S. C.

April 22, 1869

Married, March 10th, 1869, at the residence of the bride's father, by Rev. R. L. Grier, Captain **S. F. Maxey** and Miss **Sallie J. McCaw** . All of Troy, Tenn.

- - - On the evening of the 14th of January, 1869, by R. L. Grier, Mr. **John Jimnerson** and Miss **Lizzie Bumpus**.

April 29, 1869

Died, March 1st, 1869, Mrs. **Margaret Simonton**, wife of R. R. Simonton, in the 42nd year of her age. . . . was the daughter of Anderson and Sarah McQuiston, and had been a consistent member of the Associate Reformed Presbyterian from her youth. She leaves a husband and five children.

Died of dropsy in Tipton Co., Tenn. on the morning of March 21st, 1869, Miss **Ann McQuiston** in the 56th year of her age. . . was born in Chester Dist., S. C., near to Hopewell A. R. Church of which her parents were members. . .[herself a member from 1833] till the fall of 1850, at which time she, with her aged parents and a goodly number of her friends, moved to Tipton Co., Tenn. near Salem, of which she was a member at her death.

Died of consumption on the 18th of October, 1868, Miss **Mary Ellen McCown** in the 21st year of her age. . . . member of ARP Church at Bethel--the late charge of Rev. Wm. M. McElwee. We now turn to her beloved mother. But a few short weeks had passed, when death claimed Mrs. **Polly McCown**, aged about 60 years.

Died at Midway, Augusta Co., Va. on the 14th day of February, Mr. **Samuel D. Nelson** in the fiftieth year of his age. This was the last member of a large family, all of whom died of hereditary consumption. . . . [H. T. (Rev. Horatio Thompson) added the following comment]: For more than a year he took upon himself the labor of urging up the congregation of Old Providence to a more zealous and united effort in paying the promised salary to the pastor; and, acting as Treasurer, held every subscriber a debtor, in honor and veracity, and a defaulter in both till the promise was redeemed.. . It would be well for every congregation, and well for the pastor, to have such a one, even though he speak from the grave.

May 6, 1869

Drowned, on the morning of the 10th of April, 1869, in the Arkansas River, **Archibald N. Wilson**, aged 31 years. . . . had been cited to appear as a witness in the U. S. Court at Little Rock on the following Monday. In obedience to this call, he left home on Tuesday morning for Pine Bluff, little thinking that he was bidding a final farewell to his family and friends. Having attended to his business at the Bluff, he took passage on the steamer *Thompson* for Little Rock on Friday evening. He expected to reach the Rock next morning. But about 2 o'clock they are said to have been running at a fearful rate of speed. The night was very dark and either through ignorance or recklessness, they ran upon a snag, which is said to have been well known to boatmen for several years. The snag ran through the boat and held it fast. It sunk in ten feet water.
The captain stilled the fears of the passengers by telling them there was no danger--that the boat was on the bottom, etc. But it was soon discovered that a quantity of unslaked lime which was on board had caused the boat to take fire. Then followed a scene which might better be imagined than described. The captain, instead of ordering the lifeboats and yawls to be manned, to try to save the lives of all on board--took one and placed in it his family and effects, and another gentleman and lady or two, and put out for the shore. Another boat was procured and loaded with person until one man, attempting to get in, turned it over. All save two out of fifteen perished. Among that number was no doubt the subject of this notice. His body was

found on the following Friday about two miles below the wreck, on a sand bar, with his clothes and boots on. He had his money about his person, a list of road hands, and two copies of the *A. R. Presbyterian*. His general appearance and the religious papers inspired the finders with a respect for his remains, which caused him to have the body cared for and buried as decently as the nature of the case would admit. The money, after paying expenses, was kept and handed over to the afflicted father, who arrived at the scene of the disaster about thirty hours after the burial. . . . [He was a] member of Monticello congregation . . . [and] left a wife and two children.

May 13, 1869

Died in Choctaw Co., Miss., February 27th, 1869, **Elijah Wilbanks**, in the sixty seventh year of his age. . . native of Anderson District, S. C. where he grew up, settled, and spent the larger portion of his life. He was happily united in marriage to Nancy Pressly--daughter of David and Ann Pressly, and blessed with a large family of sons and daughters, among whom are Henry Wilbanks of Tippah Co., Miss and Rev. J. S. Wilbanks of Arkansas. . . . [was] an elder in Generostee congregation until he emigrated to the West some eleven years ago.

Married on Thursday evening, the 6th of May, inst., Mr. **John Partlow, Jr.** of Abbeville and Miss **Susie Matthews** of Edgefield--a graduate of the Due West Female College.

May 27, 1869

Married by Rev. J. A. Lowry on the 27th of April, Mr. **Frank Snodgrass** and Miss **Lizzie Taylor**. All of Dallas Co., Ala.

January 6, 1870

Departed this life near Starkville, Miss. on the 30th of October, 1869, Mrs. **Nancy Cross**, the wife of Maj. Wm. H. Cross, aged 51 years. Her disease was pneumonia . . . [she] became a member of the Associate Reformed Presbyterian church in Starkville at the time of its organization about thirty years ago. . . She left a husband, four children.

Married, December 9, 1869 by Rev. S. A. Agnew, Mr. **Wm. C. Grier** and Miss **M. J. Morrow**, all of Lee County, Miss.

- - - at the residence of the bride's father, December 2d, 1869 by Rev. L. R. Burris, Mr. **James A. Haddon** and Miss **Rosa M. Davis**. All of Tippah County, Miss.

- - - on the 16th of November, 1869 by Rev. David Pressly of Starkville, Miss., Mr. **J. F. Mills** and Miss **Martha J. Dunlap** at the residence of the bride's brother near Abbeville, Lafayette County, Miss.

- - - on the 24th of November, 1869 by the Rev. H. H. Robison, Mr. **R. J. Duff** of Pontotoc County to **Miss S. C. Stuart**, of Tippah County, Miss.

- - - on the 2d of September, 1869 by Rev. Jas. H. Peoples, Mr. **J. M. Anderson** to **Miss M. J. Lusk**. All of Maury County, Tenn.

- - - by the same on the 30th of September, Mr. **John E. Walker** to **Miss Melvin A. Williams**. All of Maury County, Tenn.

- - - by the same on the 5th of October, Mr. **Wm. J. Goas** to Miss **Mary E. Scott**. All of Maury County, Tenn.

- - - by the same on the 30th of November, Mr. **Reese P. Thomas** to Miss **Tennie Fleming**. All of Maury County, Tenn.

- - - by the same on the 9th of December, Mr. **Leroy W. Scott** to Miss **Isadora Perry**. All of Maury County, Tenn.

- - - on the 17th of November, 1869 by the Rev. G. W. Johnston at the residence of the bride's aunt (Mrs. Jane Lewis), Mr. **Jno. W. McKinstry** to Miss **Pinkie E. Parrot**. All of Fayette County, Tenn.

- - - December 14th, 1869 by Rev. J. C. Chalmers, Mr. **John B. Swan** to **Miss J. E.**, daughter of A. **Grier**. All of Mecklenburg Co., N. C.

- - - December 23rd, 1869 by the same, Mr. **James Miller** to **Miss M. A. Harris**, daughter of Mr. H. C. Harris. All of York County, S. C.

- - - near Due West, December 21st, 1869 by Rev. W. E. Walters, Dr. **J. Robinson** to Miss **Amanda Pratt**.

- - - December 21st, 1869, by Rev. Mr. Trapp, Mr. **W. Kinard** to Miss **Katie Allen**. All of Edgefield County, S. C.

- - - in Edgefield County, S. C. by Rev. W. T. Farrow, Mr. **Scott Shepherd** to Miss **Ida Devore**.

- - - in Due West, December 30th by Professor Young at his residence, Mr. **Wm. Bryson** of Laurens County, S. C. to Mrs. **Mary Bryson** of Mississippi.

February 17, 1870

Died in Newton Co., Ga., Jan. 10th, 1870, Mr. **Samuel Aiken** in the 56th year of his age. . . . consistent member of Hopewell (A. R.) Church. . . left a large family.

- - - in Monticello, Ark. on the 28th of January, 1870, **Leonidas Johnston McCain**, eldest son of Wm. R. McCain of Tipton Co., Tenn. . . . member of Salem church until the fall of 1866, when he and several others went with Rev. J. A. Dickson at Monticello into the Presbyterian church . . . his death was occasioned by the re-amputation of a limb which had been amputated during the war.

Married, January 20th, 1870 by Rev. D. W. Reid, Mr. **J. D. Johnson** to Miss **E. M. Carmical**. All of Coweta Co., Ga.

March 31, 1870

Died of dropsy, December 30, 1869, **Mary Ann McBride**, wife of Joseph McBride, after a long illness leaving a husband, children . . . member of the A. R. church at Long Cane.

Departed this life, February 5th, 1870, **William Patton Laird** in the 22nd year of his age. . . .Although born and reared in the church [Cedar Spring and Long Cane], and attending upon the preaching of the Gospel, he had not made a profession of religion.

Died suddenly, almost instantly, Mrs. **Sarah McFarlin**, in the 55th year of her age, on the night of the 18th of February, 1870 . . . member of church at Long Cane.

[Also, at Long Cane] **Eva Lillian Lites**, youngest daughter of R. W. and Mary J. Lites, was born April 7th, 1868, and departed this life, February 25th, 1870.

James Franklin Boyd, son of the late Archy Boyd, received his summons March 9th, 1870. He would have completed his 16th year the 15th of June, proximo. Early deprived of his parents, he found a kind, Christian home in the house of A. Wideman, Esq.

Died in Due West, 26th inst. of an affection of the heart, Mrs. **M. Luvenia**, wife of Professor J. P. **Kennedy**, of the Due West Female College.

Miss **Isabella E. Jordan**, daughter of Jonathan and Mary Ann Jordan, died in great peace and comfort, January 20th, 1870.

In memory of **George Bryson Johnson**, son of Mr. and Mrs. J. S. Johnson, who died on the 5th inst., in the fourth year of his age. . . . Bryson was one of the lambs of the Prosperity congregation.

Died, January 26th, 1870 of chronic dysepsia in Old Providence, Augusta County, Va., **Wm. J. Callison**, in the 73rd year of his age. He was a native of Virginia, a man peculiarly of his own instinct; with faults and foibles; with virtues and excellencies, deeply laid in early education. He was fearless of remark, whether in the language of praise or dispraise, and formed his own opinions regardless of others. By strong affinities he was Associate Reformed; by other affinities he was of the world, and he died, as he said "with a strong hope of salvation through the merits of Christ [Horatio Thompson]."

Died on the 20th of February, 1870 in Old Providence of cancer, Col. **Arthur M. Moore**, aged 65 years. . . . born in Lewisburg, West Virginia. . . He has left a wife and ten children. . . He was an abiding friend of the Associate Reformed church, and could not abide innovations upon her well-defined principles.

April 14, 1870

Died on the 6th day of March, 1870 with pneumonia after an illness of ten days, **Fannie Lee**, at the age of three years and fourteen days. She was the 6th daughter of John and M. A. **Parkinson**, members of the Associate Reformed church.

Married on the 6th inst. by Rev. W. R. Hemphill at the residence of Mrs. Brewton, **R. R. Hemphill**, Esq. of Abbeville to Miss **Eugenia C. Brewton** of Spartanburg, S. C.

- - - on the 15th of March, 1870 by Rev. L. McDonald, Mr. **E. J. Lynn** and Mrs. **Maria Millen**, all of Chester County.

April 28, 1870

Died at his residence in Jefferson County, Ga. on the 11th of April, 1870, Mr. **Thomas A. McBride**, ruling elder in Bethel church.

Married on the 12 of April, 1870 by the Rev. H. H. Robison, assisted by the Rev. E. P. McClintock, Mr. **William Sanders** and Miss **Mary Ann Martin** of Tippah County, Miss.

May 12, 1870

[Miss **Jane Alexander**] was born in Rockbridge County, Va., June 10th, 1796. Her parents were A. R. Presbyterians who publicly worshipped God at Timber Ridge church and at Old Providence. In 1799, they, with all their family, emigrated to Kentucky, settled in Shelby County, and became members of an A. R. P. congregation there. In 1830, they moved to Lincoln County, Missouri. . . Miss Jane . . . [died] February 9, 1870.

Died in Chester County, S. C., December 1, 1869, Mrs. **Lititia Adams**, aged 75 years and 9 months. She professed religion in the A. R. church in 1815, and died a member of Union congregation.

Died in Laurens County, April 15, 1870, **Henry F.**, infant son of John and Jane **Wilson**, not quite four months old.

Died in Laurens County on the night of the 26th of April, 1870 at the old homestead near Bethel church, Miss **Martha Fleming** in the 72d year of her age. . . . connected herself in early life with the A. R. church at Bethel.

Died in Lancaster, Gerrard County, Ky., March 17th, 1870, Mrs. **Desdemonia**, wife of Walter C. **Bailey** . . . . born in 1811, and united herself with the A. R. church in 1834 in Shelby, Ky. . . . she leaves a husband, two sons and three daughters . . . She spent the last years of her life in connection with New Hope congregation, Madison County, Ky.

May 19, 1870

Died at his residence in York County, S. C., May 6th, 1870, Mr. **Wm. Boyce**, in the 59th year of his age. . . In his youth, Mr. Boyce professed religion in the A. R. church at Sardis, N. C., and had been a ruling elder at Blackstocks' and in the united congregations of Blackstocks' and Little Steel Creek about 32 years. . . He has left an affectionate wife, two daughters, two sons, several grandchildren.

Died of dropsy, Sabbath evening, May 8th, 1870, Mrs. **Jane Sloan**, widow of the late James Sloan, Sr. of Cannon's Creek, Newberry, S. C., aged 67 years, 3 months and 24 days. The deceased was the eldest daughter of Henry and Hannah Thompson, and was married to Jas. Sloan, son of Archibald and Fanny Sloan, December 14th, 1820. She was the mother of nine children, all of whom were dedicated to God in infancy and raised up in the nurture and admonition of the Lord. Five of her children and her husband preceded her to the tomb.

Married at the residence of the bride's father, R. G. Craig, Esq., in Dallas County, Ala, on the 10th of May, 1870 by Rev. W. J. Lowry, Rev. **J. A. Lowry** and Miss **Kittie Craig.**

May 26, 1870

Married, Tuesday morning, 17th inst., by the Rev. R. C. Grier, Rev. J. C. Boyd assisting, Rev. **E. P. McClintock** of Laurens and **Miss E. J. Young** of Due West, S. C.

- - - on the 11th inst. at "Hill Side," the residence of the bride's father, near Versailles, by Rev. N. M. Gordon, Dr. **J. Gilbert Gordon** and Miss **Emma A. Hutchison**, both of Woodford County, Ky.

July 14, 1870

Died on Monday, the 13th ult., **Nancy Stack**, daughter of F. J. and

Mary Stack, aged 15 months and some days.

Died, June 10th, 1870, **William Matthew**, son of W. J. and Sarah **Henry** of Chester County, S. C. in the 2d year of his age.

Departed this life, July 5th, 1870, **Bartholomew Jordan**, in the 84th year of his age. He was born January 10th, 1787, and spent his whole life near the spot where he breathed his last. . . . He had long been a consistent member of the Cedar Spring church. . . . His companion and most of his large family preceded him to tomb. Two children and a number of grandchildren survive.

Died on the 18th of June, 1870, **infant son** of Franklin **Young**, aged 11 months and 14 days.

Died in Abbeville village, June 17th, 1870, **Josiah Cason**, Esq. in the 83d year of his age. . . . A few years before his death [as an invalid] I [Rev. H. T. Sloan] baptized him after a sermon at the house of his son-in-law . . . [and] a few years later, and only about six months before his death . . . this aged servant of God partook of the [Lord's] Supper for the first and last time on earth.

July 28, 1870

Died, June 15th, 1870 in Pontotoc Co., Miss. at the residence of John R. Hill, Miss **Sarah S. Buchanan** in the 52d year of her age. The deceased was a native of Bedford County, Tenn. Having resided in Tuscaloosa, Ala. several years, she came to Pontotoc County more than twenty years ago. Here she lived and ministered to an aged and pious mother, who was removed by death some five years ago, since which time she has resided with a sister. For more than ten years she has been a member of the A. R. P. church at Hopewell.

September 1, 1870

Died on Tuesday, August 2d, 1870 in Freestone Co., Texas, **M. Irene**, daughter of Dr. T. J. and Martha **Bonner**, aged 17 years, eight months and a half.

Died suddenly of convulsion, July 24th, 1870, **Mary Francis**, youngest daughter of Mr. and Mrs. James L. **Morrow**.

Died in Newton County, Ga., August 15th, 1870, Mr. **John W. Aiken** in the 54th year of his age. The deceased was for many years a member of Hopewell church.

Married, August 4th, 1870 by Rev. H. T. Sloan, assisted by Rev. J. E. Boyd, Mr. - - - - - - - **Cole** and Miss **Mary Ann**, daughter of Daniel **Adkins**, all of Cedar Spring, S. C.

- - - at Abbeville C. H., on the 25th of August, 1870 by Rev. J. O. Lindsay, Mr. **White Agnew** and Mrs. - - **Knox**.

September 8, 1870

Died, July 13th, 1870 in Thomas County, Ga., **Samuel St. Clair**, only child of Bradford and Sallie **Weldon**, aged 1 year, 6 months and 24 days.

Died of flux and chills about midnight, August 2d, 1870, the day and hour of his birth, at the age of 23, **Robert I. Haithcy (?)**, member of the A. R. church at New Perth.

Died in Mecklenburg County, N. C., July 27th, 1870, Mrs. **Sarah Elizabeth Ranson**, wife of Rev. A. Ranson and daughter of Wallace and Mary Shannon. She was born near Shelbyville, Ky., April 26, 1825 and was raised near Flemingsburg and in the A. R. church at that place.

October 20, 1870

Married at Honea Path, S. C., October 13th, 1870 by Rev. W. F. Pearson, Mr. **Robert Brownlee** and Mrs. **Jane C. Glenn**.

- - -13th September, a. m. by Rev. H. L. Murphy, Mr. **Riley Wylie** and Miss **M. E. Dilahunty**.

- - - also, by the same, September 13th, p. m., Mr. **Samuel McClung** and Miss **J. M. Cooper**, all of Tipton County, Tenn.

November 3, 1870

Died of congestive chill, October 15, 1870, little **Fannie Agnes Morris**, the only daughter of the late James H. and Mrs. A. E. Morris of Hopewell, Abbeville County, S. C.

Died, August 18th, 1870, **Sarah Alice**, daughter of J. M. and R. W. **McLerkin**, aged 1 year and 9 months.

Mr. **James Gillmer** departed this life suddenly on Friday, September 3, 1870, aged 67 years, 9 months and 27 days. . . [left] a widow and a large family.

Died in Mecklenburg Co., N. C. on the 8th of August, **James Wright**, son of Rev. I. G. and Mrs. M. W. **McLaughlin**, in the 11th year of his age.

Died on the 12th of August, 1870 in Ebenezer, Miss., Mrs. **Mary Henderson**, aged 82 years, 8 months and 25 days. . . . was a native of

County Antrim, Ireland, came to America at a very early period of life, and settled in the neighborhood of Generostee, S. C. At this place she cast her lot with the church.

Died near Portersville Tenn., after a painful illness of several weeks, on September 15, 1870, **Mrs. M. A. Faulkner**, wife of John Faulkner and daughter of James and Martha McCain, in the 31st year of her age. . . . A most affectionate wife and a devoted step-mother to three little children of her husband by a former marriage.

November 17, 1870

Died of inflammation of the brain, September 25th, 1870, **Harriet Hibernia**, daughter of R. S. and Martha J. **Strange**, aged 3 years and 5 months.

Died in Chester County, S. C. on the 20th of October last after a short and painful illness, Miss **Mary**, eldest daughter of Robert and Elizabeth **Boyd** in the 43d year of her age. She had been a member of the A. R. P. church of Hopewell from her youth.

Robert M. Brown, eldest son of Mr. John Brown, departed this life November 1, 1870, aged 21 years, 9 months and a few days.

Died on the 14th of September, 1870, Mrs. **Elizabeth Stevenson**, relict of the late Andrew Stevenson, a ruling elder in Concord church. The subject of this notice was born January 29th, 1797, and had more than filled her three score and ten years. She was born and spent the whole of her long life within the bounds of the Concord congregation.

John Wideman, Esq. departed this life after a brief illness, October 28th, 1870, in great peace, aged 75 years and 4 days. . . . [earlier belonged to the Methodist church, but] in the fall of 1849, he cast his lot with the A. R. Presbyterian church at Long Cane. . . .[survived by] his aged widow, two children and a number of grand-children.

Married, Tuesday morning, 25th ult. by Rev. O. T. Porcher, **W. A. Lee**, Esq., Editor of the Abbeville *Press & Banner* and **Miss V. D. Cade**. All of Abbeville, S. C.

- - -at Aylmer East, Quebec on the 25th October, 1870, **James Aylen**, Esq., M. D. and **Celestine Jane**, daughter of the late George **Bolton**, Esq. by Rev. William Freeland, member of the A. R. Presbytery of New York and minister of the Presbyterian congregation of Aylmer.

December 1, 1870

Died in Chester County, S. C. on Sabbath, the 2d of October last, **Abigail Jane**, daughter of Maj. E. M. and Martha **Miller**, in the 8th year of her age.

Died of consumption, October 28th, 1870, Miss **Jane A. Gardner**, in the 24th year of her age. She was a member of Hopewell.

Died in Laurens County, S. C. on the 26th of July, 1870, Mrs. **Martha Compton**, in the 73d year of her age.

Died in Laurens County, S. C. on the 17th of October, 1870, Miss **Mary Swan** in the 88th year of her age. The subject of this notice was a native of County Antrim, Ireland, but emigrated to this country at an early period of life, and settled in the bounds of Cannon's Creek church, Newberry, S. C. After a brief sojurn there, she with other relatives, moved to Laurens where she passed the remainder of her days.

Died of congestion of the brain, October 18th, 1870, **Sarah Agnes**, eldest child of W. C. and I. S. **Robinson**, aged 3 years, 9 months and 12 days.

Married on the 22d ult. by Rev. J. C. Chalmers, Mr. **L. M. McAlister** of Mecklenburg County, N. C. and Miss **Addie Whisonant** of York County, S. C.

- - - at Abbeville C. H., S. C. on the 23d of November, 1870 by the Rev. J. I. Bonner, Mr. **R. M. Haddon** and Miss **Lou**, daughter of Dr. I. **Branch**.

- - -October 6th, 1870 by Rev. S. A. Agnew, Mr. **James E. McCarley** and Miss **Marrietta Haddon**. All of Union County, Miss.

- - - in Laurensville, November -- by Rev. P. F. Kistler, **Thomas B. Crews** of the *Laurensville Herald* and Miss **Celia R. Ballew**, daughter of the late Rev. David L. Ballew.

- - - on the 10th inst. by Rev. D. F. Haddon, Mr. **John Wasson** and Miss **Carrie I. Reid**, all of Laurens.

- - - the 6th of October, 1870 by Rev. D. F. Haddon, Mr. **M. C. Wright** of Spartanburg and Miss **Sarah F. Bryson** of Laurens, S. C.

December 15, 1870

Died very suddenly of congestion, December 8th, 1870, **Willie H. Dickson**, a student of Erskine College from Tipton County, Tenn. in the 18th year of his age.

Married, November 24th, 1870 by Rev. A. Ranson, Mr. **J. J. Ranson** and Miss **R. E. Hunter**, daughter of Mr. R. W. and R. B. Hunter. All of Mecklenburg County, N. C.

<u>May 25, 1871</u>

Departed this life, May 1st, 1871, after a long and painful illness, **Geo. Pressly Chiles** in the 29th year of his age. . . His mother had only preceded him a few months. . . deceased was a gallant soldier in the war.

<u>February 8, 1872</u>

Departed this life on the 8th of December, 1871 in the 4th year of her age, little **Mary McFadden**. Little more than a year ago, her father (Mr. Craig McFadden) was taken.

- - - this life in Union Co., Miss. on the 11th of September, 1871, Mrs. **Mary Ellen Newton**, wife of J. C. Newton and daughter of James and Isabella Jones, aged 19 years, 1 month and 13 days.

- - - on the 25th of November, 1871, departed this life, **Mrs. E. R. Hanna**, wife of Thomas M. Hanna, aged 44 years, 5 months and 5 days. . . . member of Associate Reformed Church, Pisgah. . . . leaves a husband and six children.

<u>February 29, 1872</u>

J. Glazier Rabb. Another citizen of Due West has fallen! On last Sabbath, the 25th, he was present at the morning and evening services of the church, apparently in good health. But before day the next morning he was dead. . . . Mr. Rabb was about 58 years of age. . . . was born in Fairfield County and lived there until some five or six weeks ago, at which time he moved to Due West to educate his two sons and two daughters. The remains of the deceased were taken on Tuesday to the family burying grave at the Brick Church, Fairfield. . . . There are two grown sons in Fairfield.

<u>October 24, 1872</u>

Died on the 13th of July, 1872 of cholera morbus, **William Arthur**, son of Nathan and Agnes **Murray**, aged about two years.

Also, on the 15th of September, 1872, **Flora E.**, daughter of Zebedec and Amanda **Morris**, aged about three years and two months.

<u>February 5, 1874</u>

Died, January 22d, 1874, **David Jamison**, in the 61st year of his age. He was born in Chester County, S. C. in 1813, came to Giles County, Tenn., where he married a Miss Anderson, thence he moved to Tipton County, whence he went to the world where there is no change of place. He leaves a widow, five sons and one daughter.

Died in Dallas County, Ark., October 4th, 1873, Mr. **Wm. Gardner,** aged 68 years. . . born in Chester County, S. C., and in early life united with the church at Hopewell., then in charge of Rev. W. Flennekin [sic]. From thence he moved to Georgia, and in 1870, he located in Arkansas, where unfortunately he could not enjoy the privilege of his church. . . . He lived to see all of his children, ten in number, united with the church of their father.

Died in Iredell County, N. C., September 12th, 1873, Mr. **Neel McAuley,** aged 63 years, after a confinement of several weeks. He was one of the fathers of the church, having served about forty seven years as a ruling elder in Coddle Creek congregation. His name is connected with the good days of olden time, and is associated with those of Boyce, Witherspoon, Grier, and many other great and good men who sprang up in Sardis congregation of Mecklenburg County, N. C. during the ministry of Rev. Isaac Grier. . . . He left behind a widow, six daughters and three sons.

Married at the residence of the bride's father on Monday, 21st January, 1874 by Rev. D. G. Phillips, Rev. **W. J. Lowry,** pastor of the Presbyterian church, Selma, Ala. and Miss **Mamie C. Dixon,** daughter of Dr. R. K. Dixon of Jefferson County, Ga.

- - - at the residence of the bride's father, December 2d, 1873 by Rev. Calvin Pressly, Mr. **W. C. Spence** and **Miss S. C. Anderson,** all of Lafayette County, Miss.

- - - in Jessamine County, Ky. on the 27th of January, 1874 by Rev. J. F. Baker, Mr. **John Rennick** and Miss **Thorna Dewerson.**

- - - in Columbia, S. C. on Tuesday evening the 27th ult., at the residence of the bride's mother by Rev. J. H. Bryson, Mr. **E. Eugene Pelot** and Miss **Ella S. Nixon.**

May 7, 1874

Died, March 2d, 1874, Mrs. **Hannah Kibler,** in the 47th year of her age. Mrs. Kibler connected herself with the A. R. Presbyterian church at Prosperity, Newberry County, S. C. in early life and maintained a good confession up to the day of her death.

Died in Anderson County, S. C., April 28th, 1874, Miss **Margaret Stevenson,** aged about 74 years. This is the third time that death hath visited the family of John Stevenson within eleven months, causing him to mourn the loss of a wife and two sisters. The last deceased connected herself with the A. R. P. church in her youth, under the pastorate of Rev. Robert Irwin.

John Jamison, a ruling elder of Hopewell, died at his residence in Chester County, S. C. on the 3d of April, 1874 in the 78th year of his age.

. . . more than thirty years ago elected ruling elder in [Hopewell A. R. P. church].

May 28, 1874

Died in Tipton County, Tenn. on the 20th of March, 1874, Mr. **James Wright, Sr.**, aged 82 years. Mr. Wright was born in Lancaster County, S. C., but removed with his family some forty years ago to Tennessee. They were among the first Associate Reformed people who came seeking their fathers in the Great West. . . . He was present at the organization of the Salem church, and was among the petitioners calling for the pastoral services of the Rev. John Wilson.

Married, May 20th, 1874, near Belton, S. C. by Rev. W. P. Martin, Mr. **J. L. Norrell** and Miss **Dora J. Kuhlmann**, all of Abbeville County, S. C.

- - - on the 21st of May, 1874 by Rev. R. W. Brice, Mr. **Robert B. Mills** and Miss **E. R.**, daughter of Dr. S. W. B. **McClurkin**. All of Chester County.

- - - May 26th, 1874 in Newberry County, S. C. by Rev. E. P. McClintock, **Milton A. Carlisle**, Esq. of Okolona, Miss. and Miss **Rosa A. McMorris** of the former county.

June 4, 1874

Died near Yorkville, York County, S. C., May 8th, 1874, **infant daughter** of J. R. and M. A. **Miller**, aged about 5 hours.

Died of "croup' or 'hives,' March 1st, 1874, **Oliver Haden,** son of J. A. and S. Jane **Craig**, aged 4 years, 8 months and 14 days.

Died near Blackstocks' church, York County, S. C., May 24th, 1874, Mrs. **Mary Harris**, widow of the late Hugh Harris, Sr., aged nearly 74 years. . . . for the last twenty three years an active member in the united congregation of Blackstocks and Little Steel Creek.

Died, May 17th, 1874, Mrs. **Isabella Jane McCrum**, wife of Mr. John McCrum, aged 23 years, 2 months and 7 days. Mrs. McCrum connected herself with the A. R. P. Church at Ebenezer, Tippah County, Miss., in the morning of her existence . . . . leaves a husband and little daughter.

July 30, 1874

Margaret Cabeen, infant of Robert and Nancy C. **Stevenson** of Edgefield County, S. C., died on the 24th of June, 4 months and 15 days old.

Sarah K. Fennel, wife of Robert H. Fennel, departed this life, January 24th, 1874. . . . She was the mother of three children: two of these preceded her to the grave. . . . [and] one, an infant about three months old when the mother died, yet lingers.

Died in Union County, Miss., on the 17th of June, 1874, **Joseph H. Sanders**, son of Mr. William and the late Mrs. Araminta Sanders, aged 27 years and 10 days.

Died in Guntown, Lee County, Miss. on the morning of Wednesday, July 15th, 1874, at 15 minutes before 9 o'clock, Mrs. **Mary Melinda (Agnew) Richey**, aged 29 years, 2 months and 5 days. The subject of this notice was a daughter of the late Dr. E. Agnew, and was born in Due West, S. C., May 10th, 1845. In 1852, her father removed to Mississippi, and here Mary grew up to womanhood, and fulfilled the mission of her short life. She graduated at the Presbyterial Female Collegiate Institute at Pontotoc in 1862. . . . In 1867, she was married to Mr. L. A. Richey of Guntown . . . [leaves] husband and two little children.

Married on the 9th of July by Rev. R. W. Brice, Mr. **John Simpson** of Chester, S. C. and Miss **Nancy Lathan**, daughter of Samuel Lathan.

August 6, 1874

Died near Crowder's Mountain, N. C., May 2d, 1874, **Joseph Boyce Pearson**, son of Wm. Pearson, in his 21st year.

Departed this life in Union County, Miss., on the 19th of June, 1874, Mrs. **Sara F. Jones**, consort of Robert O. Jones and daughter of Mr. John Carlisle.

Died, June 29th, 1874 at the residence of her son, Wm. Miller, Mrs. **Ann Montgomery**, aged 84 years, 8 months and 28 days. . . . During her earlier and later days she was in connection with the Presbyterian (O. S.) church; but throughout the middle and greater portion of her life was in the communion and fellowship of the A. R. P. church.

Died at 5 o'clock, a. m., July 19th, 1874, Miss **Nancy Hannah McKemy**, aged 52 years, 2 months and 19 days.

August 13, 1874

Mrs. **Addie McKelvey**, daughter of Samuel Jordan, Esq. of Abbeville, S. C. and wife of Mr. McKelvey of Augusta, Texas, died at home, June 9th, 1874. . . . As a girl we knew her best, once an inmate of our house, we remember her as a sprightly, amiable, lovely girl. during a revival season at Long Cane, Abbeville, S. C. in August, 1858, she professed faith in the Lord Jesus. In December following she was united in marriage to Mr. H. McKelvey, and some time after they moved to Texas.

August 20, 1874

Died at his residence near Fredonia, Union County, Miss., July 6, 1874, **Obadiah Buchanan**, in the 64th year of his age. Mr. Buchanan was the son of John Buchanan and was born in Bedford County, Tenn., in 1811. He joined the church at Head Springs, under the ministry of Rev. H. Bryson, about the year 1828. He removed to Tuscaloosa, Ala. in 1832, and to Pontotoc (now Union) about 1848. When Hopewell church was organized--May 24th, 1851-- he was one of the persons elected to be a ruling elder over that congregation. He was married to Miss Eliza Hunt of Bibb County, Ala in 1834. His widow with four sons and five daughters, are left.

Mrs. **Jane Robinson McBride**, wife of Mr. Thomas McBride, departed this life after a brief illness, May 12th, 1874, in the 67th year of her age.

August 27, 1874

Died, July 14th, 1874 in Yorkville, S. C. of cholera infantum, an **infant daughter** of W. S. and Mary E. **McClelland**. Aged 27 days.

Died, July 23d, 1874 at his residence on Broad Creek, Rockbridge County, Va., Mr. **James Miller**, aged 87 years, 2 months and 26 days. For more than fifty years he was a pious and consistent member of the A. R. Presbyterian church; and for the last twenty five years a ruling elder.

Died, Sabbath evening, August 9th, 1874, near Crowder's Mount, N. C., **Mrs. A. M. Carson**, wife of Edward Carson, in the 41st year of her age. The deceased was the daughter of Samuel Torrance of Long Creek. . . . [joined] Pisgah A. R. Presbyterian church along with her first husband, Wilson Love, by whom she had two children that yet live. Mr. Love died in the battle around Richmond. . . . She leaves five children, husband.

Died, August 8th, 1874, Mrs. **Mary Patrick**, wife of Rev. John Patrick, in the 42d year of her age. Mrs. Patrick was the daughter of John Patrick of Union County, S. C. She was married on the 23d day of February, 1854, when her husband Rev. J. Patrick was exactly fifty (50) years old. In the fall of 1855, they moved to Pope County, Ark. . . . Three children, two sons and one daughter, are left behind.

Married, on Tuesday evening the 18th inst., in the Presbyterian church of Williamston by Rev Mauldin, Mr. **R. E. Hill** of Abbeville, S. C. and Miss **Mamie T. Hamilton**, of the former place.

September 3, 1874

Died of whooping cough in Jefferson County, Ga. on the 13th of August, 1874, **George Little**, infant son of George L. and Mary E. **Cain**, aged 8 months and 2 weeks.

Married, August 20th, 1874 at 10 o'clock, a. m. by Rev. W. F. Pearson, Mr. **J. L. Stewart** and Miss **J. Lillie Stewart**, daughter of Dr. J. A. Stewart. All of Ninety Six, S. C.

September 17, 1874

Died after a protracted illness in Laurens County, S. C., August 3d, 1874, Mrs. **Isabella K. Blakely**, wife of David Blakely and only daughter of Robert and Martha Sloan, in the 49th year of her age. . . .[member] of Bethel church [and] some time later she moved her membership to Providence congregation.

Died suddenly in Laurens County, S. C., August 30th, 1874, Mrs. **Mary A. Wilson**, wife of William Wilson and daughter of Silas and Jane Motes, in the 34th year of her age.

Married by the Rev. D. G. Phillips at the house of the bride's mother, Thursday the 3d of September, 1874, Rev. **A. L. Patterson** and Miss **Alice Trimble**. All of Jefferson County, Ga.

October 1, 1874

Died of dropsy, August 31st, 1874, Mrs. **Martha Gilmer**, aged 86 years. . . . member of the A. R. Presbyterian church at Generostee, Anderson, S. C.

Died in Newton County, Ga., August 30th, 1874, Mrs. **Susannah Boyd**, wife of Jas. Boyd and daughter of Samuel and Nancy Thompson. Aged 38 years. The deceased connected with the A. R. church at Hopewell in her youth.

Mrs. **Mary J. Ketchin**, aged 36 years and 19 days, departed this life, August 23d, 1874. . . . [While on the way to church] A messenger arrives, "Mrs. Ketchin's horse ran away, and in attempting to jump from the buggy, she has sustained a serious injury." Yes, so serious that she never spoke, was never conscious, and breathed but a few hours. . . . member of Union congregation, Chester County, S. C. . . . The deceased leaves a widowed mother. . . . a brother and two sisters, and an only child, a son - - to mourn her loss, her husband having preceded her some years.

Married on the 15th of September, 1874 at the parsonage by Rev. R. F. Bradley, Mr. **John Simpson** and Miss **R. L. Harris**. All of Anderson County, S. C.

October 29, 1874

Died in Dallas County, Ala. on the 8th of October, 1874 of Yellow chills in the 11th year of his age, **Eddie A. Johnson**, only son of J. S. and G. A. Johnson.

Charles Fudge, aged 69 years and 1 month, departed this life on the 19th of September, 1874. . . . member of A. R. P. church, Union congregation.

Died at her residence in Lee County, Miss. on Tuesday evening, September 22d, 1874, Mrs. **Elizabeth Ann Bryson** in the 86th year of her age. The subject of this notice was the daughter of Thomas and Margaret Blakely, and was born in Laurens County, November 14th, 1788. In 1804, she was married to James Bryson and soon after joined the Associate Reformed church at Bethel. Early in the year 1833 her husband died and she was left a widow with thirteen children to care for. In 1836, the church at Providence was organized by Rev. E. E. Pressly, and Mrs. Bryson then transferred her membership from Bethel to that place. In 1851, she, in company with several of her children, emigrated to Mississippi and settled in Itawamba (now Lee) County. Her pastor, Rev. J. L. Young, moved at the same time, and when Bethany church was organized June 5th, 1852, Mrs. Bryson was one of the little band that entered that organization. . . . of her fifteen children, seven survive her.

Married, October 8th, 1874 by Rev. C. B. Betts, Mr. **S. A. Rodman** of Lancaster County, S. C. and **Miss S. C. Waters** of Chester County, S. C.

- - - on Thursday, October 22d, 1874 in Atlanta by Rev. D. Wills, D. D., Dr. **J. W. Simpson** and Mrs. **John D. Williams**. Both of Laurens.

December 3, 1874

Palmyra Lavinia Purdy, the only child of Mr. and Mrs. R. R. Purdy, was suddenly cut down, September 20th, 1874, aged 1 year, 7 months and 20 days.

Mrs A. C. Gleghorn died of consumption on the 14th of October, 1874, at their home in Lincoln County, Tenn. in the 49th year of her age. . . . [member of] the church at Bethel.

Died of consumption in Fairfield County, S. C., May 3d, 1874, Mrs. **Margaret Jane Cabeen** in the 40th year of her age. The subject of this notice was a daughter of Samuel H. and Cynthia Stevenson. In 1860, she was married to Mr. Thomas Cabeen, who died at Richmond during the war. After the death of her husband, she returned with her only child to the home of her father, where she afterwards lived, and where she died. . . . [belonged to] the church at New Hope.

On the 31st of August, 1874, **Thomas Young Cabeen**, the only child of his deceased parents, T. and M. J. Cabeen, departed this life after several weeks of severe suffering from an affection of the brain, aged 12 years and 10 months.

- - - November 5th, 1874 by Rev. C. B. Betts at the residence of the bride's father, Mr. **J. N. Blankenship** of Mecklenburg County, N. C. and Miss **Sallie Tarborough** of Chester, S. C.

- - -- by the same, November 11th, 1874 at the residence of the bride's mother, Mr. **T. M. Allen** and Miss **Sue Cornwell**. All of York, S. C.

- - - by the same, November 12th, 1874 at the residence of the bride's father, Mr. **Harris Williams** and Miss **Mary Anderson**. All of York County, S. C.

- - - November 24th, 1874 at Mrs. Mill's, the bride's mother by Rev. W. F. Pearson, Mr. **John G. LeGare** and **Mrs. Charlie M. Hamilton**. All of Abbeville, S. C.

Married at Varennes, November 26th, 1874 by Rev. W. F. Pearson, assisted by Rev. E. E. Frierson, Mr. **John W. Thompson** and Miss **Mattie L.**, eldest daughter of Col. J. W. **Norris**. All of Anderson, S. C.

- - - at the parsonage on Oak Hill on the 29th ult. by Rev. David Pressly of Starkville, Miss., assisted by Rev. John Miller, D. D., Prof. **C. S. Dale** and Miss **Janie P. Miller** of Wilcox County, Ala.

December 17, 1874

Died in Laurens County, S. C., September 23d, 1874 of diptheria, little **Walter Hill**, son of Mr. B. M. and S. A. **Hill**. Aged 5 years.

Also, October 1st, 1874, **Nancy Elizabeth**, daughter of Mr. James and Mary **Nabors**. Aged 18 months and 25 days.

January 7, 1875

Capt. **John Cowan** was raised within a mile of Due West, and spent his days in the vicinity. For fifteen years he had been a sufferer, although only occasionally confined to his bed. His affliction was thought to be either cancer or ulceration of the stomach. . . . after a great deal of suffering, he was released on the morning of the 27th of December. . . . was a member of the Greenville (Presbyterian) Church. . . . was twice married--the last time to the youngest daughter of the late Abram Haddon of Due West who with three children survive him. Several children of the former marriage remain to weep over his grave. Some of them are far away. One who went to the far West has not been heard from for ten or fifteen years.

Died, July 18th, 1874 of cholera infantum, **Lilly Quinn**, daughter of James Q. and Mary E. **Falls**, aged 19 months and 21 days.

Died of diptheria on the 18th of November, 1874, **Henry White**, son of Samuel and Hannah **Wells**, in the 4th year of his age.

On the 4th of December, 1874 of the same disease, **Mary Wells**, daughter of the same. [M. Oates].

Died on the 22d of October, **Jannie B.**, infant son of J. A. and M. J. **Moore**. . . . born on 25th of June.

Died in Fairfield County, S. C., December 6th, 1874, Miss **Cynthia Isabella**, daughter of Samuel H. and C. **Stevenson**. This is the third time in the last eight months that death has entered that household.

Died at his residence in Charlotte, N. C., December 25th, 1874, Dr. **Wm. A. Pressly**. . . . member of Steel Creek (ARP), but having removed to Charlotte, he united with the mission church there. . . . leaves a widow, four daughters and one son.

Married in Lincoln County, Tenn. on the 9th of December, 1874 by Rev. J. B. Muse, Mr. **Robert Stewart** and Miss **Lizzie Good**.

- - - December 17th, 1874 on Long Cane by Rev. H. T. Sloan, Mr. **James Pucket** and Miss **Sarah Crawford**, oldest daughter of Mr. Robt. Crawford.

- - - December 24th, 1874 on Long Cane by Rev. H. T. Sloan, **Mr. Wells** of Mt. Carmel and Miss **Joanna Brown**, second daughter of Samuel Brown.

- - - on the 11th of December, 1874 by Rev. M. Oates, Mr. **J. M. Ferguson** and Mrs. **Martha A. Oates**.

- - - by the same on the 10th of December, 1874, Mr. **J. G. Ferguson** and Miss **Jane Sinclair**. All of Pope County, Ark.

- - - on the 17th of December, 1874 by Rev. C. B. Betts, Mr. **W. C. Abernathy** and Miss **Mary Daniel**. All of York County, S. C.

- - - by the same on the 22d of December, 1874, Mr. **J. C. Dickey** of Chester County and Miss **Jennie Crook** of York County.

- - - by the same on the 24th of December, 1874, Mr. **James Curry** of York County and Miss **Mary McElroy** of Chester County, S. C.

- - - by the same on the 24th of December, 1874, Mr. **John Dickey, Sr.** and Miss **M. J. Simpson**. All of Chester, S. C.

- - - on the 23d of December, 1874 in Due West, S. C. by Rev. W. L. Pressly, Mr. **J. D. Brownlee** and Miss **M. A. Bonner**, daughter of the editor of the *A. R. Presbyterian*.

- - - on December 15th, 1874 at the house of John O. Crawford, York

County, S. C., uncle of the bride, by Rev. E. E. Boyce, Mr. **A. C. Pursley**, son of Wm. Pursley, and Miss **Lizzie Crawford**.

- - - by the same, December 17th, 1874, near Crowder's Mount, N. C., Mr. **John Crawford** and Miss **Mary Whitesides**, daughter of Edward Whitesides.

September 23, 1875

Died, September 13th, 1875, **Hattie Young**, infant daughter of E. P. and E. J. **McClintock**, aged 9 days.

- - - in Prosperity congregation, Mecklenburg Co., N. C., **George Franklin**, son of Jas. W. and Margaret L. **Smith**. Aged 2 years, 6 months and 11 days

Mr. **Samuel Gladney** died at his residence near Auburn, Lincoln Co., Mo. on the 13th of August, 1875. Aged 86 years. . . . born in Fairfield District, S. C., July 9th, 1789, where some of his relatives still reside. He came to Missouri in 1819, and settled upon the place of his death, when this part of the State was little less than a wilderness. When quite young, Mr. Gladney united himself with the O. S. Presbyterian Church and continued in that communion, though his wife and children connected themselves with the Associate Reformed Presbyterian Church at Mt. Zion.

Married, on the 4th of August, 1875 by Rev. T. J. Bonner, Mr. **Calvin Shanks** and Miss **Lucinda Dawson**. All of Freestone County, Texas.

- - - at the residence of the bride's father on the 2d of September, 1875 by Rev. C. S. Young, Mr. **W. A. Prosser** and Miss **Mollie C. Leonard**. All of Marshall Co., Tenn.

- - - at Newberry, S. C. on the morning of the 8th, inst., at the residence of Capt. A. P. Pifer, by Rev. R. A. Fair, Mr. **W. I. Clawson** of Yorkville, S. C. and Miss **Bettie W. Fair**, second daughter of Dr. Drury Fair of Newberry, S. C.

- - - at the residence of the bride's father, Mr. Henry Moffatt on the 9th of September, 1875 by Rev. J. P. Marion, assisted by Rev. C. B. Betts, Dr. **T. D. Marion** and Miss **Julia G. Moffatt**. All of Chester, S. C.

October 7, 1875

Died in Union County, Miss., September 13th, 1875, **Samuel James Bryson**, son of John and Mrs. Louisa Bryson in the fifth year of his life.

Died in Lee Co., Miss., September 15th, 1875, **James Cornelius**

Galloway, son of John B. and Mrs. Mollie Galloway, in the sixth year of his age.

Mrs. **Jane West Pressly**, wife of the late Rev. Samuel Pressly, D. D., died at her residence in Laurensville, S. C., on the 1st of August, 1875. . . . a native of Ireland. She came with her father, Mr. Andrew Todd, and relatives, to this country very early in life. . . . in her seventy eighth year at the time of her death. She was a widow for more than twenty years. Her husband died while a professor in Franklin College, Ga.

October 21, 1875

Departed this life on the 9th of October, 1875, **Mrs. Julia G. Marion**, eldest daughter of T. H. and Mary Moffatt. . . . born August 8th, 1859. [had been married only 4 weeks].

November 25, 1875

Died of diptheria at Princeton, Ark., September 14th, 1875, **Addie Lee Reid**, daughter of Dr. Chas. Reid, aged 6 years, 1 month and 28 days.

Mrs. **Nancy McElwee**, daughter of Wm. McElwee of Bethany, S. C. . . . [died] September 20th, 1875, at her brother's house, J. N. McElwee of York. . . . For many years she kept a tidy house for her widowed father and for seventeen years, her husband, James McElwee enjoyed her extraordinary diligence.

Died on Saturday, 18th of September, 1875, at the house of J. N. McElwee, **Catherine Bell**, in her 4th year. . . . only daughter of Robert and Mattie McElwee of diptheria.

Died in York County, S. C., October 13th, 1875, Mrs. **Mary Quinn**, wife of John Quinn, in her 84th year. . . . last of her father's family, Thos. Ferguson, Pisgah. In her early youth, nearly sixty years ago, she married and came to Seven Mile post on the Kings Mountain road above Yorkville. . . . reared a family of twelve children, ten of whom are in their graves. Five sons were victims of the war. . . . thirty four grand children [member of Bethany].

Died of consumption on the night of the 16th September, 1875, Mrs. **Martha Jane Smith**. . . . daughter of Steven W. and Mary Byrn. . . . raised in Benton Co., West Tennessee. . . . [married] V. B. Smith on the 21st of December, 1859, and in 1866, they moved to the southern part of Kentucky. . . . in 1873, she and her husband moved to Lafayette Co., Miss. A Methodist. . . leaves four children.

Died of diptheria on the 5th of August, 1875, **Maggie J. Whitesides** in the 8th year of her age; on the 20th of September, of the same disease, **Mary J. Whitesides**, in the 6th year of her age; on the

26th of September of the same disease, **Jailey A. Whitesides,** in the 4th year of her age. All children of Mr. and Mrs. R. G. Whitesides.

Died in Fairfield Co., S. C. on the 20th day of October, 1875, Mrs. **Martha,** wife of James **Dunbar,** in the 62d year of her age. . . . member of New Hope . . . leaves an aged husband and seven children.

Died in Wilcox Co., Ala., October 2d, 1875, Rev. **A. Rosser Purifoy,** in the 36th year of his age . . . . brother minister of the Methodist Episcopal church and connected with the A. R. Presbyterian church of Oak Hill, Ala. by marriage and ties of Christian conscience.

Married, on the morning of the 21st October, 1875 by the Rev. J. A. Lowry, **A. P. Young,** Esq. of Selma, Ala. and Miss **Julia W. Craig,** youngest daughter of R. G. Craig.

- - - by the same on the night of the 21st October, 1875, Mr. **Thomas Chisolm** and Miss **Sallie McCullough.**

December 2, 1875

Married by Rev. W. L. Pressly, Thursday, the 25th of November, 1875, Mrs. **John Wren** and Miss **Euphemia,** daughter of Mr. Jno. M. **Bell** of Due West, S. C..

- - - by Rev. W. L. Pressly, assisted by Rev. W. M. Grier, D. D., at 11 a. m., Wednesday, the 1st of December, 1875, Dr. **Lester Hunter** of Sardis, N. C. and Miss **Mattie,** daughter of Rev. J. **Boyce,** D. D. of Due West, S. C.

- - - by Rev. J. I. Bonner, at 11 a. m., Wednesday, the 1st December, 1875, Mr. **R. A. Bryson** of Guntown, Miss. and Miss **Bettie,** daughter of Mrs. Jane **McDill** of Due West, S. C.

- - - on the 23d of November, 1875, by Rev. H. T. Sloan, Mr. **John W. Harvely** and Miss **Katie,** youngest daughter of Mrs. Jane A. **Davis.** All of Long Cane, S. C.

- - - November 25th, 1875 in Blackstock's church, York Co., S. C., by Rev. J. C. Chalmers, Mr. **Lewis M. Grier** and Miss **Emma S. Elms.** Both of Mecklenburg Co., N. C.

December 9, 1875

Died in Mecklenburg Co., N. C., Back Creek congregation, **William Baxter,** third son of I. M. and M. A. Grier, aged 5 years and 5 months.

- - - at her residence in Jefferson County, Ga., on the 17th of November, 1875, Mrs. **Mary Lowry,** relict of Rev. Joseph Lowry, former pastor of Bethel and Ebenezer. . . . daughter of David Pressly, Esq. of Cedar Spring, S. C. and sister of Drs. J. T. and J. P. Pressly, Drs. S. and G. W. Pressly in her seventy ninth year . . . widow for thirty five years.

December 16, 1875

Married, December 7th, 1875, at 9 o'clock, a. m., at the bride's mother, by Rev. W. F. Pearson, Mr. **James L. Little** of Anderson and Miss **Gustava Bowen** of Abbeville, S. C.

- - - on the 25th of November, 1875, at the residence of the bride's father, by Rev. R. A. Fair, Mr. **Alan Johnstone** and Miss **Lilla R.**, daughter of Dr. T. B. **Kennerly**.

- - - on Thursday, November 25th, 1875 by the Rev. E. P. McClintock at the residence of the bride's mother, Mr. **Jas. P. Sligh** and Miss **Fanny Cameron**. All of Newberry, S. C.

- - - on Thursday, November 25th, 1875 at the residence of the bride's father, by the Rev. W. D. Rice, Mr. **J. Henry Dorroh** and Miss **Dora Reeder**. All of Newberry County, S. C.

December 23, 1875

Married on the evening of the 2d of December, 1875, at the residence of the bride's father, by Rev. C. B. Betts, Mr. **James Glasscock** and Miss **Fannie McFadden**. All of York County, S. C.

- - - at the residence of the bride's mother on Tuesday, December 7th, 1875, by Rev. L. Broaddus, Mr. **Wm. C. Latimer** of Abbeville, S. C. and Miss **Susie J. Mobley** of Edgefield, S. C.

- - - November 3d, 1875 by Rev. S. A. Agnew, Mr. **D. A. Caldwell** of Lee County and Miss **Belle Griffin** of Prentiss Co., Miss.

- - - November 24th, 1875 by Rev. S. A. Agnew, Mr. **John W. Bryson** of Prentiss and Miss **Maggie E. Young**, daughter of Mr. F. A. Young of Lee County, Miss.

- - - November 25th, by Rev. S. A. Agnew, Mr. **Edward Flannagan** and Miss **S. E. Murphy**. Both of Lee County, Miss.

- - - December 2d, 1875 by Rev. S. A. Agnew, Mr. **John Connoway** and Miss **S. F. Byers**. Both of Lee County, Miss.

- - - December 2d, 1875 by Rev. S. A. Agnew, Mr. **J. H. Holland** and Miss **Carrie E. Whisenant**, both of Union County, Miss.

March 16, 1876

Mrs. **A. C. McGill**, born April 7, 1829, died of a protracted and painful illness, March 1st, 1876. . . . wife of Wm. McGill of Bethany, S. C.

Died, February 20th, 1876, **Mrs. S. J. Hart**, wife of W. C. Hart, in the 48th year of her age. She leaves a husband and two daughters.

Died February 23d, 1876, **James Hogue**, infant of D. A. and Martha **Crossen**. Aged 1 year, 6 months and 3 days. The circumstances of this death were distressing. Mr. Crossen had kindled a fire in a log near his house for the purpose of burning out a feeding trough for his cattle, and had then walked over to a near neighbor to be absent only a short time. Mrs. Crossen was drawing water at the well. Their two children were playing in the yard. This little boy set his clothes on fire, and, although his mother reached him in a few moments, he was so badly burned that he survived only about half a day.

Died at Idaville, Tenn., November 25th, 1876, Mrs. **O. Caroline**, wife of John G. **McCain** and daughter of Lusk and Margaret Davis. Aged 34 years . . . [had previously] lost five tender little babes out of her own family of seven children.
Died at Prentiss County, Miss., February 13th, 1876, **Lula Ceralvo Haddon**, child of John N. and Lou Haddon. Aged 4 months and 24 days.

Died in Lee County, Miss. of meningetis, February 17, 1876, **Sarah Gertrude Gamble**, youngest child of W. G. and Mrs. E. I. Gamble, aged 1 year and 14 days.

Died in Newton County, Ga., on the 25th of January, 1876, Mrs. **Susan Cowan**, wife of J. A. Cowan and daughter of Mrs. Nancy Weir. Aged 22 years, 11 months and 8 days. Married just one year and a few days.

Died in Mecklenburg Co., N. C., March 6th, 1875, Miss **Rachel A. Goodrum** in her 35th year. . . . her body lies in the graveyard near Gilead.

Died January 3d, 1876, **William Daniel McAdams**, a son of S. H. McAdams. Aged five and a half years.

Died in Lincoln County, Tenn., January 2d, 1876, Miss **Grizelda Jane Hays** in the 29th year of her age. . . . daughter of Mr. A. P. Hays of Prosperity and grand daughter of Wm. Strong.

Died on the morning of March 5th, 1876, **Robert Whitesides**, being about six weeks over 78 years of age. . . . elected a ruling elder at Smyrna, York County, S. C. at its organization some 35 or 40 years ago. . . . benevolent to a fault.

Mattie Wylie Roddy, infant daughter of W. L. and Annie B. Roddy, departed this life November 12th, 1875. Aged 2 years and 20 days.

Mrs. **Mary Weed**, wife of A. J. Weed of Long Cane departed this life, February 9th, 1876, aged 73 years, 9 months and 1 day. . . . had been a professor of religion for fifty three years and died in the fifty second year of her married life, having lived to see her great grandchildren.

Died in Louisville, Ga., January 6th, 1876, Mrs. **Rosa Little**, wife of Mr. William Little, in the 21st year of her age -- member of a Baptist church. . . . has been but a brief year a happy bride and a month since the death of her only child.

Married by Rev. David Pressly on the 1st of March, 1876 at the residence of the bride's mother, Mr. **G. B. Arnold** and Miss **Nannie Vincent**. All of Oktibehha County, Miss.

- - - on the 8th of March, 1876, at the residence of the bride's father, by Rev. David Pressly, Mr. **H. D. Bowe** and Miss **S. L. Estes**. All of the vicinity of Starkville, Miss.

September 5, 1878

Died in Laurens Co., S. C., July 18th, 1878, **Sallie Josephine**, infant daughter of A. S. and Fannie **Nichols**, aged six months.

Died in Chester Co., S. C., on the 26th of July, 1877, Miss **Anna McDaniel** in the 91st year of her age. . . . oldest member of Hopewell Church.

Died in Tippah County, Miss., April 12th, 1878, **Joseph Allen**, second son of J. W. and Mattie **Sanders**. Aged 7 years, 2 months and 2 days.

Died in Laurens Co., S. C., July 4, 1878, **Maggie P.**, daughter of Robert F. and Josephine **Bryson**. Aged 6 years and 6 months.

Died in Statesville, N. C., July 28th, 1875, Mrs. **Esther White**, wife of W. W. White and daughter of the late John Kistler. Aged 41 years. . . . leaves husband and children.

Died May 14th, 1878, near Yorkville, S. C., Mrs. **Catherine Jenkins**, wife of L. Jenkins, in the 57th year of her age. . . . long member of Sharon. . . leaves husband and children.

Died in Union County, Miss. on Monday morning, July 28th, 1878, Miss **Eliza Jane Branyon**, daughter of Henry and Margaret Branyan. Aged 25 years, 5 months and 7 days. . . . born February 23d, 1853. In 1866 joined Bethany Church.

Departed this life in Union County, Miss., June 11th, 1878, Mrs. **Jane R.**, wife of J. H. **Wright** and daughter of Mrs. Jane Stewart, in the 42nd year of her age. Mrs. Wright connected herself with the church at Ebenezer more than twenty years ago, while visiting relatives in that congregation. Soon after this she returned to the home of her father (Mr. Isaac Stewart) in Wilcox County, Ala. and united with Lebanon Church. In 1865, she was happily united in marriage to Mr. J. H. Wright. A few years after she with her husband and other relatives moved to this section and enrolled as a member of Ebenezer. She leaves five children.

Mr. **James Stewart** of Newton County, Ga. departed this life, July 18th, 1878, in his 81st year. Born and reared in Chester County, S. C. where he married December 23, 1819, and about the same time connected with the ARP church. He moved to Georgia in 1825, and entered into the organization of the church at Hopewell, Newnan County. Five children and many grand children survive.

Died July 23d, 1878, Mrs. **Lizzie Raymond** in the 24th year of her age. . . . spent most of her life in Pope County, Ark., there she connected herself with the Old Style Presabyterian church, of which she was a member until March, 1877, at which time she and her husband moved to Shelby County, Tenn. There they connected themselves with the same denomination at Atoka, from which they and others drew their certificates about four months ago for the purpose of organizaing a new church on Big Creek, Shelby County. . . . leaves a husband and two children.

July 10, 1879

Died June 19, 1879, **Rebecca Elizabeth**, daughter of Mr. R. P. **Clinkscales**, aged 14 months and 10 days.

Died at Old Providence, Augusta County, Va., June 11th, 1879, Mrs. **Mary Callison**, wife of George Callison in the 53d year of her age.

Died at her residence in Augusta County, Va. at 9 o'clock on Sabbath morning, June 1st, 1879, Mrs. **Margaret Carson**, relicit of the late E. Carson, in the 90th year of her age. . . . In her death a light has been extinguished which has been a beacon in Old Providence for well nigh fivescore years. . . belonged to a family (Rowans) of whom she was the last upon the scroll--dating back in the origins of Old Providence Church. H. T.

Mrs. **Mary Boyd** departed this life March 8th, 1879, aged 81 years, 8 months and 8 days. . . . was born in Ireland, County Londonerry; was married there in her 23d year, and in 1825 emigrated to this country, landing in Charleston. Thence she joined her husband at Winnsboro, S. C., who it seems, had preceded her a short while. Here they remained only for a time, and finally settled within the bounds of Neely's Creek congregation. Here they lived and died, her husband preceding her by a number of years. . . . She leaves four children and many grand children.

July 24, 1879

Died at his home inDeKalb County, Ga., on the first day of April, 1879, Mr. **Joseph Stewart**, who was born in Mecklenburg Co., N. C., December, 1797, joined the ARP Church at Tirzah about the year 1819, was first married to Mary Burlison, June 20th, 1822, moved to this county the winter of 1826, wher, with a few other families, organized the ARP church in this county. He was for more than forty years a Ruling Elder. . . .His wife dying, September 29th, 1848, he was again on the 3d of January, 1850, married to Elizabeth B. Pickens, who is still living and with three of his children and many grand children. J. E. E.

Died in Union County, Miss., April 30th, 1879, Mrs. **Jane Liddell**, aged 77 years, 3 months and 2 days. . . . born in Old Pendleton District, S. C. . . . a daughter of Samuel and Sarah Roseman. In her 17th year, she was married to Col. J. S. Liddell, who preceded her to the grave about ten years. . . . in youth joined Roberts Presbyterian church. In the first settlement of north Mississippi by the whites, she came with her family to this section, and when Ebenezer (ARP) church was organized she was one of the original number . . . three daughters and one son survive.

April 29, 1880

Died on the 6th of March, 1880, **Innis Josephine**, daughter of W. J. and Josephine **Miller** of York County, s. C. . . . only two and one half years old.

Died at his home in Chester, S. C. on the 30th of March, 1880, **Thomas Torbit**, aged 76 years, 3 months and 1 day. . . . He was ordained a ruling elder in the Hopewell Church in October, 1847. . . . He was twice married. First to Miss Nancy McCullough, by whom he had two children, both of whom are dead; his last wife was Mrs. Warren Flenniken, who survives him.

May 5, 1881

Died near Troy, Tenn., about February 1st, 1881, **Myrtha Kate**, daughter of Samuel and Rizpah **Curry** . . . not quite three years old.

Mrs. **Nancy Wilson** died of consumption, April 26, 1881 in Newberry, S. C. in the 84th year of her age. This severs the last link that bound Kings Creek congregation to the distant past. She was received into that church by Rev. Charles Strong. . . . Her son being keeper of the Poor House she resided at that place and exerted a most wholesome influence on the paupers.

Died January 28th, 1881 in Rockbridge County, Va., Miss **Isabella M. Poague** in the 63d year of her age. . . . she leaves three sisters and a brother.

Departed this life in Augusta County, Va., January 30th, 1881, Mrs. **Margaret Smiley**, aged 71 years, 5 months and 28 days. About forty two years ago, the deceased joined the church at Old Providence. . . . she leaves a husband and two sons.

Died at his residence near Troy, Tenn., April 20th, 1881, Mr. **Adam Dunbar** . . . . was born in Ireland, May 5th, 1826, when about twenty one years of age he moved to White Oak, Fairfield County, S. C. There he connected with the Concord Presbyterian church and was elected an elder. He enlisted in the army, passed through the war unhurt, excepting that disease had laid seige to his system. Sometimes after the war, he located near Troy, Tenn. and was received as an elder in the A. R. Presbyterian church at that place. . . leaves a wife and six children.

Mr. **Alexander Chesnut**, husband of Mrs. Mary Ann Chesnut (lately deceased) of Prosperity church, DeKalb Co., Ga., died on the 18th of April, 1881 in the 73d year of his age. . . . was born in Chester Co., S. C., August 27, 1809, of pious parents, Mr. David and Jane Chesnut. His father David moved to the State of Georgia in 1826 or 1827, and settled close to where Hopewell Church now stands in Newton County, when the subject of this notice was quite young. He was united in marriage with Mary Ann McDill, March 22nd, 1836. In 1851, Mr. Chesnut with his family, of three sons and two daughters moved from Hopewell, Newton County to Prosperity Church in DeKalb County.

Married on the 20th of April, 1881 by Rev. Horatio Thompson, D. D., at the house of the bride's mother on Mill Creek, Timber Ridge, Mr. **Harry E. Moore** and Miss **Mary Alice**, daughter of the late Wm. A. **McClung**. All of Rockbridge County, Va.

November 1, 1883

Died of consumption in Pope County, Ark., October 1st, 1883, Mr. **R. A. Ferguson**, aged 33 years, 3 months and 17 days.

Died in Pope County, Ark., June 27th, 1883 of consumption, Miss **Mary E.**, daughter of John M. and S. R. **Ferguson**, aged 24 years and 2 months. . . member of Bethany. Survived by mother, two sons and one daughter.

Died of consumption at his home in Abbeville County, S. C., Mr. **Robt. Link** on the 29th day of September, 1883. . . . about forty years of age. . . was a member and ruling elder at the ARP church at Lodiment. . . . survived by wife and four smll children.

Departed this life at the residence of his father, four miles southeast of Starkville, Miss. on the 17th of July, 1883, **David Percy Bell,** a son of W. C. and Sallie Bell and a grandson of Mr. F. A. and Jane Ware. Aged 16 years, 5 months and 18 days.

Died of consumption in Pope County, Ark., September 29th, 1883, Mr. **A. D. Oates**, aged 64 years, 11 months and 1 day. . . . twice married. First to a Miss Ferguson, second to a Miss Beattie, daughter of the late Francis Beattie of Pisgah, N. C. By the first marriage, there were two children, by the second ten. All are living except one. And all are members of the church except three, who are minors.

Departed this life in Starkville, Okitebbeha County, Miss on the 10th of May, 1883, Mr. **Thomas Gladney**, aged 55 years, 5 months and 15 days. . . . was born in Fairfield County, S. C. When ripening into manhood, he removed west and located in Oktibehha County. . . joined ARP church. . .About this time, he was married to Miss Celia Watt, daughter of the late Mr. Charles M. and Wyatt Watt. . . . He was a farmer by profession. . . four sons and two daughters survive.

Married October 18th, 1883, at the residence of the bride's brother by Rev. W. O. Cochran, Mr. **Joseph R. Guyn** and Miss **Bettie Yeagle**. All of Woodford County, Ky.

- - -October 17th, 1883, by Rev. James A. Lowry, assisted by Rev. C. S. Young, Rev. **James L. Young** of Monticello, Ark to Miss **Jennie P. Young**, daughter of the late Rev. James M. Young of Dallas County, Ala.

January 3, 1884

Died, November 23d, 1883, **Willie Doak**, infant child of A. A. and Emma **Cousar**. Aged 8 months.

J. R. Williamson departed this life October 19th, 1883, aged 60 years. . . . leaving a wife, four sons and one daughter. . . . member of the A. R. church at Little Steel Creek.

Died in Shelby County, Tenn., November 6th, 1883, Mr. **John Parkison**, aged 63 years, 2 months and 26 days. . . . brother to Rev. Thos. Parkison (deceased) and was born in Lincoln County, Tenn. He came to this county twenty five years ago.

Died at the home of her brother at White Oak, S. C., November 19th, 1883, Miss **Eliza Patrick**, aged 66 years, 5 months and 21 days.

Died, November 7th, 1883, of cancer, Mr. **Robert Jackson Patterson**, at his home in Ebenezer, Ga. He was nearly 78 years old. . . . Born and reared in Bethel church, he in due time became a ruling elder there, and continued to discharge actively the duties of his office; first, at Bethel, afterward at Ebenezer, for more than forty years. He married a daughter of Rev. Joseph Lowry, and leaves her and six children, five sons and one daughter. After the war, like many others, he was left poor in worldly goods; but by hard struggling he succeeded in having all five of his sons graduated at Erskine College. And four of them are actively engaged in the ministry.

Died, December 3d, 1883, of old age at his home in Lincoln County, Tenn., Mr. **Samuel Gleghorn**, in the 89th year of his age. The deceased was a venerable man. It is not thought that he ever was sick. He raised and cultivated with his own hands seventy eight crops consecutively. . . . He was born on Rocky Creek, Chester, S. C., where he lived until he was about thirty. . . . There he married Mary Crawford and emigrated to Tennessee about sixty years ago, casting in his lot with Dr. Bryson and the Prosperity congregation. Thence he moved to Morton's Creek and was ordained an elder in the Zion congregation (an organization that was disbanded about thirty years ago because most of the membership migrated West) when he connected with the Bethel congregation.

Married by Rev. W. H. Millen, December 18th, 1883, Mr. **John Watson** and Miss **Anna Hall**. Both of Union County, Miss.

- - - on December 4th, 1883 at the residence of the bride's mother in Winnsboro, S. C. by Rev. Jno. T. Chalmers, Mr. **W. T. Blakely** of Laurens, S. C. and Miss **Effie Lauderdale** of Fairfield, S. C.

- - - by Rev. G. R. White, December 11th, 1883 at the residence of the officiating minister, Mr. **A. H. Griffith** of Mecklenburg County, N. C. and Mrs. **Margaret M. Smith** of York County, S. C.

- - - by Rev. D. F. Haddon, December 11th, 1883, Mr. **T. P. Bryd** and Miss **Corrie Blakely**. All of Laurens, S. C.

- - - in the Presbyterian church of Asheville, December 25th, 1883 by Rev. J. P. Gammon, Rev. **Mason W. Pressly** of Chester, S. C. and Miss **Annie C. Worth** of Asheville, N. C., daughter of the late Dr. T. C. Worth.

- - - at the residence of Dr. E. D. Harriss, December 18th, 1883, by Rev. H. M. Henry, Mr. **J. F. Jones** and Miss **Annie Harriss**. Both of Oak Hill, Wilcox County, Ala.

- - - in the Cumberland Presbyterian church, Camden, Wilcox County, Ala., December 18th, 1883, by Rev. David Pressly of Starkville, Miss., **A. G. Brice**, Esq. of Chester, S. C. and Miss **Sallie L. Miller**, youngest daughter of Mrs. Sarah Miller of Camden, Wilcox County, Ala.

- - - by Rev. D. F. Haddon, December 27th, 1883, Mr. **H. L. Jones** and Miss **N. E. Coleman**. All of Laurens, S. C.

- - - at the residence of the bride's father, Mr. David Chestnut, December 27th, 1883, by Rev. C. E. Todd, Mr. **J. M. G. Henderson** and Miss **J. L. Chestnut**. Both of DeKalb County, Ga.

- - - by Rev. S. A. Agnew, December 19th, 1883, Mr. **R. Palmer Lyon** of Union County, Miss. and Miss **Maggie J. Galloway**, daughter of Mr. A. M. Galloway of Lee County, Miss.

Married by Rev. S. A. Agnew, December 19th, 1883, Mr. **S. Walker Snipes** of Union, and Miss **Mary J. Galloway**, daughter of Mr. A. M. Galloway of Lee County, Miss.

January 10, 1884

Died in his home in Anderson County, Texas, December 8th, 1883 of typhoid fever, Mr. **Thomas Chestnut** in the 77th year of his age . . . . [leaves] two single daughters.

Died near Covington, Tenn. on the 22d of November, 1883, Miss **Euphemia I.**, daughter of Rev. J. K. and Mrs. M. R. **Boyce**. Aged 28 years. . . . only daughter of an enfeebled and widowed mother.

Mrs. **Mary Jane Rogers** departed this life, December 5th, 1883, aged 42 years, 7 months and 22 days. . . . was a native of Newberry, S. C., but about two years immediately preceding her death, made her home with her brother-in-law, Mr. William Cherry, Chester County, S. C. . . . member of A. R. Presbyterian church of Newberry. . . . Mrs. Rogers was married in 1867. Her married life was short. . . . Three children were the fruits. . . . one died in infancy, the other two, a son and daughter, survive.

Departed this life, October 3d, 1883, in Dallas County, Ala., Mr. **Patrick Chisolm** in the 83d year of his age. . . . born in Ireland, emigrated to South Carolina in 1818, where he remained about two years. In the month of August, 1820, he walked from Fairfield county, S. C. to Dallas County, Ala. In 1822, he married Catherine Craig, who survives him, and with whom he happily lived for 61 years. He was the father of nine children, thirty grandchildren and eleven great grandchildren, none of whom ever removed from the community in which they were born and reared, all uniting with the church of their fathers, living honest and honorable lives. In 1822, Prosperity church was organized by Dr. Isaac Grier, under two large and beautiful oaks on the bank of the Cahaba. Thomas Craig and Bernard Johnson were elected ruling elders, and about fifteen names were enrolled, most of whom were Moores, Craigs and Chisolms. . . Mr. Chisolm was elected ruling elder in 1847. For sixty one years a member, and for thirty six an efficient elder.

Married on the 12th of December, 1883, by Rev. R. Lathan, Mr. **R. S. Hanna** to Miss **J. C. Sadler**, both of York County.

- - - by the same, on the 26th of December, 1883, Mr. **Robert Ross Love** to Miss **C. Amanda Moss**, both of York County, S. C.

- - - by the same on the 27th of December, Mr. **Robert Neely** to

Miss **Julia M. M. Adkins**, both of York County.

- - - on the 17th of December, 1883, by Rev. C. B. Betts, Mr. **T. M. Collins** to Miss **M. J. McCants**. All of York County, S. C.

- - - by the same on the 1st of November, 1883, Mr. **W. Samuel Boyd** to Miss **Annie Williams**. All of York County.

- - - by the same on the 18th of December, Mr. **N. B. Williams** to Miss **N. Josie Leslie**, All of York County.

- - - by the same on the 20th of December, 1883, Mr. **J. R. Collins** to Miss **M. J. McCreight**, the former of York County, the latter of Chester County, S. C.

- - - by the same on the 25th of December, 1883, Mr. **A. T. L. Sweat** to Miss **Fannie Bigham**. All of Chester County, S. C.

- - - by the same on the same day, Mr. **J. F. Proctor** to Miss **Fannie L. Vaughn**. All of Chester County, S. C.

- - - at the residence of Mrs. Lizzie Pharr, in Charlotte, N. C., by Rev. W. T. Waller, Mr. **C. A. McConnell** and Miss **Maggie McConnell**. All of Mecklenburg County, N. C.

January 17, 1884

Died in Hamburg, Wilcox County, Ala., November 27, 1883, Mrs. **Regenia E. Purifoy**, wife of J. Edgar Purifoy and daughter of William and Lillie Jones, aged 36 years, 7 months and twenty days. . . . was mother of four children, only one of whom, a little daughter of two summers, survives.

Died near Smyrna in York County, S. C., on the 7th of January, 1884, little **Frankie**, infant son of R. M. and M. C. **Whitesides**, aged 1 year and twenty two days.

Married, December 27th, 1883, by Rev. J. L. Young, Mr. **W. F. McQuiston** of Tipton County, Tenn. and Miss **M. E. Wilson** of Monticello, Ark.

January 24, 1884

Mrs. **Elizabeth Brownlee Lowry**, wife of Maj. J. G. Lowry of Lowrysville, S. C., died at her home, January 11th, 1884. She was born November 27, 1827 at Due West, S. C. and was married to Maj. J. G. Lowry, December 2d, 1847. . . . Early member of Greenville Presbyterian church in Abbeville County, S. C. . . . her name was one of the first enrolled at Zion Presbyterian church, Chester County, S. C.

Married on the 5th of November, 1883 by Rev. R. A. Ross, D. D., Rev. **W. A. M. Plaxco** and **Miss M. E. Whitesides**.

Married on the 6th of December, 1883, at the residence of the bride's mother, by Rev. J. E. Martin, Mr. **R. L. Cowan** to Miss **Nannie Wear**. All of Newton County, Ga.

- - - at the residence of the bride's mother, January 14, 1884, by Rev. W. H. Millen, Mr. **Samuel O. Huey** of Tipton County, Tenn. and Miss **Savanna P. Ellis** of Union County, Miss.

January 31, 1884

Little **Mattie**, infant daughter of William and Bettie **Little**, died at their home in Ebenezer, Ga. on the third Sabbath of December, 1883. Aged about 11 months.

Died near Troy, Tenn., January 16th, 1884, Mr. **Edward A. McCaw**, in the 64th year of his age. . . . born in Chester County, S. C., July 11th, 1820, within the bounds of Hopewell congregation. There he connected with the church and afterwards was elected ruling elder. In 1851, with his family, he moved to Obion County, Tenn. where he has lived since that time. . . . Five children, all grown and connected with the church [survive].

John Lindsay, Sr. died at his home on Elk River, Lincoln County, Tenn., on the 14th of January, 1884, in the 84th year of his age. . . . born in the vicinity of Lower Long Cane church, Abbeville County, S. C. in 1800. . . . married Miss Patsy Pressly, sister of the late Dr. E. E. Pressly. . . . Seven children, all grown to maturity and honored Christians [survive]. . . . More than fifty years ago he emigrated to this country and connected himself with the Prosperity congregation. . . . afterwards went with the colony which formed New Hope congregation.

Married at Oak Hill, Wilcox County, Ala., January 17, 1884, by Rev. W. W. Carothers, assisted by Rev. H. M. Henry, Prof. **Wm. Carothers** to **Mrs. J. C. McWilliams**. Both of Oak Hill.

- - - November 15th, 1883, at the residence of the bride's mother, by Rev. T. P. Pressly, Mr. **G. W. Harris** and Miss **Nannie Buchanan**. All of Troy, Tenn.

- - - by the same at the same place, January 10th, 1884, Mr. **J. C. Harris** to Miss **Maggie Buchanan**.

- - - at the residence of the bride's father, January 10th, 1884, by Rev. J. C. Galloway, Mr. **J. T. Smith** and Miss **Della Scruggs**. All of Jefferson County, Ga.

- - - in Louisville, Ga., at the residence of Mrs. Jesse Leaptrot, January

16th, 1884, by Rev. J. C. Galloway, Mr. **Angus Keith** and Mrs. **Sallie Newsome**.

Married at the residence of Mr. Walter Seager in Burke County, Ga., December 20th, 1883, by Rev. J. C. Galloway, Mr. **C. Pennington** and Miss **Mittie Sykes**.

- - - January 15, 1884, by Rev. S. A. Agnew, Mr. **T. P. Tapp** of Prentiss and Miss **Bettie Smythe** of Union County, Miss.

- - - on the evening of December 19th, 1883, at the residence of the bride's father, Mr. W. W. Sprouse, Troy, S. C. by Rev. H. T. Sloan, D. D., Mr. **J. A. McClain** and Miss **Ettie Sprouse**.

- - - January 1st, 1884, at the residence of Mr. W. W. Sprouse, by Rev. H. T. Sloan, D. D., Mr. **Henry White** and Miss **Alice Sprouse**.

- - - on the 22nd of January, 1884, at the residence of Mr. J. H. Davis in Bradley County, Ark., by Rev. J. S. A. Hunter, Mr. **David Neal** and Miss **Mary E. Leslie**.

February 7, 1884

Died at his home in Chester County, S. C., January 15th, 1884, **Robert Boyd**, aged 84 years, 11 months and 11 days. . . . for more than thirty years he had been a ruling elder in Hopewell church. . . . He leaves two widowed daughters and a son, the Rev. Warren Boyd, an honored minister in the Presbyterian church.

Died at his home in Chester County, S. C., December 14th, 1883, Col. **Jas. McDill**, aged 77 years, 6 months and 10 days. . . . for nearly forty years he was a ruling elder in Hopewell church, having been ordained in October, 1847.

Died in Lamar County, Texas, September 25th, 1883, Mr. **John Campbell** in the 48th year of his age. When quite a young man in 1850, he left his mother-land, the "Emerald Isle," and crossed the ocean, settling in Rochester, N. Y. Here he met and wedded his "Mary," who now is left a lonely widow. Attracted to the South, in 1877 we find him in Texas, where he hunted up and pitched his tent among a group of Psalm-singers. Here we find him ere long enrolled as a ruling elder in the Lamar church.

February 14, 1884

Died at her home in Chester County, S. C., January 17th, 1884, Mrs. **Jane Bigham**, relict of Thos. G. Bigham, aged 65 years, 10 months and 26 days. . . . only about three months elapsed between her death and that of her husband. They lived together for nearly a half century.

Thomas Grier Wylie was born July 12th, 1810. He died December 27, 1883... early [became] clerk in dry goods store.... After he had accumulated considerable money, he married Emily, a daughter of Christopher Strong, Esq. and removed to Hickory Grove in York County, and there he opened a store about thirty five years ago... [since the Civil War] he has given his attention chiefly to farming... member of A. R. P. church at Smyrna.... He leaves a widow, a son and six daughters, all but one living in the bounds of and members of Smyrna.

Married, January 24th, 1884, at the residence of Mrs. J. R. Gardner, the bride's sister, in Yorkville, S. C., by Rev. W. G. Neville, Rev. **W. T. Matthews** of Lowrysville, Chester County, S. C. and Miss **Sue F. Lowry**, daughter of Dr. J. M. Lowry.

- - - at the residence of Dr. J. M. Strong, January 30th, 1884, by Rev. C. E. McDonald, Mr. **W. F. Moore** and Mrs. **Elva E. Boyce**. All of Mecklenburg County, N. C.

February 21, 1884

Died, February 4th, 1884, at the residence of J. L. Cooper, Siloam, Clay County, Miss., **Silas Cooper**. He was born December 28th, 1804 . ... united with the A. R. P. church when a young man at Cedar Springs, S. C., moved to Mississippi in 1848, connected himself with Rev. D. Pressly's church in Starkville, and lived a member of same until his death. He leaves two daughters and one son.

Died, January 3d, 1884, of pneumonia, Mrs. **Alice McCalla**, wife of Silas McCalla, in the 28th year of her age.... early connected herself with the A. R. P. church at Blanche, Tenn.... She leaves a husband and three children.

Died, January 14th, 1884, of heart disease, Mrs. **Sallie J.**, wife of Rev. J. A. **Myers**, in the 50th year of her age.

Died at his residence near Wallerville in Union County, Miss., Sabbath morning, December 30th, 1883, **Robert Reid**, Esq. in the 73rd year of his age.... son of William and Mary (Caldwell) Reid, and was born in the bounds of the A. R. church at Gilder's Creek in Newberry District, S. C., November 4, 1811. His father removed to Anderson, S. C. in 1819, when he was a child, and there Robert grew to manhood. He married Miss Eliza Skelton, December 22nd, 1831, and during a season of considerable religious interest in 1833, he, with his wife, joined the Presbyterian church at Roberts. He moved to Pontotoc (now Union) County, Miss. in the fall of 1848, and soon joined the Presbyterian church at New Albany. In the year 1863, probably, he was elected ruling elder of that church. . . . For several successive terms he was elected Justice of the Peace in Pontotoc County.... He was the father of nine children, six of whom survive.

Married at the residence of Mrs. H. B. Clark, February 7th, 1884, by Rev. S. A. Agnew, Mr. **J. O. Caldwell** of Union County, Miss. and Miss **Mattie S. Holloway**, late of Shelby County, Tenn.

Married, February 14th, 1884, in Due West, S. C., by Rev. W. F. Pearson, Mr. **C. T. Burnett** of Tennessee and Miss **E. Ellen Putman** of Georgia.

- - - February 12th, 1884 at the residence of the bride's father, Henry Harris, Esq., by Rev. J. H. Peoples, Mr. **E. C. Fleming** and Miss **Mattie Harris**. All of Maury County, Tenn.

February 28, 1884

James Leroy McCain died of consumption, February 4th, 1884, at the home of his father, A. L. McCain, near Lacona, Iowa, in the 27th year of his age. He was a member of the United Presbyterian church in Des Moines.

Died in Winnsboro, S. C., January 3d, 1884, **infant son** of Mr. J. W. and Mrs. Maggie **Bolick**.

Died at her home in New Stirling, N. C., January 21st, 1884, Mrs. **Mattie Allen**. Born January 21st, 1797, she was just 87 the day she died. . . . By her former marriage to Mr. Jas. Moore, she was the mother of five children.

Miss **Lou Fleming** died in Louisville, Ga. at the residence of Mr. J. C. Little on the 27th of January, 1884 . . . . typhoid fever. . . . The deceased was born in the city of Columbus, Ga. on the 19th of July, 1863, and was in her 21st year. She was left motherless when only six weeks old and was reared by her aunt.

March 6, 1884

Died at his residence in Augusta County, Va., January 2nd, 1884, Mr. **John McCutcheon**, aged 84 years, 10 months and 16 days. . . . [ruling elder of Old Providence church] leaves a widowed daughter-in-law, two grandchildren and a brother.

Died in Tipton County, Tenn., February 15th, 1884, Mrs. **Mary (Strain) Kirk** in the 61st year of her age. . . . born in Lancaster County, S. C. . . . [member] of A. R. P. church at Shiloh.

Died at the residence of her son-in-law, Mr. W. H. Young, in Perry County, Ark., on Sabbath, December 9th, 1883, Mrs. **Martha Elizabeth McGee** in the 55th year of her age. . . . daughter of John and Sarah (Turner) Watt and was born in Anderson District, S. C., February 13th, 1829. . . joined Associate Reformed church of Little Generostee in 1844. In

January, 1845, she was married to Mr. W. H. McGee and removed to Tippah County, Miss in 1847. When Bethany church was organized, June 5th, 1852, Mrs. McGee was one of the little band of twenty one white members who entered into that organization. Her husband also joined that church. He entered the Confederate service, was captured at Perryville, Ky., and died in Vicksburg, Miss., November 22d, 1862, just after he had been exchanged from a Federal prison. For more than twenty years she was a widow with a family of daughters... and her daughters grew up, married and all now live west of the Mississippi. On December 20th, 1882 ... she left her Mississippi home and removed with her youngest daughter to Perry, Ark. ...she was the mother of six children, four of whom survive, all married and living in Texas and Arkansas.

Married in Bradley County, Ark., February 7th, 1884, by Rev. J. S. A. Hunter, Mr. **E. P. Carmical** and Miss **Ollie Ederington**.

- - - January 31st, 1884, by Rev. J. N. Bradshaw, Mr. **Samuel Stewart** and Miss **Lou Lee**. All of Newton County, Ga.

March 13, 1884

Died in Izard County, Ark., January 5th, 1884, Mrs. **Eliza Cooper**, wife of Mr. Silas H. Cooper and a daughter of Mr. William A. Gault, an elder in the A. R. church.

Died near Cross Hill, Laurens County, S. C., January 7th, 1884, Mrs. **Ada Hollingsworth**, wife of Robert Hollingsworth and daughter of James and Ann Jones, in the 33rd year of her age... left a babe only a few days old, and three other children.... [as well as a] husband ... [member of] Head Springs since 1862.

Died at the residence of his father in Lee County, Miss., January 22nd, 1884, Mr. **Langdon Augustus Richey**, aged 31 years, 2 months and 2 days. ... son of Robert C. and Nancy E. (Hill) Richey, and was born in Anderson District, S. C., November 20th, 1852. His father removed to Itawamba (now Lee) County, Miss. in the fall of 1859 ... [attended] school at Cooper Institute in Lauderdale County, Miss. ... on returning home he joined the Presbyterian church at Gaston.

March 20, 1884

[Died] on the 17th of January, 1884, **Wm. Carmical** .... born on the 8th of October, 1808, in Newberry County, S. C. ... son of Abram and Nancy Carmical. On the 10th of December, 1835, he and Margaret R. Hunter were united in marriage. In the spring of 1836, they joined the A. R. P. church at Prosperity, S. C. ... In December, 1852, they moved to Coweta County, Ga. where they lived with the exception of about two years residence in Illinois ... leaves wife and children.

Died of consumption in Pope County, Ark., February 15th, 1884, **Mrs. E. A.**, wife of Mr. C. G. **Oates** and daughter of Robert and Mary Ferguson . . . leaves a husband and three sons.

Died near Troy, Tenn., October 6th, 1883 of disease of the lungs or liver, **Hannah Elizabeth Ratterree** in the 18th year of her age. Lizzie was . . . a member of the A. R. P. church at Troy.

Departed this life, November 25th, 1883, Mrs. **Elizabeth Brown**, wife of R. O. Brown, Esq. in the 64th year of her age. . . . born March 7th, 1820 in Rowan County, N. C. . . . married September 30, 1841, and settled with her husband at New Perth, Iredell County . . . husband [is] a ruling elder . . . [survived by him and] three daughters.

Jonathan McFaddin departed this life, February 14th, 1884, aged 78 years, 6 months and 4 days. . . born in Chester County, S. C. . . . member of A. R. P. church for over fifty years, and also a ruling elder in Union congregation for about forty years . . . leaves a widow by second marriage with six children.

Married, February 6th, 1884, by Rev. C. B. Betts, Mr. **W. B. Adams** to **Mrs. D. A. Reed**. All of Chester County, S. C.

- - - by the same, February 13th, 1884, Mr. **H. J. Lock** to **Miss M. A. Simpson**. All of Chester County, S. C.

- - - by the same, March 4th, 1884, Mr. **J. W. Ferguson** to Miss **Hattie Strait**. All of York County, S. C.

- - - at the residence of the bride's father, December 7th, 1883, by Rev. Jas. Boyce, Jr., Mr. **James Bain** and Miss **Elizabeth Meikle**. All of Louisville, Ky.

- - - by the same, March 10th, 1884, Mr. **Anson S. Cornell** and Miss **Sallie M. Maxey**. All of Louisvillee, Ky.

- - - February 5th, 1884, by Rev. W. H. Millen, Mr. **E. C. Boyd** of Lafayette County and **Miss S. F. McCurry** of Union County, Miss.

March 27, 1884

Married, March 5th, 1884, by Rev. J. L. Young, Mr. **James L. Thompson** and Miss **Mattie B. Dickson**. Both of Drew County, Ark.

April 3, 1884

Little **Bessie**, infant daughter of Thomas and Lizzie **Reid**, died near Auburn, Mo., December 29th, 1883, aged 14 months and 13 days.

In the morning of March the 7th, 1884, Mr. **James Patterson** died in his home in Ebenezer, Ga. of which church he was born a member on the 3d of February, 1800, and with which church he has been in active communion from youth. . . though he lived fifteen miles from the church, as long as he was able to ride, he was regularly there.

Married, March 16th, 1884, at the residence of Mrs. Woods, by Rev. E. E. Patterson, Mr. **Jas. Childers** and Miss **Ida Goodman**. All of Roxton, Lamar County, Texas.

April 10, 1884

Married, April 2d, 1884, by Rev. W. L. Pressly, Mr. **J. D. Taylor** of Lancaster, S. C. and **Miss M. B. Edwards** of Due West, S. C.

April 17, 1884

Died of pneumonia at his home in Drew County, Ark., April 1st, 1884, Mr. **Robert Shanks** . . . . born near Long Cane, Abbeville County, S. C., October 31st, 1808. He moved to Alabama about the year 1839, and settled in Lowndes County in 1843. His next move was in 1859 when he came to Drew County, Ark. . . . [joined] the church of his fathers at Long Cane. . . . One son in Texas, two daughters in home, the wife of his youth, and a widowed daughter-in-law, with seven children, survive him.

Died at his home in Dallas County, Ala., April 7th, 1884, Mr. **Samuel Brice**, in the 75th year of his age. . . . born in Fairfield County, S. C., baptized and brought up in the New Hope congregation . . . in 1867, he removed to Dallas County, Ala., identifying himself with the Prosperity church. . . . He leaves behind a widow, two children, numerous grandchildren and great grandchildren.

April 24, 1884

Died, April 15th, 1884, in New Edinburgh, Ark., **infant son** of Rev. J. S. A. and Mrs. E. **Hunter.**

May 1, 1884

Dr. **A. T. Wideman**, son of Esq. John and Sarah Wideman, was born on Long Cane, Abbeville County, S. C., November 8th, 1824, near where his life was spent. . . . [died] at his home, April 16th, 1884 in the 60th year of his age. . . . received his literary education chiefly at Cokesbury. . . . graduated in the Medical College of Charleston in 1846, and successfully practiced his profession for a few years, after which he retired to attend to his planting interests. He married (1847) Miss Rebecca Patton, daughter of William and Jane Patton, sister of Dr. E. L. Patton and others of scarcely less distinction. They had five children, the three youngest of whom survive. . . . Elder of A. R. P. church of Cedar Spring and Long Cane from

April, 1860. . . . He entered the army a Lieutenant in Capt. Lites Company, 19th Regiment, S. C. V., but could not long endure the marches and fatigues of army life; returned home and went to the coast as superintendent of salt works.

May 8, 1884

Died at her home in Cobb County, Ga., April 16th, 1884, Mrs. **Catherine McDonald**, in the 70th year of her age. . . . wife of John McDonald and daughter of John and Mary McCartney . . . . born in Abbeville County, S. C., May ---, 1814. . . . [joined Cedar Springs]. In 1851, she moved to Cobb County, Ga. where she spent the remainder of her life. . . leaves an aged companion and four children.

Mrs. S. J. Strain, wife of Mr. W. L. Strain of Tipton Co., Tenn. died at her mother's in Lincoln County, Tenn., April 7th, 1884, in the 52d year of her age . . . . In 1873, she was married. . . united with the A. R. congregation of Bloomington, of which her husband was an elder.

Died in Belton, Bell County, Texas, January 22d, 1884, Mr. **Joseph Elijah Willbanks**, aged 30 years, 10 months and 5 days. . . son of Henry M. and Mrs. Nancy (Moore) Willbanks, and was born in Anderson County, S. C., March 17, 1853. When he was . . . five years old, his father removed to Tippah County, Miss. . . . Joseph . . . was reared in the bounds of Bethany congregation. . . . which he joined in 1873. . . . A few years thereafter he moved to Johnson County, Texas, and he was one of the little flock at Prairie Valley in that county. He married Miss Mary Bell Lackey, October 1st, 1879 in Johnson County. A year or two ago, he removed to Belton. . . . leaves a wife and little son.

Died near Statesville, N. C., April 21st, 1884, **Lula King**, daughter of Mr. J. Alston and Mrs. L. D. **Davidson**.

[Died] on the early morning of March 24th, 1884, at his residence at Flat Creek, Bath County, Ky. . . . **James C. Hamilton, Sr.** in the 68th year of his age.

May 15, 1884

Died in Statesville, N. C., April 11th, 1884, **Bessie Brevard**, youngest child of J. D. and M. E. **Patterson**, aged 21 months and 11 days.

Departed this life, March 17th, 1884, at his house near Belfast, Tenn., **William S. McAdams**, in the 80th year of his age. . . . was born July 12th, 1804. His parents were among the earliest settlers of the State, coming here from North Carolina when William was only six years old. . . . He lived and died on the farm which his father originally settled. He married May ---, 1824 to Lavinia McLain, daughter of Jesse McLain, one of the first four elders of Head Spring church. The fruits of this union were fifteen children, all living now except four. His grandchildren number seventy-five, and his great grandchildren twelve. It is a source of deep regret that none of them are members of the A. R. P. church.

May 29, 1884

Died at Chester, S. C., May 11th, 1884, **Margaret Gaston Gage**, aged 19 months and 1 week. . . . daughter of George W. and Janie Gaston Gage.

Died at his home in Chester County, S. C., April 8th, 1884 in Garrard County, Ky., **Mrs. P. Gillespie**, in the 92d year of her age. . . . born in Rockbridge County, Va. near Broad Creek, and came to Kentucky among the first settlers when only three years old. . . [member] New Hope A. R. Presbyterian church . . . leaves an only son.

Departed this life, April 19th, 1884, at her home near Belfast, Tenn., Mrs. **Sallie Ledford**, daughter of James H. Glenn, in the 19th year of her age. . . Some weeks previous to her death, she received an injury by being thrown from a horse. Then followed an attack of slow fever, then a premature birth, then death to the young mother and her infant.

Married, May 6th, 1884, by Rev. S. W. Haddon, Mr. **John Lotts** of Augusta County, Va. and Miss **Estiline McCormick** of Rockbridge County, Va.

- - - May 7th, 1884, by Rev. S. A. Agnew, Mr. **Ludy P. Bryson** and Miss **Eliza Norton**, daughter of Mrs. Jane Norton. All of Lee County, Miss.

June 5, 1884

Died, May 22d, 1884 in Due West, S. C., Miss **Julia Henry**, the youngest child of Dr. Nathan and Mrs. Rosannah Henry.

Died in Mecklenburg County, N. C., March 21st, 1884, Mrs. **Margaret Alexander**, wife of Mr. E. B. Alexander . . . . born April, 1827 . . . a member of Gilead church.

Died in Shelby County, Tenn., May 2d, 1884, Mrs. **Mary Brown Penny** . . . born in Chester County, S. C., daughter of Samuel and Martha Sloan, was brought up in the bounds of Prosperity church, Lincoln County, Tenn., but removed to Shelby County in the fall of 1872. Mrs. Penny was twice married; first to Jesse Morton, January 14th, 1836; afterward, February 15th, 1854 to H. P. Penny. . . left an aged husband and only daughter.

William Clarkston, infant son of J. Wylie and Alice **Roddey**, aged 15 months and 26 days. . . departed this life, April 22d, 1884.

June 12, 1884

Mrs. **Sarah Simonton** died May 20th, 1884, at the home of W. B. Simonton. . . born in 1789, and was 95 years of age. Her maiden name was Weldon. She married John Simonton, Sr. in 1831. . . . belonged to A. R. church at Winnsboro . . . [buried] in graveyard at New Hope.

Mrs. **Margaret C. McElroy** died at her home in DeKalb County, Ga., May 18th, 1884, aged 72 years, 3 months and 2 days. . . [left] an aged companion and only son. . . She was born in Chester County, S. C., February 15th, 1812, daughter of George and Margaret McDill . . . in 1825, Mr. McDill with his family moved to Newton County, Ga. In 1831 . . . [she] was married to Mr. (Rev.) Jno. McElroy, and moved to DeKalb County, where for more than half a century [they lived].

Maude Eugenia and **Austin Flint**, children of Dr. T. D. and Ella **Marion**, aged respectively, 1 year, 8 months and 16 days; and 4 years, 2 months and 13 days, departed this life, the former April 25th, the latter May 4th, 1884.

June 19, 1884

Miss **Fannie E. Conner**, youngest daughter of Mr. and Mrs. A. P. Conner. . . just blooming into womanhood . . . [died] June 4th, 1884. . . The fall which she received some eighteen months ago from their burning house shattered her nervous system . . . [and she died just as she was] on the eve of visiting her brothers and sister in the West.

Died at his residence on Rufer St., Louisville, Ky., May 20th, 1884, Mr. **James Tilley**, aged 34 years, 2 months and 2 days. . . . was born in Perthshire, Scotland. When he was three years old, his parents emigrated to America and settled in this city where they have ever since resided. They at once became identified with the Associate Reformed church. . . . On October 25th, 1881, Mr. Tilley was happily married to Miss Ella Gordon, formerly of Madison, Ind.

Mr. **William F. Watt** was born and raised in Fairfield County, S. C. He married Miss Sallie J. Bell of Mississippi and moved to Lind Grove, La. about 1849 where for thirty three years he made his home. Two years ago he moved to Starkville, Miss where he died the 29th of May, 1884.

Married, May 27th, 1884 by Rev. H. T. Sloan, D. D., Mr. **James Crawford** and Miss **Mattie Cresswell**. Both of Troy, S. C.

- - - June 5th, 1884, by Rev. T. P. Pressly at the residence of Mr. T. B. Moffatt, the bride's father, Rev. **T. D. Latimer** of Oxford, Miss. and Miss **Jennie Moffatt** of Rives, Tenn.

June 26, 1884

James Carson died at his residence in Rockbridge County, Va., March 4th, 1884, aged 77 years, 6 months and 11 days. . . member of the A. R. church. He never married and died where he was born and raised.

Died at his home in Drew County, Ark., May 24th, 1884, Mr. **Samuel P. Davis** . . . of measles. . . . born November 19th, 1858 in Lafayette County, Miss., but while still in his infancy was brought with his parents to Drew County. . . member of Saline church. . . . left wife and three little ones.

July 3, 1884

Died in Houston City, Texas, December 5th, 1883 of ovarian dropsy, Miss **Evie Sloan**, daughter of Mr. E. M. and Mrs. Maggie M. Sloan. . . . was a member of Mt. Carmel church, Marshall County, Miss. Her father and family moved to Houston County the first of November, 1882.

Died in Steel Creek, N. C., June 6th, 1884 of typhoid dysentery, Mrs. **Ann Knox**, in the 77th year of her age. . . . The widow of the late Samuel Boyce Knox and for many years a member of Steel Creek A. R. P. church.

[Died on June 10th, 1884] **Joseph K. Lowry**, son of Maj. J. G. Lowry of Lowrysville, S. C. The deceased was 17 years, 3 months and 25 days old. . . in school at the Lowrysville Academy.

Died near Steel Creek, N. C. June 8th, 1884, Miss **Margaret E. Grier** in the 64th year of her age. . . . daughter of Alexander and Mary Spratt Grier. She was born and raised in Steel Creek, and at an early age connected herself with the A. R. P. church at Steel Creek.

July 10, 1884

Mrs. **Kate Kirkpatrick** died in Rockbridge County, Va., April 19th, 1884. ... had passed, by several years, her three score and ten [years]. She leaves a husband, and a large circle of children.

Mr. **William Miller** was born in Rockbridge County, Va., March 25th, 1823. . . . deacon in A. R. church since 1871. . . . died May 20th, 1884, aged 61 years.

Died in Woodford County, Ky., June 17th, 1884, Mr. **Robert Guyn** in the 43rd year of his age.

Died at her residence in the bounds of Amity congregation, Iredell County, N. C., on Sabbath, June 22d, 1884, from the effects of a stroke of paralysis, Mrs. **Jerusha Morrison**, widow of the late J. N. Morrison, aged 71 years, 11 months and 3 days.

July 17, 1884

Died in Bethany, York County, S. C., June 8th, 1884, **infant** son of E. B. **Faulkner** . . . [died at the age of] one month and twenty four days.

Died near Shiloh church in Lancaster County, S. C., on the 24th of June, 1884, **A. B. Craig**, son of N. B. and J. E. Craig, aged 3 years, 11 months and 24 days.

Died at his home in Chester County, S. C. on June 7th, 1884, Mr. S . **Harvey McDaniel**, aged about 37 years. . . . About two years ago, he was married to Miss Janie McFadden, who survives him, together with a little boy.

Mrs. **Rhoda Conner** of Newberry, S. C., was born January 22d, 1805, and died May 13th, 1884. . . . member of the A. R. P. church at Head Spring. . . . was a member of that excellent family of Hunters, whose history stands prominent in the records of Newberry County. In early youth she was married to Mr. Abel Conner . . . [who died] several years ago. These years of widowhood she spent with her only son, Capt. Thompson Conner and family.

Died, July 14th, 1884 near Due West, S. C. in the 29th year of her age, Mrs. **Jane Eleanor Harris Todd**, wife of Mr. Jas. E. Todd. . . . was the youngest daughter of the late Robt. C. Grier, D. D. . . . Mrs. Todd left a devoted husband, two children.

July 24, 1884

Died in Prentiss County, Miss. on Wednesday evening, July 9th, 1884, **Addis Elizabeth Caldwell**, daughter of George R. and Sarah A. (Osborn) Caldwell, aged 2 years and 7 months.

July 31, 1884

Died near Cotton Gin, Freestone County, Texas, May 18th, 1884, Mrs. **Mary J. Shanks**, widow of R. M. McK. Shanks, born May 22d, 1822 in Newberry District.

Died at Lancaster C. H., S. C. on the morning of July 2d, 1884 of typhoid fever, Miss **Sarah Isabella**, third daughter of Rev. E. E. and Mrs. E. H. **Pressly**, aged 13 years and 11 days.

The A. R. congregation of Due West mourns the loss of another of its cherished members. On the morning of the 28th inst., Mrs. **Alice Todd**, wife of J. Mc. Todd. . . [died]. Mrs. Todd was raised in the bounds of the New Hope congregation, Fairfield County, S. C. . . . leaves bereaved husband and orphaned children.

Died at her residence in Lancaster County, S. C., June 27th, 1884, Mrs. **Elizabeth (Montgomery) Caskey**, in the 82d year of her age. . . . was born in the community in which she lived and died. . . . member of A. R. P. church; first at Perry's church near Lancaster C. H., afterwards at Gill's Creek. . . . she was the mother of eleven children, and in the providence of God she was called upon to provide for them, as she was a widow for many years. Seven of her sons were Confederate soldiers; two of whom never returned . . . Five children still survive.

Died in Winnsboro, Fairfield County, S. C., March 15th, 1884, Miss **Eliza Jane McDowell**, in the 76th year of her age. . . . was first a member of Jackson Creek, O. S. Presbyterian church in Fairfield County. In the year 1833, her mother died, and she remained a member of her father's household until 1861.

August 7, 1884

Died, July 25th, 1884 in Charlotte, N. C. of diptheria, little **Frederick Nathaniel**, son of Rev. W. T. and K. B. **Waller**, aged 1 year, 8 months and 12 days.

Died at his residence in Lee County, Miss. on Wednesday evening, July 16th, 1884, Mr. **Alexander Millen Galloway**. Aged 70 years, 8 months and 13 days. . . . son of William W. and Nancy Galloway, and was born in York District, S. C., November 3d, 1813. When he was a lad, his parents removed in 1825 to Maury County, Tenn., where his uncle, Rev. Robert M. Galloway, had recently settled as pastor of Hopewell congregation. . . . He married Miss Nancy Wiley of Prosperity, Lincoln County, Tenn., March 13th, 1838 and soon thereafter removed to that congregation where he lived until 1855, when he removed to Mississippi, settling in Pontotoc (now Lee) County at the place where he died, in the bounds of Bethany congregation. His first wife died in Lincoln County, Tenn., April 27th, 1852. He again married October 19th, 1852, Lincoln County, Tenn., to Miss Martha E. Spence. She died ten months before his death. By the first wife he was the father of six sons, all of whom are dead except one, John B. Galloway, a ruling elder in Hopewell congregation. By his last wife he was the father of nine children, three of whom are dead.

Died in Pineville, N. C., July 5th, 1884, Mr. **John W. Grier**, in the 34th year of his age. . . raised in Sardis, but ten years, perhaps, he had been a member of Steel Creek. . . He leaves a sorrowing wife and two children.

August 14, 1884

Died of pneumonia in Lee County, Miss. on Sabbath, July 27th, 1884, **James Wilson Gamble**, son of Dr. W. G. and Mrs. E. I. (Agnew) Gamble, aged 6 years, 2 months and 9 days.

Died in Union County, Miss. on Sabbath, August 3d, 1884, **Lawrence Byrd Holland**, youngest son of H. L. and Mrs. Julia A. (Tate) Holland, aged 4 years, 5 months and 21 days.

Died, June 8th, 1884, near Pisgah, N. C., Mrs. **Rebecca Whitesides**, in her 83d year. She had been a great sufferer for many years, and buried her husband and all her children but two daughters many years ago.

Married at the house of Mr. Anderson McElwee, Yorkville, S. C. by Rev. W. T. Matthews, Mr. **R. R. Harris**, Pineville, N. C. and **Miss M. H. Blankenship**, daughter of Dr. J. N. Blankenship, Rendlesburg, N. C.

August 21, 1884

Died in Mecklenburg County, N. C., June 16th, 1884, **Ethel Mabel**, daughter of Houston and Annie **Alexander** . . . . Aged 8 months.

John H. McClinton, only son of the late Samuel B. McClinton, died of typhoid malarial fever, on Friday night, August 8th, 1884, after twenty two days sickness, aged 35 years, 6 months and 25 days. . . [leaves] wife and little children, four sons and one daughter. . . . buried by his father in old Cedar Spring graveyard, near where he was born, lived and died.

August 28, 1884

Died in Mecklenburg County, N. C., August 1st, 1884, **Grier Caldwell**, son of J. M. and Nannie **Alexander**, aged 2 years.

Died at Hot Springs, Ark., June 23d, 1884, Miss **Elizabeth T. Reid**, aged 49 years . . . born and reared in Mt. Zion congregation.

Miss **Maggie Drennan**, daughter of Mrs. Mary Drennan of Long Cane, S. C., died from typhoid malarial fever on Sabbath night, August 3d, 1884. The deceased was about twenty six years of age. . . . She taught school for some time in her own neighborhood. . . . Her father, Robert Drennan, fell in the War Between the States.

Robert Williams departed this life, July 19th, 1884, at his home, Belfast, Tenn. He was born in Greenville County, N. C., May 3d, 1806. Early in life his parents came to this place. . . . He took the place of his father who was a country merchant, and for more than half a century pursued faithfully his business at the same place.

September 4, 1884

Died, August 10th, 1884, **Sarah Ellastine**, youngest child of R. P. and M. F. **Creswell**, aged 3 years, 3 months and 27 days.

John D. Upson was born in Abbeville County, S. C., near Long Cane, September 13th, 1837, and died at Cartersville, Ga., July 16th, 1884. He leaves a widow and two little children. . . . connected with A. R. Presbyterian church in South Carolina, and after removal to Georgia he connected himself with the Presbyterian church at Cartersville.

Died in Pope County, Ark., June 24th, 1884, Mrs. **Martha**, consort of the late J. G. **Hays**, in the 63d year of her age. . . . was brought up in Lincoln County, Tenn. . . . has been a consistent member of the A. R. church at Pisgah, Ark. for twenty one years. . . . She was left a widow with four daughters.

Little **Jimmie McClinton**, oldest son of the late John H. McClinton and Mrs. Mattie McClinton, died one week after his father, aged 12 years.

Died at the residence of her son-in-law, Mr. James A. Moore, near Idaville, Tenn., July 31st, 1884, Mrs. **Martha McCain**, in the 75th year of her age. . . . was born in Chester County, S. C., but since 1837, when in the bloom of womanhood, she has been a resident of Tipton County, Tenn. . . . Mrs. McCain is the youngest sister of the late Rev. John Wilson. . . . In 1838, she was married to Mr. James McCain, an esteemed deacon of Salem. . . .[three children with son and daughter surviving] husband died in 1859.

Married, August 27th, 1884, at the residence of the bride's father, Mr. H. P. Helper by Rev. J. E. Pressly, D. D., assisted by Rev. Mason W. Pressly, Prof. **W. D. Vinson** and Miss **Lizzie E. Helper**. Both of Davidson College, N. C.

September 11, 1884

Mrs. **Ella Wyatt** died at her father's house in Lincoln County, Tenn., July 19th, 1884, of anemia in the 25th year of her age. . . . Two years ago she married and accompanied her husband to West Tennessee.

Died, May 17th, 1884 in Iredell County, N. C. in the 82d year of her age, Mrs. **Nancy B. White**, widow of R. R. White . . . [a member of A. R. P. churches consecutively at Cambridge, New Perth and Statesville] . . . . she leaves two children, a son and a daughter.

Died, December 18th, 1883, in Statesville, Iredell County, N.C., Mrs. **Sarah Tryphena**, wife of M. F. **Freeland**, Esq., aged 67 years. Her maiden name was Wills. Early in life member at New Perth . . . [later at] Statesville.

Died on the 2d of January, 1884 at the residence of her son, J. K. Morrison, in Statesville, Iredell County, N. C., Mrs. **Mary L. Morrison** in the 70th year of her age. . . . widow of William A.

Morrison and daughter of Wm. Knox, Esq. . . . [early member of the A. R. church at Gilead] . . . After her marriage with Mr. Morrison, they moved West, and finding none of their profession, they connected themselves with the Baptist church. After her husband's death, she moved back to North Carolina and connected herself with Coddle Creek.

Died, March 22d, 1884, **M. C. Phillips**, in the 27th year of his age. . . . second son of L. D. and M. Phillips and was born in Anderson County, S. C. . . . member of the M. E. church at Honea Path. . .leaves a companion, three little children.

Died, August 25th, 1884, after an illness of five weeks, **Mrs. M. Phillips**, relict of L. D. Phillips in the 58th year of her age. . . . was the second daughter of D. and L. Greer, and was born in Anderson County, S. C., May 3d, 1827 . . . She leaves two sons, an only daughter.

Died at Duffton, Erath County, Texas, at the residence of her son-in-law, Rev. D. W. Leath, on Friday, August 15th, 1884, Mrs. **Sara Jane Lyon**, aged 56 years, 1 month and 25 days. . . . was the last surviving child of James B. and Mrs. Martha (Brownlee) Richey and was born in Abbeville District, S. C., June 20th, 1828. She was married January 12th, 1848 to James A. Lyon, then a merchant in Due West, S. C. When a town was established at Donnaldsville, on the Greenville & Columbia R. R., they removed to that place and resided there until the fall of 1859, when they came to Tippah (now Union) County, Miss., and here Mr. Lyon engaged in farming. During the war Mr. Lyon became a member of the 32nd Mississippi Regiment, and fell victim of disease, dying in a hospital at or near Tullahoma, Tenn., April 8th, 1863. Mrs. Lyon remained at her Mississippi home, excepting a few years subsequent to the death of her husband when she "refugeed" to South Carolina. In May last, she went to Texas to visit her eldest daughter . . . she leaves four children.

Married, August 31st, 1884, at the residence of the bride's by Rev. Calvin Pressly, Mr. **T. J. Ellis, Jr.** of Hodges and Miss **Mollie McGill** of Due West, S. C.

- - - September 2nd, 1884, at Lambertville, N. J., by Rev. P. A. Studdiford, D. D., Rev. **Henry Drennon Lindsay**, pastor of First Presbyterian church, Wilmington, Delaware and Miss **Isabella Wynkoop**, daughter of **Griffith Williams**, Esq. of Lambertville.

- - - May 7th, 1884, at the residence of the bride's mother, by Rev. H. M. Henry, Mr. **A. C. Jackson** of Escambia County, Ala. and Miss **Florie Bonham** of Wilcox County, Ala.

- - - May 7th, 1884, in the Methodist church at Rehobeth, by Rev. H. M. Henry, Mr. **W. R. Dunham** and **Miss S. A. Welsh**. Both of Wilcox County, Ala.

<u>September 18, 1884</u>

Died, August 9th, 1884, **William Jasper Lessly**, son of Robert and Margaret Lessly, aged 2 years and nearly 2 months.

Died of congestion of the brain on the 7th of September, 1884, **William Pressly**, infant son of Rev. W. M. and Mrs. Monica **Hunter**, aged 9 months and 6 days.

Nannie Lillas, infant of Mr. and Mrs. E. W. **Watson**, died on Sabbath night, September 7th, 1884, aged nearly 2 years.

Died at his home near New Stirling church, Iredell County, N. C., July 25th, 1884 of paralysis, Mr. **Joseph Maxwell Alexander**, aged 80 years, 7 months and 17 days.

Died near Pineville, N. C., August 12th, 1884, **Katie Belle McClelland**, aged 1 year and 10 months.

Died in Ripley, Miss., June 18th, 1884, Mrs. **Nancy E. Dickson**, at the time of her death in the 61st year of her age. . . . some sixteen years ago she connected with Ebenezer church . . . removing from the bounds of the church, she took out her letter and united to the Cumberland Presbyterian church with her husband.

<u>September 25, 1884</u>

Died, August 25th, 1884 on Crowder's Creek, Gaston County, N. C., **William Benton Ferguson**, in the last day of his 5th year, son of Alford and N. E. Ferguson.

Died, September 8th, 1884, near Bethany, S. C., **William Lowry Plaxco**, son of John B. Plaxco and grandson of Maj. J. B. Lowry. . . . three months and twenty days old.

Mrs. **Nancy Amelia Williams**, wife of A. J. Williams, Esq. died at her home at Pope Hill, in Jefferson County, Ga. on the 22d of August, 1884 in the 47th year of her age. . . . a consistent member of Ebenezer church, a pious mother of a large family of children.

Died in Bradley County, Ark., at the residence of her son-in-law, W. T. Barry, on the 5th of September, 1884 of typhoid malarial fever, Mrs. **Mary B. Pierce**, aged 71 years, 11 months and 12 days. . . was born October 23d, 1812 near Ebenezerville, York County, S. C. About fourteen years ago she moved to this State with her children and grandchildren.

On last Thursday, the 28th August, 1884, was the sad occasion of the death of Mrs. **Elizabeth K. Anderson**. She had reached the advanced age of 73 years, and the greater number of those years were spent in the ancestral home in Fairfield. . . was the eldest daughter of Col. Wm. Kincaid.

Samuel Alexander Marion, son of Rev. J. P. and Mrs. M. E. Marion, born September 12th, 1872, died September 4th, 1884, at Greenwood.

Married, September 9th, 1884 at the residence of the bride's stepfather, Mr. J. J. Figg, by Rev. H. Rabb, assisted by Rev. J. S. Mills, Mr. **John C. McCalla** and Miss **Laura Crom**. Both of Shelby County, Tenn.

October 2, 1884

Departed this life on the 16th of September, 1884, in Dallas County, Ala., in the 75th year of her age, Mrs. **Margaret Cochran**. . . . Mrs. Cochran, with her husband, came from Cedar Springs, S. C. to Dallas County, Ala. in 1831.

Died of anasarca, in Lincoln County, Tenn., July 19th, 1884, Mrs. **L. Ella Wyatt**, aged 25 years, 2 months and 4 days. . . . was the fourth daughter of Mr. A. B. and Mrs. S. J. Sheffield of Lincoln County, Tenn. . . . . early member of Prosperity church. September 21st, 1882, she was happily married to H. W. Wyatt of this (Shelby) County. . . . her membership was transferred to Richland church.

October 9, 1884

Died in Pontotoc County, Miss. on Friday, August 29th, 1884, **Elizabeth Myrtle Agnew**, youngest child of John D. and Mattie E. (McGee) Agnew. Aged 5 years and 1 day.

John R. Patton departed this life August 13th, 1884, aged 66 years, 5 months and 8 days . . . was born, lived and died in York County, S. C. [elder in Neely's Creek] . . . the deceased was twice married. A devoted wife and fourteen children survive him.

October 16, 1884

On the 31st of August, a little **daughter** was born to W. M. and M. E. **Whitesides**. . . . [died] eleven days later.

Died in Laurens County, S. C., August 29th, 1884, Mrs. **Mary Cowan**, daughter of Abram and Nancy Thomson and relict of F. R. Cowan in the 64th year of her age.

Died in Lee County, Miss. at 6:15 o'clock on the evening of Friday, September 26th, 1884, Mrs. **Laura Letitia Mahon**, wife of Capt. J. G. Mahon, aged 41 years, 8 months and 9 days. . . . was a daughter of Rev. J. L. and Mrs. Margaret (Todd) Young, and was born in Laurens District, S. C., January 17th, 1843. Her father removed to Mississippi in the fall of

1851, and here in the bounds of Bethany congregation, she grew up, married, lived and died. . . graduated at the Atheneum in Columbia, Tenn. in 1861. . . . February 27, 1867, married Capt. John G. Mahon. . . mother of seven children, two [have died].

Married at the house of the bride's father, by Rev. C. B. Betts, assisted by Rev. D. R. Perry, Mr. **John M. Simpson** of Chester County, S. C. and Miss **Lizzie Dunbar** of Fairfield County, S. C.

- - - at the house of Mr. C. E. Bell in Mecklenburg Co., N. C. on Wednesday, the 10th of September, 1884, by Rev. J. Boyce, D. D., assisted by Rev. G. R. White, Mr. **Christopher Brice** of New Hope, Fairfield County, S. C. and Miss **Mattie J. Bell** of Mecklenburg County, N. C.

October 23, 1884

Died in Dorsey County, Ark., October 8th, 1884, of cholera infantum, **Roy Carmical**, son of Mr. C. L. and Mrs. Sue Carmical, aged 14 months and 14 days.

Died in Newton County, Ga., July 10th, 1884, Mrs. **Martha Chestnut**, widow of James Chestnut in her 74th year. . . . was born in Spartanburg County, S. C. and moved to Georgia in her younger days. . . [member] of A. R. P. church.

Died in Newton County, Ga. on the 17th of August, 1884, Mr. **James Y. Thompson.** He had passed, by several years, his four score. . . . member of Southern Presbyterian church.

Died in Prentiss County, Miss., of croup, on Thursday, October 9th, 1884, **Elizabeth Jane Tapp**, child of W. L. and M. J. (McDill) Tapp, aged 3 years, 10 months and 22 days.

Married, October 23, 1884, by Rev. H. T. Sloan, D. D., Mr. **John S. McLean** and Miss **Sallie L. Traylor**, daughter of A. A. Traylor of McCormick, Abbeville County, S. C.

- - - October 14th, 1884, at the residence of the bride, by Rev. C. E. Todd, Mr. **W. A. Chesnut** and Miss **J. M. Chesnut.** All of DeKalb County, Ga.

October 30, 1884

A little three year old so n of Mr. and Mrs. John **Brown**, Jr. of Long Cane, S. C., died of typhoid dysentary, Monday night, October 20th, 1884.

Died at her home in Fairfield County, S. C., August 27th, 1884, Mrs. **Janie E. Bankhead**, wife of John W. Bankhead, aged 27 years, 1 month and 14 days. . . . the little babe, **Mary Eunice**, which was about two months old at her mother's death, passed away on October 12th.

Mrs. **Anna Stewart** died July 18, 1884 . . . . was daughter of Dr. David and Mrs. Mary Young Black and was born in Wilcox County, Ala., September 17th, 1846; removed with her parents to the State of Mississippi, was married to D. A. Stewart.

Dr. **Joseph Hearst Bonner** was born in Abbeville County, S. C. on the 15th of February, 1820, and died in Camden, Ala., June 20th, 1884. He was in his 65th year. . . . was educated in literature and the sciences at Oxford, Ohio, and was graduated in medicine at Charleston, S. C. He was married in 1845 to Miss Sarah J. Young of Wilcox County, Ala. Of this union, eight children were born of which only one survives. He was left a widower in 1865 and never married again.

Rev. **Charles E. Todd** of Doraville, Ga. and Miss **Leila P. Cowan** of Due West, S. C. were happily married last Wednesday evening at six o'clock at the residence of the bride's mother, Mrs. T. C. Cowan. The pastor of the bride, Rev. W. L. Pressly, and the brother of the groom, Rev. C. L. Stewart, officiating.

Married, October 1st, 1884, in Mecklenburg County, N. C., by Rev. D. G. Caldwell, Mr. **W. L. McCoy** and Miss **Mary J. Alexander**.

- - - October 8th, 1884 in Mecklenburg County, N. C., by Rev. D. G. Caldwell, Mr. **Robert Blythe** and Miss **Mattie Kirkpatrick**. All of Mecklenburg County, N. C.

- - - October 16th, 1884 at the residence of the bride's father, Paint Lick, Ky., by Rev. Jas. Boyce, Jr., Mr. **W. A. Todd**, formerly of Due West, S. C. and Miss **Mary B. Guyn**.

November 6, 1884

Mr. **Robert C. Brown** died of typhoid fever near Millboro, Va., August 21st, 1884. He was the youngest son of Col. R. H. Brown of Monmouth, Rockbridge County, Va., was born March 29th, 1861 and therefore in the 24th year of his age.

Died near Unity church in Lancaster County, S. C. on the 29th of August, 1884, **John Hunter Nisbet**, son of Mrs. M. J. Nisbet, aged 15 years, 10 months and 7 days.

November 13, 1884

Died of consumption in Shelby County, Tenn., October 4th, 1884, Mrs. **Elizabeth Miller**, aged 81 years, 9 months and 5 days. . . . was born and reared in Chester County, S. C. . . . in 1878, she came with her daughter and grandchildren to make her home in Tipton County, Tenn.

Again in November, 1883, she removed with them to Shelby County, where she lived in the house of Mr. J. S. Kirkpatrick till the time of her death.

Born in Edgefield County, S. C., February 29th, 1810; and died August 24th, 1884, **William Jennings**, aged 74 years, 6 months and 5 days. When a young man, Mr. Jennings moved to Anderson County, S. C. and there married Miss Malinda Patterson. In 1844 they emigrated to Mississippi and settled in Tishomingo County. There they remained four years. In 1848 they moved to Tippah, now Union County. . . . he left behind an aged widow, several children.

Died at the residence of her son, Capt. W. P. Stewart, in Union County, Miss., September 2nd, 1884, Mrs. **Elizabeth Stewart**. . . . was born in the vicinity of Old Generostee congregation in Pendleton District, now Anderson County, S. C., in the year 1804, December 1st, and was at the time of her death in her 80th year. When quite young, she was united in holy wedlock with Mr. Stewart. In the year 1843, they emigrated to Mississippi, settling first in Tishomingo County, and afterward, and finally in 1847 in Tippah, now Union County.

Married, October 31st, 1884, at the residence of the bride's father, by Rev. W. H. Millen, Mr. **J. A. Johnson** and Miss **Callie Ayers**.

November 20, 1884

Died in Lancaster County, S. C. on the 25th of October, 1884, Mr. **Samuel Robinson**. Aged 80 years and 2 months . . . [survived by] two children, seventeen grandchildren, twenty two great-grandchildren.

Died at his residence in Lee County, Miss. on Friday morning, October 31st, 1884, **John Milton Bryson**, aged 31 years, 1 month and 26 days. . . . was a son of Samuel and Jane (Milam) Bryson, and was born in Itawamba (now Lee) County, Miss., September 5th, 1853, and his whole life was spent in the same neighborhood. He married Miss Viola J. Braden, January 2d, 1873, and joined the A. R. church at Bethany . . . leaves wife and four little children.

Married, October 29th, 1884, at the residence of the bride's father, Mr. Jno. A. Steele, by Rev. J. E. Pressly, D. D. , assisted by Rev. Wm. W. Pharr, Mr. **Sammie J. Pressly** of Cabarrus County and Miss **Emma Steele** of Iredell County, N. C.

- - - November 5th, 1884, by Rev. C. E. Todd, Mr. **John Sullivan** and Miss **Rebecca Castles**. Both of Newton County, Ga.

- - - November 12th, 1884, by Rev. W. L. Pressly, assisted by Rev. W. F. Pearson, Mr. **R. P. Blake** of Greenwood, S. C. and Miss **Gussie Hood**, daughter of Prof. Wm. Hood of Due West, S. C.

- - - November 13th, 1884, by Rev. W. L. Pressly, Mr. **W. J. Donnald** and Miss **Corrie Agnew**. Both of Donnaldsville, S. C.

November 27, 1884

Died, November 19th, 1884, in Due West, S. C., of diptheria, **Lucy Armathine**, daughter of Mr. and Mrs. Donald **Brownlee** [aged six years].

Died in Hamburg, Wilcox County, Ala., October 31st, 1884, Mrs. **Lillie A. Jones**. She was born in Sumter County, S. C., September 25th, 1814. . . . daughter of David and Susannah Mitchel and wife of William Jones, once an elder of Bethel church, but now deceased. . . . mother of eight children.

Died of dropsy, November 10th, 1884, at Doraville, Ga., **Robert Ezra**, son of D. A. and S. E. **Chesnut**, aged 21 year, 11 months and 22 days.

December 4, 1884

Died at her home in Iredell County, N. C., November 13th, 1884, Mrs. **Elizabeth Morrison**, aged 73 years, 3 months and 2 days. . . . was a member of Amity congregation.

Died at the residence of her son-in-law, Mr. R. M. Huey, in Winnsboro, S. C., August 6th, 1884, Mrs. **Margaret Jane Shaw**. . . . was born in March --, 1830, in County Antrim, Ireland, and came to the United States in 1850, landing at Charleston in the month of November, and locating soon after in Winnsboro. . . [joined church at Bally-castle in Ireland, and in S. C.] transferred her membership to Bethel Associate Reformed Presbyterian church, of which Rev. Thomas Ketchin was then pastor. On the 21st of January, 1853, she was married to James Warnock Shaw, who departed this life August 3rd, 1858. Mrs. Shaw was left thus early a widow with two children, aged respectively six months and three years. In February, 1861, Mrs. Shaw removed to Illinois, remaining there with relatives until September, 1865, when she returned to Winnsboro. Here she remained until the day of her death, with the exception of two years (1875-76) spent in Due West where her daughters were receiving instruction in the Female College.

Married, November 26th, 1884, 8:30 p. m., at the residence of the bride's father, 516 Gray St., Louisville, Ky., **S. F. Blakely**, M. D., and Miss **Millie M. Jones**, Rev. J. H. Morrison of the Southern Presbyterian church officiating.

- - - December 2nd, 1884, in Gastonia, N. C., by Rev. H. T. Sloan, D. D., assisted by Rev. E. E. Boyce, Mr. **William P. Wideman** of Abbeville, S. C. and Miss **Rebecca E. Boyce** of the former place.

December 11, 1884

Died, November 23d, 1884, in Dorsey County, Ark., **infant** daughter of Mr. and Mrs. J. T. **Hunter**. Aged 1 day; its twin brother survives.

Little **Walter Leslie**, son of Jno. M. and Laura M. **Moore** of Lincoln County, Tenn. died of tetanus 4th October, 1884 . . . in fifth year.

Died in Newberry, S. C., November 23d, 1884, Mrs. **Sarah Bushardt**, in the 72d year of her age. . . member of A. R. P. church at Cannon's Creek for nearly forty years . . . leaves five children.

Died in Winnsboro, S. C., September 8th, 1884, **Robert Todd**, son of Mr. and Mrs. Thos. H. **Ketchin**, aged 2 years and 1 month.

Married, November 25th, 1884, at the residence of Dr. Davis, in Bradley County, Ark. by Rev. J. S. A. Hunter, Mr. **O. P. Coplinger** and Miss **E. E. Henmore**.

- - - October 22d, 1884, by Rev. W. W. Orr, at the residence of the bride's mother, Mrs. M. M. McAuley, Mr. **Wm. Bradford** of Cabaarrus County and **Miss M. Grier McAuley** of Mecklenburg County, N. C.

- - - October 30th, 1884, by Rev. W. W. Orr, at the residence of the bride's father of Huntersville and Miss **Alice V. Overcash** of Cabarrus County, N. C.

- - - - November 12th, 1884, by Rev. W. W. Orr in the A. R. P. church of Huntersville, Mr. **Jno. O'Brien** and Miss **T. C. Alexander**. All of Mecklenburg County, N. C.

- - - - November 27th, 1884, by Rev. W. W. Orr in the A. R. P. church of Huntersville, Mr. **Jno. R. Hunter** and Miss **Newlie L. Ross**. All of Mecklenburg County, N. C.

December 18, 1884

Died in New Sterling congregation, on the 27th of November, 1884, Miss **Sophia McKay**. Aged 83 years, 10 months and 13 days.

Amelia Craig, daughter of Mr. T. J. Craig of Prosperity church, Dallas County, Ala., died October 21st, 1884.

Mrs. **Mary Beard** was born April 24th, 1812 in Rockbridge, and died in Augusta County, Va., October 1st, 1884. . . mother of six children, all of whom she dedicated to God in baptism at Old Providence church, Va.

Mr. **R. B. Wright** died in Tipton County, Tenn, October 1st, 1884, in the 33rd year of his age.

Mrs. **Jane McCaslan**, widow of the late A. L. McCaslan, Esq. and sister of Gen. P. H. Bradley, died in Troy, S. C. on Sabbath night, November 16th, 1884 in the 68th year of her age.

Married, November 26th, 1884, at the residence of S. M. Rice, Esq., brother-in-law of the bride, by Rev. John E. Carlisle, Rev. **Hugh R. McAuley** of Woodruff, Spartanburg County to **Miss Thompson Carlisle**, daughter of the late T. A. Carlisle of Union County, S. C.

- - - - December 4th, 1884 in the Associate Reformed church in Troy, Obion County, Tenn. by Rev. David Pressly, assisted by Rev. Thomas P. Pressly, Dr. **W. C. Pressly** of Marshall County, Miss. and Miss **Maud M. Moffatt**, only daughter of Mrs. Mary B. Moffatt of Troy, Tenn.

January 1, 1885

Mrs. **Sallie M. McQuiston** died in Tipton County, Tenn., November 26th, 1884, in the 48th year of her age. . . . was born in Fairfield County, S. C. . . . was first happily married to J. C. Chisolm, who afterwards became a ruling elder in New Hope congregation. In 1869, they moved to Tipton County, Tenn., and became identified with Salem congregation. In about a year afterwards the husband died, leaving to his devoted wife the responsible charge of rearing and educating six small children. . . After remaining a widow five or six years, she was again married to Dr. W. C. McQuiston, an elder in Salem. This husband lived but a few years . . . She left two sons and three daughters.

Died on the 2d of October, 1884, Mr. **David Hood**, aged 73 years, 1 month and 26 days. . . was born the 6th of August, 1811. . . . was ruling elder in Shiloh church [Lancaster County, S. C.] for about forty five years.

Died at his home in Huntersville, N. C., on the evening of the 28th of November, 1884, Mr. **J. Nixon Hunter**, aged 50 years, 8 months and 4 days. . . . first connected with the church under the ministry of Rev. John Hunter at Prosperity (A. R. P. church). A few years afterwards he moved to Charlotte where he did business for a number of years. . . . Some fourteen years ago he moved his family to this place [Huntersville] (it was no town then), and opened up a stock of goods; thus he was one of the founders of our little town. . . For the past twelve years he has been our postmaster. . . [buried] in Elmwood cemetery in Charlotte.

Married, December 3rd, 1884, at the residence of the bride's father, Mr. J. H. Walker, by Rev. G. R. White, Mr. **Sidney Long** of Charlotte and **Miss C. E. Walker** of Mecklenburg County, N. C.

- - - - December 4th, 1884 in Charlotte by Rev. G. R. White, Mr. **E. P. Griffith** of Mecklenburg County and Miss **Minnie L. Blackwelder** of Charlotte, N. C.

- - - - December 17th, 1884, near Due West, S. C., by Rev. W. F. Pearson, Mr. **John P. Hawthorn** and Miss **Nannie B. Nance**. All of Abbeville County, S. C.

- - - - December 17th, 1884, at the home of the bride, by Rev. E. L. Patton, LLD, assisted by Rev. H. T. Sloan, D. D. and Rev. R. F. Bradley, **W. P. Addison**, M. D. and Miss **Sallie T. Wideman**. All of Abbeville County, S. C.

- - - - December 11th, 1884, by Rev. W. M. Hunter, assisted by Rev. J. B. Marsh, at the residence of the bride's father in Alexander County, N. C., Mr. **Kelly Overcash** of Statesville, N. C. and Miss **Alice Alexander**.

- - - - December 18th, 1884, at the residence of the officating minister, Rev. John E. Pressly, D. D., and assisted by Rev. Neill E. Pressly of Tampico, Mexico, Mr. **J. L. McCall** amd Miss **Cornelia L. Overcash**, daughter of Mr. Neal Overcash. Both of Cabarrus County,N. C.

- - - - December 23d, 1884, at the residence of the bride's father, Mr. L. H. Walthall, by Rev. C. E. Todd, Mr. **Thomas W. McDonald** and Miss **Sallie L. Walthall**. Both of Coweta County, Ga.

<u>January 8, 1885</u>

Died, November 22d, 1884, **Jennie Roseborough**, daughter of Mr. and Mrs. R. B. **Mills**, aged about thirteen months.

Died, September 12th, 1884, **Samuel Moffatt**, son of Dr. and Mrs. S. M. **Wylie**. Aged 2 years and 15 days.

Died of membranous croup in Pope County, Ark., December 3d, 1884, **Wade Bonner**, son of Dr. T. D. and L. J. **Whitesides**. Aged 12 years, 3 months and 19 days.

Died of consumption in Pope County, Ark., September 19th, 1884 in the 24th year of her age, **Miss I. J.**, daughter of J. M. and S. R. **Ferguson**.

Mrs. **Margaret Jane Hughey**, wife of James Hughey, died suddenly at Bradley's, S. C., Monday evening, December 15th, 1884, aged about 45 years, leaving two small children . . . consistent member of the church at Cedar Spring.

Mrs. **Mary M. Brown** died near Brussels, Mo., December 4th, 1884, in the 45th year of her age. For five years she was afflicted, periodically, with asthma. . . [leaves] bereaved husband and motherless children.

Died in Union County, Miss., November 28th, 1884, **George**

Johnson Falkner, youngest child of Mr. E. G. and Mrs. R. F. Falkner, aged 12 years, 11 months and 3 days. . . . was born in Walker County, Ala., January 25th, 1872. His parents, after living some years in Laurence County, Ala., removed to Mississippi three years ago and settled in the neighborhood of Bethany.

Married, December 23d, 1884, at the residence of the bride's mother, by Rev. S. W. Haddon, Mr. **William Beard** and Miss **Iola McCutcheon.** All of Augusta County, Va.

- - - December 3d, 1884, at the home of the bride's mother, Mrs. Mary Bigham, by Rev. J. A. White, Mr. **Robert McElroy** and Miss **Lizzie Bigham.**

- - - December 23d, 1884, at the residence of Mr. Andrew Oates, by Rev. J. S. Mills, Mr. **L. A. Williams** and Miss **J. C. F. Oates.**

- - - December 17th, 1884, by Rev. W. L. Pressly, Mr. **E. W. Nance** and Miss **Mollie Young** of Level Land, S. C.

- - - December 18th, 1884, by Rev. W. L. Pressly, Mr. **J. G. Baird** of Chester, S. C. and Miss **Laura Johnston** of Due West, S. C.

- - - December 10th, 1884, in Drew County, Ark., by Rev. J. L. Young, Mr. **Theodore C. Boles** and Miss **Cinthia Shanks.**

- - - December 18th, 1884, in the Christian church at Union City, Tenn. by Rev. T. P. Pressly, Mr. **Lee Nolen** and Miss **Neelie Wade.** All of Obion County, Tenn.

- - - December 16th, 1884, at the residence of the bride's father, Mr. W. B. Simpson, by Rev. C. B. Betts, Mr. **T. F. Lesslie** of York County and Miss **Sallie E. Simpson**, of Chester County, S. C.

- - - December 18th, 1884, in Lewisville, S. C., by Rev. C. B. Betts, Mr. **J. M. Parris** of Chester C. H., and **Mrs. M. J. Hamilton** of Chester County, S. C.

- - - December 25th, 1884, at the parsonage, by Rev. C. B. Betts, Mr. **T. E. Hudson** and Miss **D. C. Orr.** All of Chester County, S. C.

- - - December 24th, 1884, at the residence of the bride's father, Mr. D. P. Waters, by Rev. C. B. Betts, Mr. **S. W. Garrison** of York County and Miss **J. Irene Waters** of Chester County, S. C.

- - - December 30th, 1884, at the residence of the bride's father, by Rev. C. B. Betts, Mr. **T. D. Burnadore** and Miss **Ida R. Mobley.** All of Chester County, S. C.

- - - January 1st, 1885, by Rev. H. T. Sloan, D. D., Mr. **Andrew Young** and Miss **Minnie Young**, daughter of Mr. S. O. Young. All of Long Cane, S. C.

January 15, 1885

Died in Alexander County, N. C., December 31st, 1884, **John Mason**, son of Mrs. Lizzie and the late John **Alexander**, in his 6th year.

Died, October 4th, 1884, **Walter Leslie Moore**, aged 4 years, 6 months and 9 days, son of John and Laura Moore of Prosperity, Lincoln County, Tenn.

Louis Bryson Wiley died of consumption at his home in Fayetteville, Tenn., on the 16th of December, 1884, and in the 58th year of his age. He was a Christian gentleman of culture, who graduated from Erskine College in 1846, but whose health was so precarious that he never embarked in the profession [as an artist] for which he was educated. . . a devoted wife and little daughter sorrow.

Died, January 10th, 1885, of capillary bronchitis, Mr. **H. M. Johnson** of Due West, S. C. . . . was a native of Tennessee, but while yet a young man married in this State and settled in the lower part of this [Abbeville] County. In 1873, attracted to its educational advantages, he came to our place [Due West], and was, at the time of his death, an honored citizen of our town. In April, 1875, he was received by certificate from the Methodist church into the communion of the A. R. church of Due West.

Miss **Mary Steele Finley** died at Auburn, Mo., December 5th, 1884. . . . was born in Shelby County, Ky., March 30th, 1816. Her father, Mr. Jas. Finley, removed to Missouri more than half a century ago, and settled in Lincoln County. He was one of the founders of Mt. Zion church, and at its organization was elected ruling elder. Even before the erection of a house of worship, there was "a church in his house."

On Sabbath morning, October 19th, 1884, **Mrs. E. F. Henry** departed this life. . . . was born January 28th, 1820. . . . In the year 1850 she was married to Mr. J. H. Henry, and in the fall of the same year she joined the A. R. P. church at New Hope in Madison County, Ky. Afterwards she removed to Bath County, and until her death lived a consistent member of Mt. Olivet church.

Died, August 26th, 1884, in Cabarrus County, N.C., Mr. **Andrew Bell**, in the 69th year of his age. . . . faithful member of the A. R. church at Coddle Creek for about forty years.

Married, December 11th, 1884, at the residence of the bride's father, by Rev. Mr. Clark, Mr. **Jno. C. Turnage** of Covington and Miss **Eugenia E. Reid** of Kerrville, Tenn.

- - - January 8th, 1885, by Rev. W. L. Pressly, Mr. **J. W. Gillespie** of Kentucky and Miss **Mattie Sharp** of Due West, S. C.

- - - January 8th, 1885, by Rev. C. E. Todd, Mr. **George W. Harnor** and Miss **Emma Nash**. All of DeKalb County, Ga.

- - - January 8th, 1885, in the A. R. church at Starkville, Oktibbeha County, Miss., by Rev. David Pressly, Mr. **David Packer** of Camden, Wilcox County, Ala. and **Miss M. Bell Pressly** of Starkville, Miss.

January 22, 1885

Infant son of Mr. Joseph and Mrs. **Huey** was born the 24th and died the 25th of December, 1884.

Died in Union County, Miss., December 21st, 1884, **Thompson Millen Snipes**, child of S. W. and Mary J. (Galloway) Snipes, aged 2 months and 1 day.

Died in Tipton County, Tenn., December 10th, 1884, **Lowry**, son of S. G. and J. M. **McLuney**, in the 14th year of his age.

Died in Ebenezer Township, York County, S. C., January 1st, 1885, **Mary Cathcart**, daughter of W. J. and M. J. **Miller**. Aged 11 years, 5 months and 16 days.

Mr. **Wm. H. McQuiston** died of chronic diarrhoea near Monticello, Drew County, Ark., November 8th, 1884. Born in Fairfield County, S. C., December 28th, 1813, he grew up in Hopewell church. In 1837 he moved to Tipton County, Tenn. He remained there thirty seven years, and moved to Arkansas in January, 1874. He was twice married, and the father of nine children, seven of whom are still living. His widow is also with us. Mr. McQuiston served as deacon first in Saline, then in Bloomington church in Tennessee, and afterwards in the church at Monticello, Ark. August 8th, 1880, he was ordained an elder in the Monticello church.

Departed this life at Belfast, Tenn., October 20th, 1884, Mrs. **Julia F. Williams**, in the 74th year of her age. . . . was born in Stokes County, N. C., April 19th, 1811. Early in life her parents came to Tennessee. [First joined the Cumberland Presbyterian church, then the Southern Presbyterians] . . . She was married September 2d, 1830 to Robert Williams of Belfast. . . She became the mother of three children, all daughters, two of whom still survive.

Married, January 15th, 1885, at the home of the bride's father, Mr. James Stephenson, by Rev. R. G. Miller, Mr. **Calvin C. Castles** and Miss **Maggie Stephenson**. All of Fairfield County, S. C.

- - - January 15th, 1885, at the home of the bride's father, Mr. Robert Stephenson, by Rev. J. G. Miller, Mr. **L. O. Westbrooks**, late of Texas, and Miss **Maggie J. Stephenson**, of Fairfield County, S. C.

January 29, 1885

Died, December 17th, 1884, of pneumonia, Mrs. **Joanna Reid** of Newberry, S. C. . . . She was married twice; twice left a widow. She leaves one child, a little boy two years old.

Died near Catawba, N. C., from the effect of a burn on the 18th day of January, 1885, Miss **Laura Carmichal**, only daughter of Mr. J. McLewis, aged 17 years, 10 months and 1 day.

Jane Lathem, wife of R. A. Lathem, died on the 16th of November, 1884, in the 74th year of her age. . . for many years a worthy member of Sharon.

T. K. McKnight died on the 9th of December, 1884, in the 79th year of his age. . . . Some forty years ago, or more, he was elected and ordained a ruling elder in the A. R. P. church at Olivet, York County, S. C.

Died in Guntown, Miss., at the residence of Mrs. K. D. Cole, at 8:46 o'clock, p. m., November 14th, 1884, Mrs. **Sarah McAlister**, lacking but two days of being 92 years old. . . was the daughter of Marshall and Lydia (Hinson) Diggs, and was born in Anson County, N. C., November 16th, 1792. She married Mr. George Haley, February 28th, 1809, and removed to Richmond County, N. C. He died November 12th, 1818, leaving her a widow with three little children. She was married the second time to Mr. John McAlister in 1819. He died December 24th, 1848, leaving her with two daughters. She was thus the mother of five children, only two of whom survive. She came to Mississippi in 1876, and resided with her daughter, Mrs. K. D. Cole, in Guntown. . . member of the Methodist church for sixty eight or sixty nine years.

Married, December 31st, 1884, by Rev. W. C. Bailey, Mr. **Jas. M. Matthews** and Miss **Palmetto Pinkerton**. All of Flemington, Fla.

- - - January 15th, 1885, by Rev. J. S. Mills, Mr. **W. L. McBride** and Miss **F. L. Harrell**.

- - - January 22d, 1885, at the residence of the bride's mother, Mrs. E. J. Puller, in Starkville, Miss., by Rev. David Pressly, Mr. **Geo. T. Hamilton** of Durant, Holmes County, Miss. and Miss **Lizzie L. Puller**, of Starkville, Okitebbeha County, Miss.

- - - January 21st, 1885, at the residence of Zenus Porter, in Mecklenburg County, N. C., by Rev. G. D. Parks, Mr. **Harvey Bigham** of Chester, S. C. and Miss **S. B. Porter**.

- - - - November 26th, 1884, by Rev. W. H. Millen, Mr. **L. D. Turner** and Miss **Bettie McBride**. All of Tippah County, Miss.

- - - - December 11th, 1884, at the residence of the bride's brother in New Albany, Miss., by Rev. W. H. Millen, **John W. Frederick**, Esq. and Miss **Mary E. Thompson**.

- - - - December 17th, 1884, at the residence of the bride's father, by Rev. W. H. Millen, Mr. **W. H. Harrell** of Lee County and Miss **Minnie Grace** of Union County, Miss.

- - - - January 1st, 1885, by Rev. W. H. Millen, Mr. **J. C. Newton** and Miss **Mattie F. Patterson**. Both of Union County, Miss.

February 5, 1885

Departed this life January 23d, 1885, Mrs. **Margaret Moffatt**, being in her 88th year since the 17th of July. . . . was the second child of Rev. Jno. Hemphill, D. D., one of the earlier pastors of Hopewell A. R. P. congregation, Chester County, S. C. . . . [She] was married in her twenty first year to Mr. William Moffatt, who was then settled in Union congregation, Chester County, of which Mr. Hemphill was pastor in connection with Hopewell. Mr. Moffatt was a ruling elder . . . a successful merchant, and amassed a considerable fortune, and left his widow, whom he preceded to the grave by more than thirty years, a competency of this world's goods. She was the mother of eight children. . . [three still live] Mrs. R. C. Grier of Due West, Mr. Henry Moffatt and Mrs. Roseborough of Chester County. One son Josiah. . . and two sons-in-law, were ministers of the gospel [Rev. H. Quigg and Dr. R. C. Grier].

Married, January 14th, 1885, at the residence of the bride's father, John Brown, Sr., by Rev. H. T. Sloan, D. D., Mr. **James Crawford** and Miss **Mattie Brown**. All of Long Cane, S. C.

- - - - December 10th, 1884, at the residence of Mr. H. R. Ryde, by Rev. E. E. Patterson, Mr. **John Moffatt** of Mississippi and Miss **Louila Logan** of Lovelady, Texas.

- - - - January 21st, 1885, in Newton County, Ga., by Rev. S. P. Davis, Mr. **W. W. Vinson** and Miss **Janie S. Stewart**, daughter of Turner Stewart.

February 12, 1885

Died at the home of his mother in Alexander County, N. C., on the 31st of December, 1884, **Adger Mason**, son of Mrs. Lizzie **Alexander** and the late Junius Alexander, aged 5 years, 9 months and 28 days.

Died at her home in Ebenezer, Ga., December 31st, 1884, Mrs.

Elizabeth Scruggs. She was the widow of Mund Scruggs, for many years an elder in Ebenezer church, and she survived him more than thirty years.

Died at her home in Ebenezer, Ga., on the 26th of January, 1885, Mrs. **Mary Ann Smith.** . . . was for a number of years a consistent member of Ebenezer church. These two old ladies were near neighbors, had traveled the same road to church for near half a century, were each over eighty years of age.

R. A. Lathem died on the 19th of January, 1885, in the 71st year of his age. . . member of Sharon about forty years. . . . For a good many years past he was a deacon in Sharon.

On the 13th of December, 1884, Mrs. **Elizabeth Young**, relict of the late Arthur Young, departed. . . was the third daughter of Simon Bexley. In Lowndes County, Miss., in September, 1831 she [was born]. . . For many years previous to her decease she lived in widowhood, but enjoyed the cheerful sympathy and love of a son and daughter.

Died, September 19th, 1884, in Cabarrus County, N. C., Mr. **James DeKalb Bell**, aged 38 years, 2 months and 14 days. . . member of the A. R. church at Coddle Creek. . . son of Andrew Bell. . . . left behind a youthful widow and her little boy.

Married, December 9th, 1884, at the residence of the bride's uncle, Mr. E. B. Alexander, by Rev. D. G. Caldwell, Mr. **Grier Barclay** and Miss **Mollie Blakely.** Both of Mecklenburg, N. C.

- - - - January 28th, 1885, at the residence of the bride's father, by Rev. H. M. Henry, Mr. **W. R. Chandler** and Miss **M. A. Stewart.** All of Wilcox County, Ala.

- - - - January 29th, 1885, at the residence of the bride's father, by Rev. H. M. Henry, Dr. **S. O. Jones** and Miss **Kate McConico.** Both of Wilcox County, Ala.

- - - - January 29th, 1885, at the residence of her brother, Wm. Cresswell, by Rev. H. T. Sloan, D. D., Mr. **Samuel Young, Jr.** and Miss **Sallie Cresswell.** All of Long Cane, S. C.

February 19, 1885

Died of lockjaw in Drew County, Ark., November 24th, 1884, **M. Lena Murry.** Aged 10 years, 11 months and 7 days.

Also, January 16th, 1885, **Robt. Wilson Murry** of pneumonia. Aged 15 years, 3 months and 7 days. Thus Mr. and Mrs. N. A. Murry were bereaved of their two oldest children in the short space of fifty three days.

Mr. **John Simonton** of Tipton County, Tenn., died at his residence January 29th, 1885. . . . had just entered on the 63rd year of his age. . . . was elected ruling elder in Portersville Presbyterian church.

Died in Mecklenburg County, N. C. on the 9th of January, 1885, Mr. **S. B. McLaughlin**, aged 23 years. He was a brother's son of Rev. I. G. McLaughlin and grandson of M. B. Wallace, a late elder of Sardis congregation.

Died in Chester County, S. C., February 2d, 1885, Dr. **Samuel McLurkin**, in the 64th year of his age. . . as a practicing physician, he easily stood at the head of his profession in this section. . . . To his natural skill and devotion was added a large experience of forty years of practice in Fairfield and Chester counties, and, in a large territory, perhaps forty miles square, there was scarcely a family where he had not at some time visited and administered to the sick.

February 26, 1884

Died near Shiloh church, Lancaster, S. C., little **N. Ella**, daughter of Mr. R. W. and Mrs. M. E. **Draffin**, the 3d of February, 1885. Aged 8 years, 3 months and 2 days.

Died near Shiloh church, Lancaster , S. C., on the 7th of February, 1885, **Mrs. S. S. (Craig) Draffin**, consort of Capt. Hugh Draffin, deceased, in the 73d year of her age since the 19th of Nevember . . . [married] in 1834. . . . . The fruit of this relation was five children, all of whom embraced the religion of their parents, and now survive.

Mrs. **Martha Jane Gragg** died of typhoid malarial fever, February 3d, 1885 at the residence of her son-in-law, Mr. R. M Vaughan, in Shelby County, Tenn. The deceased was born in Lincoln County, Tenn., April 24th, 1826. Her parents, David and Susan Reid, died when she was only four years old, and she was left to the care of her uncle, Wm. Blair. In 1842, she was married to J. Walker Gragg, and with him came to Shelby County two years later. . . . [joined] Salem A. R. P. church, but at the time of her death she was in connection with Bloomington, her husband being an elder in that church. . . She leaves four sons and two daughters, with the aged husband.

Died in Due West, S. C., February 19th, 1885, Mrs. **Mary A. Sharp**, wife of Mr. R. C. Sharp. . . . was the eldest daughter of Mr. George Brownlee, who settled within what is now the corporate limits of Due West, long before there was any such corporation. At the time of her death she lacked only one week of having completed her 62nd year. . . [married] in 1839 . . . member of the Associate Reformed church of Due West.

Died near Shiloh church, Lancaster, S. C., on the 27th of January,

1885, little **James Huey**, son of Mr. R. W. and Mrs. M. E. **Draffin**. Aged 3 years, 4 months and 9 days.

Died in Lee County, Miss., on Friday evening, January 16th, 1885, Mrs. **Elizabeth Ivanona Gamble**, wife of Dr. W. C. Gamble, aged 41 years and 4 days. . . . was a daughter of James W. and Mrs. E. D. (Richey) Agnew, and was born in Due West, S. C., January 12th, 1844. While she was yet a child, her parents removed from S. C. to Lincoln County, Tenn., and from thence, in 1855, to Tishomingo (now Prentiss) County, Miss., into the bounds of Bethany church. Her father died in 1856, leaving her and seven other children . . . [married on] September 17th, 1872. . . She was the mother of seven children, three of whom preceded her [in death].

Married, February 12th, 1885, at the residence of the bride's father, by Rev. W. M. Harden, Mr. **J. C. Grady** and Miss **Mary C. Rochester**. All of Union County, S. C.

March 5, 1885

Departed this life July 12th, 1884, Mr. **John Simpson**, aged 81 years, 5 months and 3 days. . . was of Scotch-Irish descent, his father, John Simpson, having emigrated to this country early in life. . . was the second child by a second marriage, but the fourth child in his father's family. His mother was an Adams. . . . He was a born mechanic, and his mind of the inventive order, but unfortunately too versatile; he could not wait to perfect one thing before it would spring to something else . . . [member of] A. R. P. church, Union congregation, Chester County, S. C. . . . . early in life married to Miss Sarah Wylie. . . . He was one of the original number who went into that organization [Union], the oldest member of the original bench of elders. . . Nine children were the fruits of his first marriage . . . [his first wife] died May 15, 1866. July 10th, 1874, he was happily married to Miss Nancy Lathan of Hopewell congregation.

Married, February 17th, 1885, at the residence of Mrs. Howell, Newnan, Ga., by Rev. Jas. Stacy, D. D., Mr. **A. H. Young** of White Oak, Ga. and Miss **Jean McRitchie** of Newnan.

- - - - February 19th, 1885, by Rev. R. M. Stevenson, Mr. **William T. Hart** and Miss **Virginia S. Hall**, daughter of the late Robert C. Hall. All of Rockbridge County, Va.

- - - - February 18th, 1885, in Mecklenburg County, N. C., by Rev. D. G. Caldwell, assisted by Rev. Osborne, Mr. **W. W. Ranson**, son of Rev. A. Ranson, D. D., deceased, and Miss **Julia E. Whitley**.

- - - - February 5th, 1885, at the Parsonage, by Rev. C. B. Betts, Mr. **J. S. Barr** of Lancaster County, S. C. and Miss **M. E. Miller** of Chester County, S. C.

- - - - February 19th, 1885, at the house of the bride's mother, Mrs. Elihu Simpson, by Rev. C. B. Betts, Mr. **T. Stuart Ferguson** and Miss **Lois Isabella Simpson**. All of Chester County, S. C.

- - - - February 11th, 1885, at the residence of the bride's mother, White Oak, Coweta County, Ga., by Rev. J. L. Hemphill, Mr. **Wm. J. Flowers** and Mrs. **Maggie J. Carmical**.

Olin Hawthorn of Chester, formerly of this place [Due West], was happily married to Miss **Emma Rowland** of Donnalds [S. C.], by Rev. W. D. Kirkland on the 25th of February last.

March 12, 1885

Died of old age, on the 19th of January, 1885, **James Stewart**. . . . born on the 11th of September, 1798, at Stony Batter, Newberry County, S. C. . . . In 1812, his father moved to the Reedy branches in the Cedar Spring congregation. [where he joined the church] . . . In 1820, he married Margary Wiley, Rev. J. T. Pressly officiating. In 1826, he moved to Tennessee and settled in the bounds of Prosperity congregation.

Mrs. E. B. Mines was born in Augusta County, Va., April 9th, 1802, and died January 20th, 1885. . . . joined Old Providence church in 1822. . . married in 1828. She was the mother of four children, for about forty years she was a widow.

Mrs. **Elizabeth Reid** died at her home near Auburn, Mo., February 20th, 1884, in the 76th year of her age. . . She was a sister of Rev. Jackson Duff, and an aunt of Rev. Barnett, lately deceased, the first foreign missionary of the A. R. P. church. She was born in Madison County, Ky. . . . [orphaned at an early age] she found a home with Mrs. Ann Wallace. . . was married about 1835 to Mr. Alexander Reid, and removed to the bounds of Mt. Zion church, Mo.

Died, December 25th, 1884, at the residence of his son-in-law, Mr. John G. McCurry, Anderson County, S. C., Mr. **John McDonald**, aged 76 years. . . was born of Scotch parents in what is now Hart County, Ga. Here, as tradition tells us, we once had a church organization sixty or seventy years ago, but the church was lost by immigration. Mr. McDonald [went to the "next of kin," the Presbyterian church] . . . was a brother of Rev. L. McDonald.

Died in Lee County, Miss., on Sabbath, January 25th, 1885, at 7:20 o'clock, p. m., Mrs. **Maria Cappleman**, aged 73 years, 1 month and 19 days. . . was a daughter of Mr. James Wilson, Sr. and Mrs. Amelia (Brown) Wilson, and was born in Newberry District, S. C., December 6th, 1811. Her father was a ruling elder of the Associate Reformed church . . . and about 1828 she joined the church at Head Spring . . . was married to Henry Cappleman, December 22d, 1836. In 1847, they removed from S. C., and living one year in Coweta County, Ga., and five in Tippah County, Miss., they settled in 1853 in Itawamba (now Lee) County, Miss. in the bounds of Bethany church. . . . Her husband died October 3d, 1880. . . She was the mother of seven children. . . with two sons and two daughters [surviving].

Married, February 19th, 1885, in Jefferson County, Ga., by Rev. J. S. Mills, Mr. **J. W. A. Causey** and Miss **Sussie A. Gordon**.

- - - - February 26th, 1885, in Burke County, Ga., by Rev. J. S. Mills, Mr. **T. A. Harrell** and Miss **Mollie Thomas**.

- - - - March 5th, 1885, at the residence of and by Rev. W. M. Hunter, Mr. **D. M. Moore** of Iredell County and Miss **Cora Little**, Tayorsville, N. C.

March 19, 1885

Died in Fairfield County, S. C., March 1st, 1885, Mr. **Robert Curry**, aged 85 years and 2 months. . . For a long time a consistent member of the "Old Brick" church, Associate Reformed . . . [his death removes] the oldest of the few remaining members of that expiring congregation.

Mrs. **Caroline Richey**, the devoted wife of Walter Richey died. . . . February 25th, 1885, in the 50th year of her age. . . was a daughter of Mr. Daniel Atkins, and has left a devoted husband and five children . . . member of the A. R. P. church at Cedar Spring.

Mrs. **Agnus J. Nelson** was born March 21st, 1826, and died January 25th, 1885 in Rockbridge County, Va. . . . She was early in life, together with her two brothers and sister, brought from Missouri by an uncle to Rockbridge County, Va., and by him raised. . . . after her marriage to Samuel D. Nelson, which took place on November 22d, 1849, she joined Old Providence by certificate.

Mr. **Joseph P. Caldwell** died of heart disease, January 13th, 1885, in the 69th year of his age. He resided near Holland's Store, Anderson County, S. C. . . . was born in Newberry County, S. C. When just a boy his parents, John and Margaret Caldwell, moved from Newberry to Anderson County, and settled near Old Shiloh. His parents some years after went West and settled in Mississippi . . . [he became a member] of old Shiloh . . . in 1840. In 1841, he was united in marriage to Miss Rebecca G. Seawright. In 1876 or '77 he was elected ruling elder at the organization of the Grove church. . . . His children having all gone before, he leaves a widow.

Died at Winnsboro, S. C., January 15th, 1885, Mrs. **Mary Jane Cummings**, in the 32d year of her age. . . . was a daughter of Henry L. Elliott, and the wife of Joseph H. Cummings . . . member of Associate

Reformed church of Winnsboro. . . . leaves a husband and four children.

Married, March 5th, 1885, at the house of the bride's father, Mr. Michael Tolbert, by Rev. H. T. Sloan, D. D., Mr. **Joseph Cresswell** and Miss **M. F. Tolbert**.

- - - - March 11th, 1885, at the residence of Mr. W. H. Goodrum, the bride's father, by Rev. L. K. Glasgow, Mr. **Eli B. Alexander** and Miss **Mary Goodrum**. All of Mecklenburg County, N. C.

March 26, 1885

Died in Fairfield County, S. C., March 12th, 1885, Mr. **R. C. Clowney**, aged about 47 years. . . . once he represented his county in the Legislature. . . . was a ruling elder in the Presbyterian church.

Died near Pineville, N. C., February 28th, 1885, Mrs. **Mary E. McClelland**, in the 37th year of her age. . . . was the only daughter of Robert and Jane Stewart, and the wife of Wm. S. McClelland. . . . Scarcely five weeks had elapsed since we buried Mrs. Stewart. . . . Mrs. McClelland . . . leaves a devoted husband with six children, the youngest only three weeks old. . . [member of] Steel Creek.

Died in Shelby County, Tenn., February 28th, 1885, Mr. **Robert Craig**, aged 38 years, 10 months and 3 days. . . . was the son of John L. Craig. . . born and reared in Lafayette County, Miss., was married March 4th, 1868, to Miss Florence B. Black of Union County, Miss., where he lived eight or ten years, and where he was ordained an elder in Ebenezer congregation. . . . returning to Lafayette County in 1880, he became an active worker in Shiloh congregation.

Married, March 17th, 1885, at the residence of the bride's father in Statesville, N. C., by Rev. R. G. Miller, Col. **J. S. Miller** and Miss **Cora L. Templeton**. All of Statesville, N. C.

April 2, 1885

Died at the residence of her son-in-law, Mr. W. S. McClelland, near Pineville, N. C., January 25th, 1885, Mrs. **Jane G. Stewart**, in the 76th year of her age. . . . widow of the late Robert Stewart and member of the church at Steel Creek.

Mrs. M. E. (Thompson) Draffin, consort of Mr. R. W. Draffin, was born on the 24th of August, 1844, and died February 25th, 1885. . . [married in] 1874. The fruit of this relation was four children, three of whom preceded her to the grave.

William Plaxco, infant son of Mr. R. W. and Mrs. M. E. **Draffin**, was born on the 1st of April, 1884, and died on the 18th of February, 1885.

Out of four children, only one survives.

Died in Newberry, S. C., 4th February, 1885, of peritonitis, **Laura N.**, wife of Robert L. **McCaughrin**, aged 41 years, 2 months and 2 days. . . . was the youngest child, but one, of the late Drayton and Mrs. Lucy W. Nance, and spent her life in her native place. . . . [has lost three children]. Her first bereavement was little **Thomas**, 19th July, 1883, aged 14 months and 16 days. . . Again on the 26th September, 1884, **Robert Lusk**, aged 12 years and 5 months. . . . only two days later on the 28th September, 1884, the baby, little **Laura Nance**, [aged] eight months.

Married, February 10th, 1885, at the residence of the bride's mother, in Lafayette County, Miss., by Rev. Mr. Gamble, Mr. **D. K. Oates** of Yell County, Ark. and Miss **M. A. McAteer**.

April 9, 1885

Died in Newton County, Ga., March 20th, 1885, Mrs. **Margaret Thompson**, widow of Wm. Thompson, in her 69th year. . . one son and five daughters and many grandchildren mourn their loss.

Mrs. **Elizabeth Jane Carmack**, wife of Mr. James T. Carmack, and daughter of Col. Wm. S. and Mrs. Rebecca J. Ryburn, of Lodi, Va., departed this life November 28th, 1884, aged 26 years, 4 months and 8 days. . . . She never attached herself to any church -- there being near her no church organization of the faith of her father and mother, to which, in principle, she was strongly attached -- the Associate Reformed Presbyterian-- was married on the 26th of December, 1883. . . . became a mother the 17th of November, 1884.

Died at his home near Matthew's Station, in Mecklenburg County, N. C., on the 21st of January, 1885, **Amzi G. Reid**, Esq., aged 57 years, 8 months and 21 days. . . ruling elder in the church for thirty years, a part of which time was in Sardis A. R. P. church and the remainder was in the Presbyterian church at Matthews.

Married, April 2d, 1885, at the residence of the bride's father, Dr. W. E. Aiken, Winnsboro, S. C., by Rev. Jno. T. Chalmers, assisted by Rev. D. E. Jordan, Hon. **Chas. A. Douglass** and Miss **Gussie Aiken**. Both of Winnsboro, S. C.

April 16, 1885

Died at Clover, York County, S. C., in the home of Zimri Carroll, Mrs. **Isabella Hemphill**, in the 88th year of her age. . . . Born on Alison Creek, York County, reared in the Associate Reformed congregation of Bethany, married before the war and moved to North Georgia, her husband died there during the war, had all the experience of being overrun and impoverished by Sherman's army, moved back to Alison's Creek and the home of a brother's son where she lived in great domestic comfort for nineteen years. . . [until death] the 25th of March, 1885. . . member of Bethany congregation.

Died at Clover, York County, S. C., and in the same house as the foregoing, **Mrs. S. E. Carroll**, wife of Zimri Carroll, in her 51st year. . . . leaves a good husband and dutiful children, three of whom are daughters.

Died on the 14th of March, 1885, at Hickory Grove in York County, s. C., Mrs. **Emily Wylie**, in the 59th year of her age. . . . was the widow of the late T. G. Wylie. . . a daughter of Christopher Strong, Esq. of Chester. Her mother was a daughter of John Hams of Steel Creek and sister of Dr. John M. Hams. . . [member of Hopewell until marriage]. Near forty years ago she, with her husband, removed to western York, and connected with Smyrna A. R. P. congregation . . . mother of one son and six daughters.

Miss **Sue M. Thorn** . . . [died] March 4th, 1885. She was in the 19th year of her age, being born December 5th, 1866. . . member of A. R. P. church of Hinkston, Ky.

Married, January 15th, 1885, by Rev. M. Oates, Mr. **J. T. Ferguson** and **Miss M. F. Oates**. Both of Pope County, Ark.

- - - - March 5th, 1885, by Rev. M. Oates, Mr. **C. C. Oates** and **Mrs. M. A. Ferguson**. Both of Pope County, Ark.

- - - - March 19th, 1885, by Rev. M. Oates, Mr. **J. B. Sinclair** and **Miss M. E. Oates**.

April 23, 1885

Mrs. **Betsy Ingraham** died in Rockbridge County, Va., about the last of February. Her age is not known to the writer, but she had past by several years that age, when the Psalmist says in the 90th Psalm. . . member of Broad Creek Church.

Died in Guntown, Miss., on Monday, March 16th, 1885, Mrs. **Lucy Ann Frances Copeland**, aged 60 years, 2 months and 19 days. . . . was a daughter of David and Mary (Rogers) Justice, and was born in Wake County, N. C. , December 27th, 1824 . . . . During 1850, she visited a brother, Dr. J. W. Justice, then residing in Fulton, Miss. Here she made the acquaintance of L. J. Copeland, Esq., a prominent citizen of that place, and was married to him August 15, 1850. In 1852, they removed to the northwestern part of the county and settled on a farm. . . Mr. Copeland died October 10, 1884. . . . She was the mother of two children.

Mrs. **Louisa N. McGill** died on the 24th of March, 1885 at her home in western York, S. C., being 68 years and 10 days old. On the 24th of January, 1837, she married Thomas McGill, Esq., who still survives.

The fruit of this union was ten children, five of whom long since passed into the spirit world. Thomas McGill and his wife identified themselves with Smyrna A. R. P. congregation and was elected a ruling elder. . . . She has left, besides her aged husband, three sons and two daughters.

April 30, 1885

Died in Allenton, Ala., March 7th, 1885, **Merlin Carlisle**, infant son of Dr. Joseph H. and Mrs. Sallie Hall **Jones**, aged 13 months and 1 day.

Mrs. **Ellen A. Patterson**, wife of A. L. Patterson, was born August 3d, 1830, and died in Louisville, Ga., April 4th, 1885.

Married, April 9th, 1885, at the residence of the bride's father, in Burke County, Ga., by Rev. J. S. Mills, Mr. **J. H. Ivey** and Miss **Jessie M. Harrell**.

May 7, 1885

John Lawson Pursly died April 8the, 1885, in the 45th year of his age, near Bethany, York County, S. C. . . . son of William Pursly. . . . was a deacon in Bethany. He leaves a wife and four children.

Mrs. **Mary C. Caldwell** died on the 15th of March, 1885, of hemorrhage of the lungs. She was in the 70th year of her age. . . was the daughter of Wm. McGill, Esq. . . in 1836 she was married to Wm. Caldwell, who survives her. . . in 1837, she and her husband . . . [joined] the A. R. P. church at Sharon. . . . She bore ten children, five of whom survive her.

Miss **Rachel N. Caldwell** died on the 26th of March, eleven days after her mother. . . [member] of Bethany A. R. P. church.

May 14, 1885

Amanthus, daughter of J. T. and Janie **Marion**, departed this life April 7th, 1885, aged 2 months and 20 days.

Died of bronchial pneumonia at the residence of Mr. Robt. Banks, Tipton County, Tenn., January 31st, 1885, Mrs. **Sophronia Hindman**, aged 60 years, 10 months and 10 days. . . . born and reared in Chester County, S. C. . . . After coming West she identified herself with the Bloomington A. R. P. church.

Mr. **Clinton Willson** died at his home on Swan Creek, Lincoln County, Tenn., on the 12th of April, 1885, in the 72nd year of his age. . . . member of Bethel congregation.

Mr. **N. B. Craig** was born the 17th of January, 1829, and died near Shiloh the 4th of April, 1885, aged 56 years, 2 months and 27 days. . . . On the 10th of January, 1860, he was married to Miss E. J. Malkinson. The fruit of this relation was seven children, six of whom still survive.

Mr. **Joseph L. Bigham** died at his home in Chester County, S. C., April 20th, 1885, aged 70 years and 20 days. . . . was born and reared to manhood in York County. . . . He reared a large family, all, except one, of which he lived to see reared to manhood and womanhood and become members of the church.

Married, May 7th, 1885, in Dallas County, Ala., by Rev. J. A. Lowry, Dr. **James M. Donald** and Miss **Kate M. Young**, daughter of the late Rev. J. M. Young.

- - - - April 15, 1885, in the M. E. church, Orange City, Fla., Mr. **F. C. Austin** and Miss **Kittie Lankester**.

May 21, 1885

Died in Newberry, S. C., April 29th, 1885, Miss **Carrie L. Reid**, daughter of James Reid, deceased, in her 54th year. . . . early connected herself with Cannon's Creek church.

Departed this life March 18th, 1885, **Mrs. R. M. Ratterree**, aged 44 years and 9 months. . . was born in Cleveland County, N. C. Her maiden name was Dickson. . . . When but a little over sixteen she gave her hand in marriage to Mr. James Ratterree of York County, S. C., who was a widower with two small children. . . . She was the mother of several children, but three however lived to be grown.

Died in Mecklenburg County, N. C. on the 18th of March, 1885, Mrs. **Louisa Kirkpatrick**, in the 75th year of her age. On the 8th of July, 1830, she was married to Mr. Hugh Kirkpatrick, who, about two years ago, preceded her to the grave. . . [member] of Ebenezer congregation. . . . Her children, some gone before, the others grown and settled.

May 28, 1885

Mrs. **Jane S. McAuley**, wife of Mr. John C. McAuley, died April 5th, 1885, aged 35 years, 9 months and 4 days. She leaves six children, a devoted husband.

Little **Droyatt**, son of Mr. and Mrs. J. M. **Holler**, died in Huntersville, N. C., May 18th, 1885, aged 1 year and 11 months.

Mr. **W. J. Stevenson** died March 8th, 1885 in Columbia, S. C. , aged 23 years, 2 months and 17 days. . raised in Chester Co. by an aunt, Mrs. E. J. Jamison. . . [member of] the A. R. church of Huntersville, N. C.

Died in her home in Abbeville County, S. C., March 12th, 1885, **Mrs. M. E. Sherard**, the beloved wife of Mr. W. C. Sherard and daughter of Mr. A. J. Clinkscales, in the 29th year of her age. . . [member of] Presbyterian church. . . graduated from the Due West Female College in the class of 1875 . . . united in marriage to Mr. W. C. Sherard, September 12th, 1877. . . she leaves her husband and two little children.

Married, April 16th, 1885 by Rev. S. W. Haddon at the residence of the bride's mother, Mr. **John Dixon** and Miss **Sallie Horne**. All of Rockbridge County, Va.

June 4, 1885

Died April 30th, 1885, Mr. **John B. Davis**, aged 28 years, 6 months and 23 days. . . . member of the Troy [S. C.] church. . . . nursed through his last illness by his mother, Mrs. Jane M. Davis.

Mr. **William Chesnut** died of bronchial affection in Fulton County, Ark., March 17th, 1885. Born February 23d, 1805 in Fairfield District, S. C., when only three or four years old his parents, David and Jane Chesnut, moved to Newton County, Ga. On the 27th of November, 1827, Mr. Chesnut married Miss Susanna Sims. Nine children were born to them, six sons and three daughters. Three sons, two daughters, the aged companion [survive] . . . . In the spring of 1839, the family moved to Henry County, Ga.; in the spring of 1848 to Cobb County, Ga.; in the fall of 1857 to Pope County, Ark.; in the fall of 1858 to Fulton County, Ark. . . . ruling elder for many years.

Mrs. **Martha Purdy**, the devoted wife of Mr. Leroy Purdy of Cedar Spring, S. C., departed this life, May 7th, 1885, after a long and painful illness, aged 66 years and 3 months. For forty six years and four months this couple had shared life. . . had lived to see their children grown and married, save one. . . . six children . . . members of church at Cedar Spring.

Married by Rev. W. L. Pressly, June 2nd, 1885, at the residence of the bride's father, Rev. J. N. Young, Mr. **James E. Todd** and Miss **Hattie Young**. Both of Due West.

Married, 9 o'clock, a. m., June 3rd, 1885, by the Rev. W. L. Pressly at the residence of the bride's father, Dr. E. H. Edwards, Mr. **J. E. Taylor** of Lancaster, S. C. and Miss **Nannie Edwards** of Due West.

June 11, 1885

My [R. H. Jennings] grandmother, Mrs. **Jane Robinson**, *nee* Elliott, died May 16, 1885, in Fairfield County, S. C. in the 88th year of her age. . . . She was married while quite young to Robert Robinson of said State and county, and had ten children, seven of whom, together with her husband, preceded her to the grave. Few persons are permitted to see so many of their own posterity as she. These amount to about one hundred and forty. She was for many years, perhaps threescore and ten or more--a consistent member of the Associate Reformed Presbyterian church.

John Chalmers McMaster, son of R. N. and Mrs. Sallie McMaster, died in Winnsboro, S. C., May 22, 1885. . . . 3 years and 6 months old.

Died in Newberry County, S. C., May 20, 1885, Mr. **Thomas Beasley Chalmers**, in the 58th year of his age. . . . active member of Head Springs church and for the last twenty five a ruling elder.

June 18, 1885

Died at his residence in Lee County, Miss., March 24th, 1885, Mr. **Robert Caldwell Richey**, aged 73 years, 1 month and 11 days. . . was a son of William and Elizabeth (Cowan) Richey, and was born in Abbeville District, S. C., February 13th, 1812. In 1818, when he was six years old, his father died, leaving him to be reared by an affectionate mother. He married Miss Nancy E. Hill, April 21st, 1836. He removed from Abbeville to the neighborhood of Pendleton in Anderson about 1854, and from thence in the fall of 1859 he removed to Itawamba (now Lee) County, Miss., and settled on the place at which he died. Mrs. Richey died June 25th, 1877. Mr. Richey contracted a second marriage with Mrs. S. C. Thompson, November 25th, 1880. . . . [member of] Gaston Presbyterian church . . . [and] ruling elder. . . . father of ten children, most of which preceded him to the tomb. He leaves a wife, three sons and one daughter.

Married, April 28th, 1885, at the residence of J. N. Bethea, Esq., by Rev. D. G. Phillips, D. D., Mr. **Thos. Hardeman** and Miss **Sussie P. Little**. Also, Rev. **J. S. Mills** and Miss **Berta H. Little**, Daughters of the late Hon. R. P. Little of Jefferson County, Ga.

- - - - May 21st, 1885, at the residence of the bride's father, Mr. T. T. Youngblood, by Rev. W. W. Orr, assisted by Rev. C. E. McDonald, Mr. **J. I. Blakely** of Huntersville, N. C. and Miss **Nannie Youngblood**.

June 25, 1885

Died in Taylorsville, N. C., May 10th, 1885, **Jacob Erasmus**, infant son of Mr. Jas. T. and Mrs. Anna **Hedric**, aged 1 year and 22 days.

Died Sabbath, the 21st instant, Mrs. **Elizabeth Ellis**, relict of the late John Eli Ellis, Esq. . . . in hrt 82d year. She was the mother of seventeen children, eleven sons and six daughters. . . . with a single exception these children all lived to be grown, the majority of them raised families of their own, so that the descendants of this good woman are quite numerous. Exactly two years before her youngest child, Miss Savannah P. Ellis, was buried. . . . [Mrs. Ellis was] member of the A. R. church at Due West.

Died at her home in Newberry County, S. C., May 17th, 1885, Mrs. **Elizabeth (Bettie) Reid**, in the 84th year of her age. . . . member of the A. R. P. church at Cannon's Creek. . . . She leaves two daughters, Mrs. Fannie Neel and Mrs. E. C. Maffett.

Married on the 17th June, 1885, at the residence of the bride's mother, Mrs. M. Galloway, by Rev. W. L. Pressly, assisted by Rev. H. T. Sloan, D. D., Mr. **John A. Devlin** and Miss **Lola M. Galloway**. Both of Due West.

July 2, 1885

Died of pneumonia in Bradley, Ark., April 15th, 1855, at the residence of Mr. Lee Martin, Mrs. **Harriet Clary**. . . . born in Lancaster County, S. C., in 1815. Moved to this state in 1860. Her maiden name was Cothran. She first married a Mr. Mason, then to Mr. Daniel Clary; both of whom preceded her to the grave. She was a devoted member of the A. R. P. church at Shady Grove.

Died in Mecklenburg County, N. C., May 24th, 1885, Miss **Sarah Wallace**, in the 53d year of her age. . . . long a communing member of Sardis church.

William Wilson was born October 16, 1821, and died May 17, 1885. . . . [member and ruling elder] at Pisgah. . . . He leaves a widow and nine children. . . . He was born, lived and died near Crowder's Mountain, Gaston County, N. C.

Died at his home near Huntersville, N. C., June 6th, 1885, Mr. **Milton Osborne**, aged 83 years, 5 months and 5 days. . . one of the founders of the A. R. P. church at Huntersville.

Died near Doraville, Ga., May 25, 1885, Mrs. **Jennie Sellers**, in the 72d year of her age. . . . was born in Chester County, S. C. in 1832. Her father moved to Newton County, Ga. In 1852, she moved to DeKalb County near Doraville. . . . for thirty years a member of Prosperity church. . . . for many years a widow.

Mrs. **Elizabeth Smith**, wife of Capt. John Smith, departed this life May 6th, 1885, aged 74 years, 5 months and 21 days. . . . maiden name was McGill. . . . member of Hopewell congregation, Chester County, S. C. . . . first married to Mr. Montgomery by whom she had two daughters [the one surviving is Mrs. Richard Peoples of North Carolina]. The married life in this case was short, covering a period of about seven years. In September, 1845, the deceased became the second wife of Mr. John Smith, with whom she lived a comfortable and happy life for over thirty-nine years. One child, a daughter.

Married, November 6th, 1884, in Lincoln County, Ark., at the residence of the bride's father, by Rev. W. L. Patterson, Mr. **J. T. Stirling** and **Miss M. E. Boyd**.

- - - December 24th, 1884, in Freestone County, Texas, at the residence of the bride's father, by Rev. W. L. Patterson, Dr. **J. D. Reid** and Miss **Bell B. Thornton**.

- - -June 17, 1885, by Rev. R. M. Stevenson, Mr. **Jno. P. Harrison** and Miss **Jennie Bowlin**. All of Rockbridge County, Va.

- - - June 24th, 1885, in the Associate Reformed Presbyterian church, at 7 o'clock, p. m., by Rev. David Pressly, Mr. **John Walker Pope** of Mobile, Ala., and Miss **Julia Alice Montgomery**, a daughter of Col. Wm. B. Montgomery of Starkville, Okitibbeha County, Miss.

July 9, 1885

Died at midnight, June 27th, 1885, in Catawba County, N. C., **Ralph**, son of Mr. Alex. and Mrs. Sallie **Yount**, aged 2 years, 9 months and 23 days.

Died in Mecklenburg County, N. C., on the 26th of May, 1885, Mr. **J. Ellis Irwin**, in the 27th year of his age. . . . member of Sardis church.

Mrs. **Mary Ann Moore** died in Newberry, S. C., May 15th, 1885, in the 84th year of her age. . . .[born in Wales] when she was a girl of about four years her parents moved to this country and settled in the Prosperity congregation. After marrying she lived in the Cannon Creek congregation . . . . and raised a family of seven children. Since the death of her husband, some twenty years ago, she has lived among her children.

Died at his residence in Troy, Tenn., May 25th, 1885, Mr. **Augustus Peden Moffatt** in the 56th year of his age. . . . the son of James S. and Martha Moffatt, was born in Greenville County, S. C., near Fairview church, March 3d, 1830. When he was but a boy, his father came to Troy. . . for some twenty five years a ruling elder. . . . Almost from infancy, he was an invalid and suffered much during all his days. . . . twice he was deprived of his bosom companion. He has left to mourn his departure an aged father, a brother and two sisters; also a daughter by his first wife, Mrs. Sallie Meacham, now in Florida, a son by his second wife, Mr. C. L. Moffatt, and his last wife with a little daughter and son.

Married, July 2d, 1885, by Rev. J. W. Abernathy, assisted by Rev. Mr. Davis, Mr. **Thomas J. Abernathy** and Miss **Lucy S. Elms**. All of Mecklenburg County, N. C.

- - - June 11th, 1885, by Rev. C. B. Betts, Dr. **E. Y. Murphy** and Miss **H. L. Crook**. All of York County, S. C.

July 16, 1885

Mrs. **Margaret (Wiley) Stewart** died on the 26th of May, 1885, in her 90th year. . . [member of] the A. R. P. church for about seventy five years; first at Cedar Springs and for the last fifty-five at Prosperity and New Hope. Her family, a large one, was as remarkable for its piety as longevity, most of whom reached more than fourscore.

Mrs. **Elizabeth S. McElroy**, wife of Mr. Robert McElroy, died June 22d, 1885, aged 27 years, 3 months and 4 days. . . married last December.

Died of measles and pneumonia, on the 14th of June, 1885, **Miss E. Isabella Young**, near Bethel church, Tenn., in the 16th year of her age. . . . Though baptized in infancy and not an unfrequent presence at the house of God, still she belonged to a small class of our youth who have not, though of proper age, professed faith in the Lord Jesus.

Born in Abbeville County, S. C., August 24th, 1814, and died at the residence of her son-in-law, Mr. John Newton, in Union County, Miss., June 17th, 1885, Mrs. **Catherine Addin Patterson**. . . . member of Methodist church. . . has left behind an aged husband, three sons and two daughters.

Died in Union County, Miss., June 17th, 1885, Mrs. **Martha Savannah Caldwell**, aged 24 years, 1 month and 3 days. . . . was a daughter and the only child of Daniel R. and Eliza (Spence) Holloway, and was born in Lincoln County, Tenn., May 14th, 1861. Her father died in February, 1862. . . . in the fall of 1880, with her mother she removed to Union County, Miss., and became members of Hopewell church. Here on February 7th, 1884, she was married to Mr. J. O. Caldwell. . . . On the 7th of June she gave birth to a dead babe, and now the mother has speedily followed her child.

July 30, 1885

Married, June 17th, 1885, in the A. R. P. church in Lovelady, Texas, by Rev. R. E. Patterson, Dr. **George Y. Mangrum** and Miss **Callie Arnold**. All of Lovelady, Texas.

- - - July 23d, 1885, by Rev. E. P. McClintock, in the Thompson Street church, Newberry, S. C., Mr. **Samuel B. Jones** of Newberry and Miss **Jessie Chalmers** of Dallas, Texas.

- - - in Washington, D. C., Tuesday evening, July 21st, **J. J. Darlington**, Esq. and Miss **E. R. Meador**, daughter of Rev. Mr. Meador, pastor of the 5th Baptist church.

August 6, 1885

Died in Back Creek congregation on the 11th of February, 1885, **Maggie**, aged 4 months and 21 days, infant of C. V. and M. I. **Furr**.

Mrs. **Mary B. Waters**, wife of David P. Waters, departed this life, July 22nd, 1885, aged 61 years, 10 months and 13 days. . . . member of Union congregation for more than forty years. . . . married November 21st, 1861, being the second wife of D. P. Waters. Thus was devolved upon her the care of five small children, just at the commencement of the war, the father and husband being in the war. . . . Of the deceased it can be said what can be said of very few. She was married and died in the same room. . . . She leaves a husband, six children.

August 13, 1885

Died at his home in Shelby County, Tenn., April 4th, 1885, Mr. **James Rodgers**, aged 69 years, 9 months and 17 days. . . . son of William and Mary (Robinson) Rodgers. He was married to Miss Mahalah Murphy, December 23d, 1842. His wife and eight children, four sons and four daughters survive him.

Married at the residence of the bride's father, in Mecklenburg County, N. C., by Rev. G. R. White, Mr. **Îsaac Bartlett** and Miss **Mollie E. Griffith**, all of Mecklenburg County, N. C.

August 20, 1885

Died at his home in Woodruffs, S. C., July 27th, 1885, Dr. **T. S. Wright**, in the 52d year of his age. The deceased was twice married. His last wife was Miss Lizzie Bryson, the daughter of Mr. Wm. Bryson of Laurens County, whose children and relatives were the founders of the A. R. P. church of this place. Dr. Wright was born, reared and spent his life almost within a stone's cast of the place he died. He practiced medicine successfully for about twenty five years in and around Woodruffs. He was a member of the Baptist church. . . leaves a widow and six children.

August 27, 1885

Died at Santa Barbara, South America, on the 24th of June, 1885, **Robert Miller**, aged 34 years, son of James and Sarah B. Miller, formerly of Lewisville, Chester County, S. C. . . .was a young man of fine promise, having had for the last seven years the superintendence of the large coffee business of Legerwood & Co. of Santas, Brazil. He leaves a young wife.

Died in Shelby County, Tenn., July 1st, 1885, **Edward Lee Garner**, aged 5 years, 9 months and 13 days. Eddie's mother died when he was only sixteen months old, but he was . . . cared for by his grandmother, Mrs. Mahalah Rodgers.

Died at her home in Monroe County, Ala., July 13th, 1885, Mrs. **Ella Dale**, in the 38th year of her age. . . was the wife of Mr. Andrew Dale, daughter of Mr. Andrew McBryde, and mother of six daughters and four sons, all of whom survive.

Mrs. **Adda Watson**, eldest daughter of Mr. and Mrs. W. G. Neil and the lovely wife of Mr. John H. Watson, died of a long and painful illness, July 31st, 1885, aged 25 years, 1 month and 20 days, leaving three small sons, husband.

"Old Aunt" Jinnie Young died August 1st, 1885, of old age, supposed to be either in the 90th or 92nd year of her age. One of the old landmarks of the church at Long Cane, and one of two sisters who had lived long and happily together until the tie was broken a few years ago by the death of the younger. After that she found a home in the house of a nephew, Mr. S. O. Young.

Lillian Leora, youngest child of Mr. and Mrs. R. J. **McCaslan**, died August 12th, 1885, aged 1 year and 5 months.

Married, August 12th, 1885, at the residence of Mr. W. J. Black, Charlotte, N. C. , by Rev. C. E. McDonald, assisted by Rev.. J. C. Galloway, Mr. **John H. Williamson** and Miss **Hattie Reid**.

- - - August 18th, 1885, by Rev. G. R. White, in Charlotte, N. C., Capt. **James E. Griffith** and Miss **Louisa Blackwelder**. All of Mecklenburg County, N. C.

- - - My - - , 1885, at the residence of Mr. E. Townsend, the bride's stepfather, by Rev. E. E. Patterson, Mr. **Wm. H. Moore** and **Miss W. B. Henderson**.

- - -August 20, 1885, by Rev. E. E. Patterson, Mr. **John W. Henderson** and **Miss A. E. Townsend**. All of Lamar County, Texas.

September 3, 1885

Died in Mecklenburg County, N. C. on the 5th of June, 1885, Mr. **James Irwin**, aged 85 years. . . . member of Sardis church from early life . . . leaves a single daughter and two grandchildren.

Mrs. **Margaret L.**, wife of Mr. Jessie **Rochelle**, died August 15th, 1885, in her 64th year. . . was the daughter of Jas. Hayes, and born in Chester County, S. C., removed to Lincoln County, Tenn. in 1833. . . . member of A. R. P. church at Prosperity for forty six years. . . leaves a husband and two children.

Died in Mecklenburg County, N. C. on the 27th of July, 1885, Mrs. **Elizabeth Smith**, wife of Mr. George Smith, aged 25 years . . . .

member of Sardis. . . left a husband and three small children, the youngest of which followed her to the grave in a few days.

Died of consumption in Bradley County, Ark. atthe residence of her son, Mr. M. Lathan, August 3d, 1885, Mrs. **Mary Lucinda (Faulkner) Lathan** . . . was born in Lancaster County, S. C., August 21st, 1817. In early life she connected with the A. R. P. church at Shiloh. . . . In 1860 she immigrated to this state with her husband who preceded her to the grave. During her sojourn here she was a member of the Hickory Springs church.

Married, July 14, 1885, near Franklin, Izard County, Ark., by Rev. J. C. McDonald, assisted by Rev. Wm. Duren, Mrs. **Robert W. Chestnut** of Fulton County, Ark. and Miss **Mary E. Meers** of Izard County, Ark.

September 10, 1885

Mrs. **Nannie D. (Perry) Knight** was born July 6th, 1849, and died July 8th, 1885. . . . was born in Mississippi where she was left an orphan ten years old. She then came to South Carolina and was reared by her grandfather, Mr. C. L. Dye, Sr. . . . She became the happy bride of Mr. W. B. Knight on the 16th of April, 1884 . . . on the 22nd of March, 1885, she was received into the full communion of the A. R. P. church at Lancaster, S. C., she being the first to enroll her name as a member of the new congregation. She leaves a husband and an infant child.

Died at her home in Catawba County, N. C., July 28th, 1885, Mrs. **Sallie**, wife of Mr. Alexander **Yount**. This devotedly pious young mother departed this life on her 26th birthday, the first anniversary of her youngest, and just one month after she buried her oldest child.

Died at her home in Fairfield County, S. C., July 19th, 1885, Mrs. **Mary Cordes**, aged about 75 years. . . left an aged husband.

Died July 9th, 1885, **infant** son of Mr. and Mrs. J. R. **Peay**, aged about 7 months.

David Chalmers, son of William and Nancy **Simpson**, departed this life August 5th, 1885, aged 19 years, 10 months and 13 days. . . . on the evening of his last day, he went out with his gun to kill some squirrels. Later, and just as the sun is about to go down, the report of a gun is heard and heard by the mother who happened to be not far away. Now a cry is heard, it is not her son's voice, but that of a colored boy who accompanied him, "Chalmers has shot himself."

Married, August 26th, 1885, by Rev. S. W. Haddon, at Raphine, Va., Mr. **Wm. I. McCormick** and Miss **Cornelia O. Rosen**. Both of Rockbridge County, Va.

Married, September 2d, 1885, at the residence of Mr. H. L. Elliott, Winnsboro, S. C., by Rev. Jno. T. Chalmers, assisted by Rev. D. E. Jordan, Rev. **J. R. McAlphine** of York County, S. C. and Miss **Lula Elliott** of Winnsboro.

September 24, 1885

Died of meningetis in Statesville, N. C. on the 8th of September, 1885, **Lewis Campbell**, son of Rev. D. G. and Mrs. Lizzie B. **Caldwell**, aged 21 months and 27 days.

Died in Shelby County, Tenn. on the 23d of August, 1885, Mrs. **Clarinda Smith**, aged 58 years. . . . native of South Carolina, but greater part of her life was spent in Tipton County, Tenn. She was the daughter of William and Sarah Murphy, and a sister of our esteemed brother, the late Rev. H. L. Murphy. . . . When quite young [joined] A. R. P. congregation at Salem. Of late years in order to be in the same ecclesiastical communion with her children, she sustained a connection with the Cumberland Presbyterian church.

Died of dropsy on the 14th of August, 1885 in Dallas County, Ala., Mr. **Robert C. Moore**, in the 73rd year of his age. In 1819 . . . with his father removed from Tennessee to Alabama. He united with the Prosperity church about 1839 . . . in 1845 was elected a ruling elder. . . . He leaves behind him a wife and five children.

Died at her home in Wilcox County, Ala., on the 15th of April, 1885, Mrs. **Martha Hines**, aged 54 years, 7 months and 29 days. . . . was the daughter of Samuel and Elizabeth Young, and was born and reared near the site of Old Lebanon on Prairie Creek, Wilcox County. In December, 1851, she was married to W. C. Smith, M. D. Four children, two of whom survive, were the fruit of this marriage. In July 1864, she was married to Mr. Robt. H. Hines, who died in January, 1885. One daughter who lives was the result of the second marriage.

Died near Ideaville, Tenn., August 7th, 1885, at the advanced age of 97, Mrs. **Jane Latham**. . . . was born in Lancaster County, S. C. . . . She leaves several families of grandchildren. All of her other near kindred have preceded her to the grave.

October 8, 1885

Died near Doraville, Ga., August 26th, 1885, **Mrs. N. J. McCurdy**, aged 31 years. . . leaves husband and three sons.

Died of flux, September 14, 1885, **William A.**, youngest child of Mr. and Mrs. J. B. **Wilson** of Monticello, Ark. Again, September 24th, **John McHugh**, only remaining son of these parents, a bright boy of about 4 years.

Mrs. **Mary E. Roddey** of Fairfield County, S. C. died September 1st, 1885 in the 49th year of her age. . . . daughter of John Simonton, deceased, and wife of David Roddey, who preceded her to the grave nineteen years. She leaves a son and two daughters.

October 15, 1885

Died, September 10th, 1885, of lung trouble, **Joseph C. Orr**, aged 72 years, 7 months and 6 days. . . . born in Marshall County, Tenn. and member of the A. R. church nearly fifty years.

Died May 30th, 1885, Mrs. **Jane Wilson**, aged 80 years, 3 months and 1 day. . . . was born in Chester County, S. C. . . . the daughter of Mr. David McAnn, joined the Associate church. . . . After her marriage she moved to Lincoln County, Tenn. in 1856, and united with the A. R. P. church at Prosperity.

October 29, 1885

Miss **Elizabeth Ann Robinson**, daughter of F. B. Robinson of Long Cane, S. C., died of congestion on the morning of September 24th, 1885, aged 51 years and 3 months.

Mrs. **Mary Pearson**, wife of Mr. William **Fair** and daughter of Col. Drayton and Mrs. Lucia Nance, was born October 16, 1846 and died of pneumonia September 22d, 1885. . . . left husband and five little children.

Married, October 21st, 1885, at the residence of the bride's parents in Fairfield County, S. C., by Rev. R. M. Stevenson, assisted by Rev. R. G. Miller, Dr. **J. E. Douglass** and Miss **Nettie E. Stevenson**.

November 5, 1885

Died in Newton County, Ga., July 13th, 1885, Mrs. **Jean Harvey** in her 86th year. It may be truly said that she died of old age. She had been for years nearly blind, deaf and dumb, and very helpless. She had been all her life a consistent member of the A. R. P. church.

Also, on September 5, 1885, **J. E. Harvey**, son of Robert and Janie Harvey, aged 2 years and 10 months.

Leonadas Faulkner, infant son of Mr. S. W. and Mrs. Lucy **Craig** was born on the 28th of October, 1884 and died September 27th, 1885.

Died in Bardley County, Ark., September 29th, 1885, with peritonitis, Mrs. **Eleanor Elizabeth (Kenmore) Caplinger**, wife of Mr. H. Caplinger, aged 28 years, 3 months and 25 days. . . . member of A. R. P. church of Hickory Springs. . . . left babe of ten days.

Died at her home in Rockbridge County, Va., September __, 1885, Miss **Sarah W. Lusk**, daughter of Wm. and Patsy Lusk, in the 62d year of her age. . . . lived with two maiden sisters. . . . lies buried in the graveyard of her mother at Old Providence.

Died in Tipton County, Tenn., October 2nd, 1885, Mrs. **Mary E.**, wife of Mr. E. M. **McDaniel**, aged 29 years. . . daughter of John and Jane Huey . . . leaves a husband and two little ones.

Married October 27th, 1885, in Huntersville, N. C. at the residence of A. J. Hunter, the officiating Justice, Mr. **Thos. A. McDonald** and Miss **Mollie Shields**. All of Mecklenburg County, N. C.

- - - - September 2nd, 1885, in Charlotte, N. C., by Rev. C. E. McDonald, Mr. **J. M. W. Elder** of Guthriesville, S. C. and Miss **Alice Parden** of Charlotte, N. C.

- - - - October 20th, 1885, near Pineville, N. C. , by Rev. C. E. McDonald, Mr. **D. F. Grier** and Miss **Mattie Williamson**. All of Mecklenburg County, N. C.

November 12, 1885

Died in Union County, Miss., August 15th, 1885, **Edgar Roscoe West**, child of Mr. T. H. and Mrs. Lucreatia (Richey) West, aged 1 month and 5 days.

Married, October 27th, 1885, in Guntown, Miss., by Rev. S. A. Agnew, Mr. **B. G. Cordes** of Union and Miss **M. J. Rose** of Lee County, Miss.

- - - October 28th, 1885 at the residence of the bride's father, in Mecklenburg County, N. C., by Rev. G. R. White, assisted by Rev. C. E. McDonald, **W. L. McDonald**, Esq. of Winnsboro, S. C. and Miss **Jessie H. Bell** of Mecklenburg County, N. C.

- - - November 4th, 1885 at the residence of the bride's parents, in Hamburg, Wilcox County, Ala., by Rev. H. M. Henry, Mr. **Thomas M. McWilliams** and Miss **Laura E. McBryde**.

November 19, 1885

Died, September 21, 1885 in Newberry, S. C. of congestion of the bowels, **Essa Iola**, aged 8 years. . . . a daughter of John and Mary **Sligh**.

Died near Due West, S. C. on the 15th of November, 1885 and in the 72d year of her age, Mrs. **Jane Martin**, relict of Robert Martin. . . . . one of the oldest members of the church at Due West -- perhaps the very oldest. . . . twenty years ago, perhaps, she was left a widow--eight or nine years ago she lost her sight--became totally blind and has [since] sat in darkness.

Died in Laurens County, S. C., September 7th, 1885, Mrs. **Jane Motes**, relict of Silas Motes and daughter of Abram and Nancy Thompson in the 75th year of her age. . . . joined the Associate Reformed congregation worshiping then at Liberty Springs Presbyterian church during the ministry of Rev. John T. Pressly.

Died near Idaville, Tenn., October 9th, 1885, Mr. **J. R. McDaniel** in the 58th year of his age. . . . born in Chester County, S. C., but spent the greater part of his days in Tipton County, Tenn. and in the bounds of Salem congregation. . . . [later] ruling elder. . . . leaves a widow and six children.

November 26, 1885

Gamble Lyle Huey was born in Brooklyn, December 11th, 1884 and died in Winnsboro, S. C., Wednesday, September 23d, 1885. . . . member of A. R. P. church of Winnsboro.

Married, November 18th, 1885 in Dallas County, Ala. by Rev. J. A. Lowry, **W. B. Chisolm** and Miss **Bettie Daniel**.

December 3, 1885

After a long illness of three months, Mrs. **Mollie Arrington**, wife of Mr. William Arrington and daughter of Hugh L. Burke, died at her home in Ebenezer, Ga. on the 31st of October, 1885. . . . She leaves a husband and infant only two or three months old.

Died in Pope County, Ark., October 1st, 1885, Mrs. **Rebecca**, wife of Mr. H. M. **Hughey**, aged 75 years. . . . brought up in Lincoln County, Tenn. . . . for the last twenty eight years a consistent member of the A. R. P. church of Pisgah, Ark.

Died June 12, 1885, **Amanda Enloe Brice**, infant daughter of Dr. Walter and Mrs. Jennie B. Brice.

Died, August 11th, 1885, at the residence of her son-in-law, Mr. W. H. Caldwell, Rives, Tenn., **Mrs. M. A. Sterling**, in the 61st year of her age. . . raised, perhaps, in Chester County, S. C., was for a long time a member of the church at Hopewell. After the death of her husband and the marriage of her children, she followed the latter to West Tennessee. . . . removed her membership to the A. R. P. church at Troy, Tenn.

Died at her home near Toy, Tenn., August 16th, 1885, Mrs. **Jane (Banks) McDonald** . . . . was born in Chester County, S. C. and for a long time a resident of Tipton County, Tenn. . . . [After marrying] David McDonald, she became identified with the A. R. P. church at Troy, Tenn. . . . eight sons survive.

Died, August 20th, 1885, **Sammie Emma Dunbar**, orphan daughter of Adam and Nancy Dunbar, about 19 years old.

Mr. **Samuel D. Barron**, a ruling elder of Tirzah, York County, S. C. departed this life, October 30th, 1885, aged 38 years.

Married in Pope County, Ark. at the residence of the officiating minister, Rev. M. Oates, Mr. **R. M. Oates** of Pope County and Miss **Annie E. Rowan** of Augusta County, Va.

Married, November 18th, 1885, at the house of the bride's father, Mr. F. Dilling of King's Mountain, N. C., by Rev. E. E. Boyce, Mr. **Geo. W. Fall** of Pleasant Ridge, Gaston County and Miss **Mollie E. Dilling**.

December 10, 1885

Died in Lamar County, Texas, November 3d, 1885, **Mattie**, daughter of Mr. Thos. W. and Mrs. Annie **Ware**, aged 8 years and 12 days.

Died in Pope County, Ark., October 27th, 1885, after a protracted illness, **Mrs. E. E.**, consort of the late J. Franklin **Oates**, aged 67 years. . . . . native of York County, S. C. . . . . [early joined] Smyrna [but] for 32 years in A. R. church at Pisgah, Ark. - - - - widow for thirty years. . . . leaves four children.

Died in Lamar County, Texas, August 20th, 1885, little **Eddie Pressly**, child of Mr. Thos. W. and Mrs. Annie **Ware**, aged 17 months and 16 days.

Married, November 12th, 1885, by Rev. E. E. Patterson, at the residence of the bride's sister, Mr. **Robert A. White** and Miss **Leona G. Hall**. All of Lamar County, Texas.

December 17, 1885

Married, December 9th, 1885, at the residence of the bride's father, R. R. Steele, by Rev. W. W. Orr, Mr. **Thos. W. Davis** of Statesville, N. C. and Miss **Ella Steele** of Huntersville, N. C.

- - - December 9th, 1885, at the residence of the Dr. J. W. Herron, by Rev. C. E. McDonald, assisted by Rev. G. L. Cook, Mr. **Price Neely** and Miss **Bessie Herron**. All of Mecklenburg County, N. C.

December 24, 1885

[Died] In Crittenden, Ky., November 20th, 1885, of laryngitis, **Mattie Lee**, daughter of Rev. W. O. and Marcie L. **Cochran**, aged 3 years and 9 months.

Died in Newton County, Ga., November 12th, 1885, Mr. **Alexander Cowan** in his 91st year. . . . was born in Chester County, S. C. on the 24th of August, 1795. He was married to Rosa Ann Wylie on the 29th of January, 1820 and they joined the A. R. P. church at Union. They removed to Newton County, Ga. in the fall of 1826 and united in the organization of a church at Hopewell of which he was elected ruling elder.

Alice Louise, infant daughter of Mr. and Mrs. F. A. **Sinquefield**, was born January 24th and died October 6th, 1885.

Died in Gill's Creek congregation, Lancaster County, S. C., October 26th, 1885, **Baxter Chalmers**, son of Mr. and Mrs. W. Q. **Caskey**, aged 3 years, 2 months and 18 days.

Departed this life on the 25th of October, 1885, Mrs. **Catherine Craig Chisolm** in the 83d year of her age. . . . . born in Chester County, S. C., removed to Alabama about 1819, was married in 1822 to Patrick Chisolm, who two years ago preceded her to the grave.

Mrs. M. M. Whitesides died of some unnamed complication of female diseases on the 5th of June, 1885. She was born in New Hope A. R. congregation in Fairfield County, S. C. on the 5th of December, 1837. . . . She was the daughter of Henry and Margaret Castles and sister of Rev. T. R. Castles and Henry Castles, M. D. . . . On the 24th of November, 1857, she married J. M. Whitesides of Smyrna A. R. P. congregation, York County, S. C. to which congregation she moved her membership. . . . She was the mother of eight children, four of whom preceded her to the grave.

Married [unreadable].

January 7, 1886

Married, December 29th, 1885 by Rev. H. T. Sloan, Mr. **J. W. Noble** of Ridge Springs, Edgefield County, S. C. and Miss **M. Eliza Shanks** of Long Cane, daughter of Mr. J. J. Shanks.

- - - November 26, 1885 at the residence of Mr. J. D. Carmical by Rev. J. L. Hemphill, Mr. **R. W. Thompson** of Coosa County, Ala. and Miss **Etta B. Davis** of Coweta County, Ga.

- - - December 22d, 1885 by Rev. H. T. Sloan, Mr. **James Long** and Miss **Isabella Young**, daughter of Mr. S. O. Young.

- - - December 22d, 1885 by Rev. H. T. Sloan, Mr. **John Cresswell** and Miss **Kate Cresswell**, daughter of Mr. John F. Cresswell. All of Long Cane, S. C.

- - - December 15, 1885, at the residence of the bride's mother, Mrs. J. C. Caldwell, by Rev. W. A. M. Plaxco, Mr. **Leonard Poag** of Chester,

S. C. and Miss **Maggie Taylor** of Lancaster, S. C.

Married, December 23rd, 1885, by Rev. W. M. Grier, D. D., assisted by Rev. James Boyce, D. D., at the residence of the bride's father, Rev. W. L. Pressly, Prof. **Paul L. Grier** and Miss **Effie L. Pressly**. Both of Due West, S. C.

- - - December 17th, 1885, in Yorksville, S. C. at the residence of the bride's parents, by Rev. J. C. Galloway, assisted by Rev. R. A. Ross, D. D., Mr. **James E. Meek** of Johnsville, Ark. and Miss **Ida**, oldest daughter of Mr. Wm. M. **Kennedy** of Yorksville, S. C.

- - - December 15th, 1885, at the residence of the bride's brother, Mr. John Wilson, by Rev. C. B. Betts, Mr. **J. J. Stroud** of Florida and Miss **Aggie Wilson** of Chester County, S. C.

- - - December 16th, 1885 at the residence of the bride's father, by Rev. C. B. Betts, Mr. **William Nickey** and Miss **Hattie Fudge**. All of Chester County, S. C.

January 14, 1886

Died, December 20th, 1885, in Navarro County, Texas, **Nellie Eliza Sloan**, little daughter of Mr. R. S. and Mrs. H. I. Sloan. . . . lacked but three days of being 17 months old.

Died, December 19th, 1885, an **infant** daughter of Mr. J. W. and Mrs. E. C. **Wilson** of Mecklenburg County, N. C., the mother until recently a member of Sardis.

Mrs. **Lizzie Little**, wife of R. P. Little, Jr., died at their house in Louisville, Ga., November 25th, 1885 . . . . married less than a year.

John B. Whitesides, Jr. died December 21st, 1885 in the 19th year of his age.

James McCutcheon was born July 12th, 1804, and died November 17th, 1885. . . . was married to Susannah Harris in 1835, and had one daughter, an only child, who is now living at the old homestead. . . . His father and brother were ruling elders in Old Providence, to which church the deceased belonged for about fifty years.

Mrs. **Anna Eliza Alexander**, oldest daughter of John and Grace Gibson, was born September 25th, 1831, and died October 17th, 1885, of inflammation of the bowels. She died within three miles of where she was born and raised in Rockbridge County, Va. She was married to John Mc. Alexander, M. D., April 25th, 1850. . . . seven children, five of whom are still living. . . . some eighteen years ago she was left a widow. . . . member of A. R. church on Timber Ridge.

Married, December 23d, 1885 at the residence of Mr. C. E. Bell of Mecklenburg County, N. C., by Rev. G. R. White, assisted by Rev. Mr. Thompson, Mr. **W. E. Younts** of Pineville and Miss **Eunice J. Bell** of Mecklenburg County, N. C.

- - - December 30th, 1885 by the same in Charlotte, N. C., Mr. **Thos. A. Smith** of Mecklenburg County, N. C. and Miss **Mary L. Propest** of Charlotte, N. C.

- - - January 6th, 1886, at the residence of the bride's brother, Mr. M. B. Alexander, by Rev. W. Y. Love, Mr. **J. D. McAulay** and Miss **I. D. Alexander**. All of Mecklenburg County, N. C.

- - - December 17th, 1885 at the Parsonage, by Rev. C. B. Betts, Mr. **T. E. Patton** and Miss **Janie Boyd**. All of Chester County, S. C.

- - -December 29th, 1885 by Rev. J. E. Martin, Prof. **S. P.. McElroy** and Miss **Mary E. Sullivan**. All of Newton County, Ga.

- - -December 9th, 1885 in Tipton County, Tenn., by Rev. J. H. Strong, Mr. **A. E. McQuiston** and Miss **M. E. Strong**.

- - -December 30th, 1885 in Tipton County, Tenn. by Rev. J. H. Strong, Mr. **J. H. Faulkner** and Miss **M. O. McCain**.

January 21, 1886

Died, November 22nd, 1885, in Dallas County, Ala., **Henry Hughes**, son of Mr. and Mrs. S. H. **White**, aged 6 months.

Died of membraneous croup in Shelby County, Tenn., December 27th, 1885, **Nina E.**, second child of Mr. R. C. and Mrs. M. E. **Parkison**, aged 4 years, 8 months and 30 days.

Died in Dallas County, Ala., December 28th, 1885, in the 32nd year of her age, Mrs. **Mary Spiva**, wife of Edward Spiva and eldest daughter of the late Rev. James M. Young . . . . [member] Prosperity church. . . . left husband and two daughters.

Departed this life in Starkville, Oktibbeha County, Miss. on the 2d of May, 1885, Mr. **James J. Bell**. Aged about 37 years. . . . was the second son of the late David and Jane M. Bell. . . [served in Civil War] left wife and two children.

Married, December 24th, 1885 by Trial Justice Jno. C. Flenniken, at the residence of Mr. Thomas Wren, Mr. **J. Avonder Wilson** and Miss **Mattie Wallace**.

- - - January 5th, 1886 at Fairview Hill by Trial Justice Jno. C.

Flenniken, Mr. **William Jackson** and Miss **Gracey McDaniel**. All of Chester County, S. C.

- - - November 19th, 1885, by Rev. S. A. Agnew, Mr. **John P. Robinson** and Miss **Martha Grier**. All of Union County, Miss.

- - - November 24th, 1885, by Rev. S. A. Agnew, Mr. **H. D. Knight** and Miss **Emma D. Bullard**. All of Guntown, Miss.

-- - - December 17th, 1885 by Rev. S. A. Agnew, Mr. **J. S. Byers** and Miss **Sudie Means**. All of Lee County, Miss.

- - - December 17th, 1885 by Rev. S. A. Agnew, Mr. **R. C. Rabun** and Miss **Lucretia Douglas**. All of Union County, Miss.

- - -January 6th, 1886 by Rev. S. A. Agnew, Mr. **Thomas E. Gordon** and Miss **M. A. McDonald**. All of Prentiss County, Miss.

- - - December 17th, 1885 by Rev. H. Rabb, Mr. **J. J. Furguson** of Tipton County and Miss **Nannie J. Smith** of Shelby County, Tenn.

- - -January 5th, 1886, by Rev. E. E. Patterson, Mr. **W. H. McMillen** of Tyler County and Miss **Sarah E. Jones** of Hardin County, Texas.

- - - At the residence of the bride's father, Mr. Thos. F. Parkison by Rev. H. Rabb, assisted by Rev. J. H. Strong, Mr. **W. H. McQuiston** and Miss **Katie B. Parkison** of Shelby County, Tenn.

- - - Also at the same time and place and by the same, Mr. **W. J. McQuiston** of Tipton County and Miss **Johanna H. Parkison** of Shelby County, Tenn.

- - - December 31, 1885, by Rev. J. C. McDonald in Izard County, Ark, Mr. **A. C. Oldfield** and Miss **Sarah J. Gleghorn**, daughter of Mr. John Wylie Gleghorn.

- - -January 7th, 1886 in the Bloomington church by Rev. David Pressly, Mr. **W. W. Owen** of Navarro County, Texas and **Miss E. J. McQuiston** of Tipton County, Tenn.

January 28, 1886

John William Carmical, son of Thomas and Susie Carmical, was born July 15th, 1885 and died December 23d of the same year.

Miss **Lizzie**, only daughter of William and Isabella **Patton**, was born November 17th, 1856, and died at the home of her grandfather, John Graham on Timber Ridge, Rockbridge County, Va., November 5th, 1885 . . . once a pupil at Due West Female College, but owing to ill health, was unable to finish her education. . . . member of A. R. P. church on Timber Ridge.

Hugh A. Galloway died on the 27th of December, 1885, in the 85th year of his age. . . . of his ancestry the earliest reliable knowledge we can get is, they were devoted members of the A. R. P. church. At the time of the Dixon and McMullen secession from the A. R. Presbytery of the Carolinas and Georgia, his parents were members of the Sharon A. R. P. congregation and refused to go with Rev. W. Dixon and his party into the Associate church. They removed their membership to Hopewell, Chester County, S. C., then in charge of Rev. John Hemphill, D. D., and though nearly forty miles distant, were generally in their place on preaching days. This was their place of worship up till the organization of Sharon as an A. R. P. congregation under the care of First Presbytery of the Carolinas. At this reorganization, probably in 1836, Rev. T. Ketchin officiating, John Galloway, Hugh A. Galloway, John Kennedy, and I. N. McElwee were elected and ordained elders. In 1843, when I [Rev. R. A. Ross] became pastor of Sharon, these four constituted the session.

Married, December 8th, 1885, in Augusta County, Va. by Rev. Dr. Vaughan, Mr. **F. M. Oates** of Pope County, Ark. and Miss **Sallie B. McClure** of Augusta County, Va.

- - - January 21st, 1886, at the residence of the bride's father, Mr. William A. Weldon, by Rev. C. E. Todd, Mr. **Robert W. McElroy** and Miss **Luda Weldon**. All of DeKalb County, Ga.

February 4, 1886

[Died] on the 24th of June, 1885, Rev. **John F. McClelland** . . . . [son of John and Lucy McClelland] . . . born in Henry County, Ga. in 1840. . . . born, baptized, and brought up in the Associate Reformed church at Hopewell church. . . only when distance had debarred him for years from enjoying the privileges of that dear old church which he loved so well and in which his dear brother George had labored as a minister that he united himself with the Presbyterian church in the United States. [taught schools in Henry and in Jasper County at Conyers [Ga.] Male and Female Academy and in 1881 was ordained as a minister. . . married] Miss Amanda E. Reagan, daughter of John Reagan, Rockdale County, Ga. . . .[survivors are his wife and] seven children, three sons and four daughters.

Married, January 24, 1886, near Raphine, Va., by Rev. S. W. Haddon, Mr. **J. Gearhost** and Miss **Maggie Helmick**. All of Augusta County, Va.

- - - January 27th, 1886, in Louisville, Ga. at the residence of Dr. Powell, the bride's father, by Rev. J. S. Mills, Dr. **J. D. Wright** and Miss **Loulie Powell**.

February 11, 1886

Mrs. **Caroline (Bell) Hanna**, the widow of Dixon Hanna, died at her home, with her son-in-law, Mr. Kerr, in Mecklenburg County, N. C., January 14th, 1886. . . . member of Gilead.

Joseph Brevard Hubbard died January 18th, 1886. Brevard was 3 years, 7 months and 9 days old.

Died of pneumonia near Coddle Creek church, Miss **Sarah E. McKnight**, in the 62d year of her age. . . . niece of the Rev. Jas. McKnight, the second pastor of the church.

Died in Oak Hill, Wilcox County, Ala., January 6th, 1886, Mrs. **Blanche Jones**, wife of Dr. W. C. Jones, aged 37 years, 7 months and 19 days. . . . She was a daughter of James and Isabella Bell, and was born and reared in Darlington C. H., S. C. In 1865, she joined the Darlington Baptist church. On the 16th of October, 1867, she was married to Dr. W. C. Jones, and in the spring of 1868 was received into the full communion of the Associate Reformed church at Bethel. . . mother of eight children, four of whom preceded her to the grave.

February 18, 1886

Died, November 2d, 1885 in Newberry County, S. C., **Caleb Daniel Cannon**, little son of Mr. and Mrs. B. F. Cannon, in his 5th year.

H. Clemens Sloan died of typhoid fever on the 4th of November, 1885 in the 23d year of his age. . . . Some two years before his death he was united in marriage with Miss Cordy Forbis, who with a bright little son [survives him]. . . . member of Prosperity church.

Mrs. **Mary Spence**, wife of Milton Spence, deceased, died at her home in Newberry County, S. C., January 27, 1886 in the 74th year of her age. . . . member of A. R. P. church at King's Creek . . . some twenty years ago left a widow. . . leaves two children.

Married, January 31st, 1886 at Fairview Hill by Trial Justice Jno. C. Flenniken, Mr. **Cuthbert B. Wilson** and Miss **Sarah Jane Goings**. All of Chester County, S. C.

- - - February 4th, 1886 at Fairview Hill by Trial Justice Jno. C. Flenniken, Mr. **Wm. Drayton Estes** and Miss **Nannie J. Wallace**. All of Chester County, S. C.

- - - February 11th, 1886 in Capers' Chapel by Rev. J. B. Traywick, assisted by the Rev. L. R. McCormick, Maj. **Jas. G. Lowry** and **Miss S. C. Anderson**, daughter of Dr. A. F. Anderson. Both of Lowrysville, S. C.

March 4, 1886

Died, January 25th, 1886, in Navarro County, Texas, **Rufus Emmerson Johnston**, infant son of Bettie A. (Davidson) and G. E. Johnston. Aged 7 months.

Died of consumption in Bradley County, Ark., February 7th, 1886, **Samuel David Lathan** . . . was born in Lancaster County, S. C., October 28th, 1848. . . . member of the A. R. P. church at Hickory Springs. . . He leaves a wife and four little daughters.

Died at Troy, Abbeville County, S. C., February 12th, 1886, Mrs. **Mary Isabella Lites**, aged 58 years, 4 months and 10 days. . . . daughter of the late Thos. W. and M. Isabella Chiles. She was twice married; first to Mr. R. A. Jordan, who lived only four months after the marriage, and the second time to Capt. R. W. Lites, January 28, 1845. . . . member of Cedar Spring congregation until the organization at Troy. . . leaves a husband and four children.

Ella Craig, eldest child of S. F. and M. E. D. **Roddy**, departed this life January 19th, 1886, aged 3 years and 3 months.

Married, December __, 1885 at the residence of the bride's father by Rev. E. E. Patterson, Mr. **George Derrick** and Miss **Evie Kemp**. All of Chicota, Lamar County, Texas.

- - - December 24th, 1885 at the residence of Mr. Robert A. Black, formerly of York County, S. C., by the same, Mr. **Robert Thompson** and Miss **Mattie Black**. All of Chicota, Lamar County, Texas.

- - - January __, 1886, at the residence of Mr. Jno. Brumley's , by the same, **Henry Pearson**, Esq. and Miss **Susie Littlejohn**. All of Chicota, Lamar County, Texas.

- - - January __, 1886, at the residence of the bride's aunt, Mrs. Baker, by the same, Mr. **George Campbell** and Miss **"Bennie" Sneed**. All of Chicota, Lamar County, Texas.

- - - February 4th, 1886 at the residence of the bride's father, Mr. Robt. A. Black, by the same, Mr. **Henry Thompson** and Miss **Mamie Black**. All of Chicota, Lamar County, Texas.

- - -February 17th, 1886, at the residence of the bride's father, Mr. Jno. Patterson, by Rev. W. W. Pharr, Mr. **Evander C. Johnston** and **Miss Joseph E. Patterson**. All of Iredell County, N. C.

- - -February 10th, 1886 in Navarro County, Texas at the residence of the bride's sister, Mrs. J. Dunham, by Rev. W. L. Patterson, Mr. **J. B. Hale** and Miss **Effie Johnston**.

March 11, 1886

Miss M. E. Clemie Milliken died of consumption at the home of her grandfather, John Anderson, on the 19th of February, 1886. Aged 20 years . . . member of Bethel church.

Joseph McConnel, only child of Mr. W. S. and Mrs. A. E. **Boyd**, departed this life February 17th, 1886, aged 1 year, 2 months and 26 days.

Married, February 23rd, 1886 in Richland church by Rev. H. Rabb, Mr. **E. P. Hill** and Mrs. **Caledonia (Taylor) Keathly**. All of Shelby County, Tenn.

March 18, 1886

Little **Rebecca**, youngest child of Mr. and Mrs. Samuel P. **Morrah**, died March 12th, 1886, in the 2nd year of her age.

Mrs. S. A. Lindsay, wife of W. P. Lindsay, died at their home near New Hope on the 8th of March, 1886, aged 45 years. . . She has left three little ones.

Little **Jennie Blair**, daughter of J. C. and M. P. Blair, died of membraneous croup on the 18th of November, 1885 in the 5th year of her age.

Died at the Sulphur Wells in Lincoln County, Tenn. on the 3rd of March, 1886, Mr. **John M. McFerrin** in the 73rd year of his age. . . . raised a large family- - was twice married and was spared to see his youngest grown. In the first revival of religion that occurred under our present pastorate he professed faith in Christ at the Prosperity church, and has ever since been regarded as a member of the church, though sometimes a suspended member, because of an infirmity (an occasional drinker to excess).

Married, February 26, 1886, at the residence of the bride's father by Rev. W. M. Hunter, Mr. **Horace Lount** and Miss **Fannie C.**, daughter of Mr. A. L. **Alexander**. All of Iredell County, N. C.

April 1, 1886

Dr. J. Q. McDavid's little girl, Kittie, died Friday night and was buried Sabbath evening in the [Due West] Baptist burying ground near Prof. McCain's. The funeral services were conducted by Rev. Carter.

Mrs. **Jane Crawford**, widow of the late Robert Crawford of Cedar Spring, died at the residence of her son-in-law on Long Cane, March 8th, 1886 in the 74th year of her age. . . . Her funeral was preached at the house and the remains deposited by those of her husband in Lebanon graveyard. She left one daughter.

Associate Reformed Presbyterian

Died at home in Abbeville County, S. C., March 11th, 1886, Mr. **Fed Cook**, aged 73 years, 3 months and 18 days. . . . was married September 20th, 1832 to Miss Sarah Cox, who survives him and with whom he lived fifty three years. He left fifty three descendants. . . . Living remotely from the church of his fathers, the deceased connected himself first with the Baptist church which was more convenient, but when the church was organized at Troy, he joined the A. R. P. church and was elected a ruling elder.

Died January 19th, 1886, **infant son** of Mr. and Mrs. J. B. **Wylie**, aged about 6 months.

Miss **Tirzah Watson** died at her home in Western York on the 12th of March, 1886. It is not certain how old she was. . . it is thought about 68 years old. . . . member of Sharon A. R. P. congregation.

Departed this life at his residence in Madison County, Miss. on the 15th of October, 1885, Mr. **Thomas Simpson**, aged 91 years. . . . was born in York County, S. C. He removed West during 1846, and located in Mississippi.

James Marion Cashion died the 8th of March, 1886, aged 2 years, 8 months and 7 days.

Married, March 10th, 1886 by Rev. S. A. Agnew, Mr. **W. L. Tapp** of Prentiss and Miss **Fannie Outlaw** of Lee County, Miss.

- - - March 10th, 1886 by the Rev. J. S. A. Hunter at the residence of the bride's father in Cleveland County, Ark., Mr. **L. C. Carmical** and Miss **Ella Wynn**.

- - - March 17th, 1886 at the residence of Mrs. Mary Dale in Oak Hill, Wilcox County, Ala., by Rev. H. M. Henry, Mr. **G. W. Welch** and **Miss S. L. Dunham**.

- - - March 18th, 1886 at the residence of Mr. Barron W. Pressly by Rev. J. E. Pressly, D. D., Mr. **John D. Croker** and Miss **Mollie Eagle**. Both of Cabarrus County, N. C.

April 8, 1886

Died, December 8th, Mrs. **Mary Kimball** at the residence of her brother, Rev. J. P. Weed near Troy, Tenn. . . was born near Starkville, Miss., and was first married to Mr. Stovall, who was killed in battle at Perryville, Ky., during the late war. Afterwards she married Mr. Kimball, and they lived in Marshall County, Miss. a number of years until December, 1885, when they came to live with her brother above mentioned. . . . Her husband and five children survive her.

Also, January 19th, 1886, after a brief existence of 19 days, an **infant** daughter of Rev. T. P. and Mrs. Dora **Pressly**.

Mrs. **Rachel Fudge** departed this life October 22nd, 1885, aged 75 years, 4 months and 4 days. . . . member of Union congregation for more than forty years. . . . She was the mother of six children; four of whom, all grown, survive.

April 15, 1886

Mrs. **Rebecca Henry**, who lived four miles from this place [Due West] on the Abbeville road, died very suddenly last Saturday. . . . buried at Upper Long Cane.

Died, April 12th, 1886, **Willie Safford**, son of Mr. and Mrs. J. H. **Wren** of Due West . . . less than two summers [old. Buried in new Baptist burying gound].

Died at her home, February 5th, 1886, Mr. **S. A. Snell** . . . . was born in North Carolina, March 19th, 1832, where he lived until 1882 when he moved to Mississippi . . . leaves a wife and seven children.

Died at his residence in Union County, Miss. on Monday night, March 22nd, 1886 at 9:10 O'clock, **Abram Thompson**, Esq., aged 63 years and 8 days. . . . was son of Abram and Nancy (Bryson) Thompson, and was born in Laurens County, S. C., March 14th, 1823. . . . He married Miss Jane E. Coleman, November 23d, 1843. In the fall of 1852, they removed to Pontotoc (now Union) County, Miss. . . . had joined the A. R. church at Head Springs in 1844, and after his removal to Mississippi [member of Hopewell] and ruling elder. . . previous to war, elected a Justice of Peace of Pontotoc County. . . . leaves a wife and four children.

Died in Mecklenburg County, N. C. on the first of March, 1886, Mrs. **Maggie Peoples**, wife of Mr. R. R. Peoples, aged 42 years. . . was raised in Chester County, S. C. Her maiden name was Montgomery. Her marriage to Mr. Peoples brought her to the Sardis congregation. . . leaves an aged wife, two sons and three daughters.

Died in Tipton County, Tenn., January 12th, 1886, Mr. **John Lyon** in the 76th year of his age. . . . born in Chester County, S. C. In 1837, and soon after his marriage, he removed to Tennessee where he died. . . consistent member of Salem congregation.

Married, March 10th, 1886 at the home of the bride's mother near Monticello, Ark. by Rev. J. L. Young, Mr. **R. B. Lesslie** of Bradley County, Ark. and **Miss M. J. McQuiston**.

April 22, 1886

Departed this life in Brighton, Tipton County, Tenn. on the 25th of

March, 1886, Mrs. **Katie M. Dewese**, wife of Mr. Robert Dewese, aged 27 years, 10 months and 18 days. . . member of the Associate Reformed Presbyterian church of Bloomington, Tipton County, Tenn. . . . leaves husband and four children (two sons and two daughters).

Married, April 15th, 1886 at the parsonage by Rev. C. B. Betts, Mr. **James A. Hyatt** of Lancaster County, S. C. and **Miss S. E. McFadden** of York County, S. C.

- - - March 31st, 1886 at the residence of the bride's mother near Rives, Tenn., by Rev. T. P. Pressly, Mr. **James A. Brown** of Morley, Mo. and Miss **Ella Wade**.

April 29, 1886

Mr. **Willie Wright** died at the residence of his aunt, Mrs. Cohen, after lingering several months with consumption on last Friday. He was seventeen years old and a consistent member of the Baptist church [buried in Newberry].

May 6, 1886

Died in the city of Greenville, S. C. on Saturday, April 24th, 1886, of measles, **Rosa Eva**, eldest daughter of Mr. C. G. and Mrs. Sallie **Haddon** [of Phoenix, S. C., buried in Due West graveyard beside a sister].

May 13, 1886

Died at White Oak, April 19th, 1886, **Ralph Madden**, infant son of Mr. and Mrs. John **Vinson**, aged about 14 months.

W. C. Mateer was born December 6th, 1815, and died in Rockbridge County, Va., April 11th, 1886. . . . has been an elder in Ebenezer congregation since February 19, 1871.

May 20, 1886

Mrs. **Jane (Sis) Alexander**, Brussels, Mo., wife of Mr. J. J. Alexander, fell asleep February 26th, 1886, aged 32 years and 5 months. . . member of Mt. Zion congregation. . . leaves a husband and two children.

Died, March 12th, 1886 in Dallas County, Ala. in the 10th year of his age, **Wyatt**, youngest son of Mr. and Mrs. E. F. **Harrell**.

May 27, 1886

Some of our readers will perhaps remember Mr. **Billy Fields** who used to dig wells in the community [of Due West] forty years ago. He died at the age of 97, week before last, at Mr. Winton Fisher's in this township.

In Louisville, Ky., Sabbath night, April 25th, 1886, Miss **Petrina McPherson** entered into rest, lacking only one hour and forty minutes of reaching her 77th birthday. . . . was born at Dulsie Bridge, Nairnshire, Scotland, April 26th, 1810. The family came to America about the year 1834 and resided two years in Montreal, Canada. They moved to Louisville, Ky., in August, 1836 . . . [earlier member of Presbyterian church] she united with the Associate Reformed church in 1885.

Died of paralysis in Yell County, Ark., December 23rd, 1885, Mrs. **Martha**, consort of T. M. **Oates**, aged 65 years . . . a native of Gaston County, N. C. Her first husband was a Mr. Lovesay. . . . left a widow with three small children. . . Her last husband was Mr. T. M. Oates.

Died in Yell County, Ark., March 26th, 1886, of typho-malarial fever, Mr. **T. M. Oates**, aged about 59 years . . . native of Gaston County, N. C., and resided near Crowder's Mt. within a mile of old Pisgah church. . . . [member of] and after coming to Arkansas he was received at Pisgah church and was elected and ordained an elder in this congregation . . . first married to a daughter of Mr. James Hanna of North Carolina. His second marriage was with Mrs. Lovesay. The fruit of his first marriage was seven children.

Married, April 29, 1886 at the residence of the bride's father, Mr. James McFadden by Rev. J. A. White, Mr. **W. H. Wylie** and Mrs. **Janie McDaniel**.

June 3, 1886

Susie Mabel, infant daughter of Mr. and Mrs. Thos. **Davis** of Jefferson County, Ga. . . . . was born August 19th, 1885 and died March 2nd, 1886

Ida Anderson, daughter of Mr. and Mrs. (Mariah) Anderson, died May 13th, 1886.

Died in Tippah County, Miss., **Mrs. Sanders**, wife of Dr. Sanders . . . . . member of Ebenezer [Mississipp].

Died at Winnsboro, S. C., Thursday, May 13th, 1886, **Freddie Bell**, daughter of Mr. and Mrs. F. A. **Sitgreaves**, aged 5 years, 6 months and 8 days.

Born in Lafayette County, Miss., December 25th, 1840, and died January 7th, 1886, Mr. **John A. Craig** . . . member of Shiloh . . . left wife and children.

Died at his residence in Garrard County, Ky., of heart disease, Col. **Edward M. Leavell**, aged 73 years, 5 months and 25 days. . . . born in

Garrard . . . married Miss Rebecca A. Sharp . . . [She] and a son survive . . . . member of New Hope.

On the night of the 26th of May, 1886, Miss **Elizabeth McQuerns** passed from our midst. . . . born the 8th of March, 1802 . . . This long life was spent largely in this community [Due West] and was devoted mainly to teaching. At least three generations received instruction at her hands.

Died at Winnsboro, S. C., March 26th, 1886, Mr. **John Kirkpatrick McCarley** in the 55th year of his age. . . . born in Craigwarren near Ballymena, County Antrim, Ireland, September 15th, 1830. His family were Scotch Covenanters and removed to Ireland in the time of persecution. In 1870, Mr. McCarley emigrated to South Carolina and located at Woodwards, Fairfield County. . . . in employ of C. C. & A. R. R., and when the depot was removed to Blackstocks he also removed and aided in building up the Presbyterian church in that place in which he was a ruling elder. . . . when hymns of human composition were introduced in place of inspired Hymns of Revelation, which had been the exclusive psalmody. . . . he determined to remove as soon as possible. This he accomplished in the fall of 1882 when he removed to Winnsboro, S. C. . . . He was elected elder in the A. R. P. church in December, 1884. . . [leaves] a wife, three daughters and one son.

Married, April 27th, 1886 at the residence of the bride's father by Rev. J. S. Mills, Mr. **Geo. Agerton** and Miss **Nellie E. Smith**.

- - - May 18th, 1886 at the residence of Mr. H. R. Vick, the bride's brother-in-law, by Rev. J. H. Strong, Rev. **David Pressly** of Brighton, Tenn. and Miss **Janie M. Grier**, the youngest daughter of Mrs. Ellen J. Moffatt of Barnesville, Marshall County, Miss.

June 17, 1886

John Beard was born on the 22d of April, 1807 and died at his home near Mt. Mourne, N. C. on the 18th of May, 1886. . . He leaves a widow and a large family of children and grandchildren.

Died in Back Creek congregation on the 22d of April, Miss **M. Lorenna Caldwell** in the 51st year of her age.

Mr. **John Barron** died at his residence on the 4th of June, 1886 . . . . was nearly 78 years old. Thirty three years ago he was ordained an elder of Tirzah church, in York County, S. C.

Died at his home in Cobb County, Ga., April 3rd, 1886, Mr. **Samuel Brown Wylie** in his 88th year. . . . born in Chester District, S. C., September 13th, 1798, and lived at his father's home till 1821 when he moved to Newton County, Ga. . . . elder in Hopewell A. R. P. . . . Moving to Cobb County, he, with others, procured preaching and soon organized

Bethesda A. R. P. church near Marietta. That terrible scourge, the late war, practically disorganized the church, and Mr. Wylie moved his membership to Doraville. . . leaves wife and six children.

Married, May 30th, 1886 in Louisville, Ga by Rev. J. S. Mills, Hon. **J. H. Polhill** and Mrs. **Sue B. Denny.**

- - - June 10th, 1886 by Rev. H. T. Sloan, D. D., Mr. **John H. Watson** and Miss **Minnie J. Cowan**, daughter of Capt. E. Cowan. All of Long Cane, S. C.

- - - May 30th, 1886 at the Christian church in Russelville, Ala. by Elder R. B. Larimore, Mr. **Robt. H. Ranson** of Waco to Miss **Aggie C. Anderson** of Russelville, Ala.

June 24, 1886

Mrs. **Louisa J. Scott** was born on the 31st of July, 1814 and died June 9th, 1885. She was the grand-daughter of Father Bothwell, one of the pioneer ministers of the A. R. church. . . [member of] Bethel, Burke County, Ga. for forty nine years. . . . She was twice married, but outlived both husbands.

Died at Shelbyville, Tenn. on the 21st of May, 1886, **Mrs. H. Bryson**, in the 76th year of her age. . . . was born in Abbeville District, S. C., near the Flatwoods, in 1810, was the daughter of Archibald McMullin and niece of Rev. Peter McMullin, the first pastor of the Due West congregation, who enjoyed exceptional Christian training, had two brothers, Robert and Porter, who became eminent ministers of the Presbyterian church, and was married to Rev. Henry Bryson about 1827. . . . four surviving children.

Died at his home in Chester, S. C., May 16th, 1886, **David Moffett**, aged about 72 years. . . . born and reared and lived the greater part of his life in the bounds of Hopewell church, in which he was for many years a ruling elder. A few years ago he moved to Chester, transferring his membership to that congregation.

July 1, 1886

Mrs. **W. A. Burke** died of typhoid fever at her home in Ebenezer, Ga. . . . on the 8th of June, 1886. . . . member of Ebenezer [A. R.P.] . . . left a husband and five little children.

Died near Auburn, Mo., April 21st, 1886, Mrs. **Lucy Reid**, in the 78th year of her age. Mrs. Reid, (*nee* Robinson) was born in Shelby County, Ky., July 30th, 1808. . . . was married to Mr. Jas. Reid about 1832, and soon afterward removed to Missouri, and settled in the bounds of Mt. Zion congregation.

Killed by lightning near Pierce City, Mo., May 27th, 1886, Mr. S. T., son of the late Rev. John **Patrick** of Arkansas. Mr. Patrick had taken an agency for a book, and had been canvassing in Benton County in this State [Arkansas]. For some reason he abandoned his agency, went into Missouri and hired to do farm work. While at work he was struck by lightning and killed instantly, we suppose. . . was first a member of the A. R. P. church, but connected with the Cumberland Presbyterian church during the great revival at Russelville last year.

Mrs. **Mary V. Little**, wife of Mr. J. C. Little and daughter of Wm. Fleming, Esq., was born August 15th, 1853, married May 9th, 1872, and died at Louisville, Ga., June 18th, 1886. She left five children, a devoted husband.

Mr. **R. M. Stevenson, Sr.** died at his home in Fairfield County, S. C., June 12th, 1886. Aged 87 years and 27 days. . . . He was, perhaps, the tallest man in the State, being six feet and nine inches and well proportioned. He was possessed of a wonderful constitution. He was not only the oldest person in this whole community, except one, but was the oldest of a large family noted for their longevity; few, if any of them, died under four score years. . . . member of church at New Hope . . . leaves a widow and four children, the eldest of whom is Rev. R. M. Stevenson.

Married April 7th, 1886 in the Presbyterian church, Fairfield, Va. by Rev. Alfred Jones, assisted by Rev. S. W. Haddon, Mr. **J. G. Alexander** and Miss **Mary P. Patton**. All of Rockbridge County, Va.

- - - June 9th, 1886 at Raphine, Va., by Rev. S. W. Haddon, Mr. **J. H. Humphries** and Miss **Amanda Wheeler**. Both of Rockbridge County, Va.

July 8, 1886

Died of consumption in Shelby County, Tenn., May 28th, 1886, Mrs. **Mary L. Hearlston**, aged 19 years, 6 months and 10 days. . . . was daughter of Marion Reese and born and reared in Lincoln County. In July, 1882, she married W. N. Hearlston and moved to this county. . . . [leaves] husband and little child.

Married, June 30th, 1886, in Cabarrus County, N. C. at the residence of the officiating minister, Rev. J. E. Pressly, D. D., Mr. **J. O. Witherspoon** of Cabarrus and Miss **Cora L. Patterson** of Iredell County.

July 22, 1886

Departed this life in the vicinity of Bloomington church, Tipton County, Tenn. on the 8th of April, 1886, **Spurgeon H. Simonton**, a son of the late Mr. Romain and Mrs. Mary (Huffman) Simonton. Aged 8 years, 10 months and 22 days. Disease, pneumonia.

Mr. **Charles F. Griffith** died of cancer of the stomach, June 5th, 1886. Aged 50 years, 4 months and 2 days. . . . youngest of six brothers who were members of Ebenezer church [N. C.] leaves a wife and seven children. . . five brothers and three sisters.

Died in Shelby County, Tenn., July 1st, 1886, **Maggie Bell**, infant daughter of John Bell and Maggie (McLaury) **Wylie**. . . . 15 months old.

Died in Camden, Ala., June 6th, 1886, Mrs. **Sarah Pressly Miller**, in the 59th year of her age. She was one of the daughters of Dr. Samuel and Elizabeth (Hearst) Pressly, born in Abbeville County, December 24th, 1827, and removed with her parents to Wilcox County, Ala. in 1836. She completed the course of her academic studies in Due West under the tuition of the late Dr. J. I. Bonner and the late Miss Elizabeth McQuerns. . . After this she returned to Alabama and was married on the 25th of August, 1846 to the late Dr. John Miller who was called from the labors of the holy ministry about eight years ago. . . . She was the mother of ten children, eight of whom are living. Of these eight, five are sons and three are daughters. Her daughters are married; one living in Oak Hill, Ala.; one at Gadsden, nothern Alabama; one at Chester, S. C. Of her five sons, only one is married--the eldest, and engaged in the practice of law in Camden, Ala.; one is a Professor of Mathematics in Erskine College; one is engaged in the pursuit of agriculture in Wilcox County; one is teaching in his native county, also; one is a student at Erskine College.

July 29, 1886

Mr. and Mrs. John **Brown**, Jr. lost an interesting **child** of two years, July 1st, 1886 [Long Cane & Cedar Spring].

Mr. **G. R. Shillinglaw** died at his home on the 5th of July, 1886 . . . . was an elder in the A. R. church at Yorkville, S. C.

"Old Aunt Mattie Davis," widow of William Davis and sister of F. B. and Rev. D. P. Robinson and Mrs. Jane Lindsay, died of old age, July 8th, 1886. . . . being about 83 years old. . . . long been a member of the Associate Reformed church at Long Cane and Cedar Spring.

Died at Doraville, Ga., June 28th, 1886, **Rachel L. Stewart**, daughter of Mr. and Mrs. T. T. Stewart, aged 6 years, 11 months and 14 days.

Charles DeArmond Porter, son of James and Annie Porter, born April 20th, 1884, died of flux, August 3d, 1885.

Joseph Walker Long, son of W. M. and M. E. Long, died of meningetis, aged 1 year, 8 months and 22 days.

John B. Walker, born November 8th, 1868, died December 13th, 1885 . . . the son of Jas. H. and Margaret J. Walker.

Mrs. **Margaret J. Walker** was born November 3d, 1839, and died of flux July 4th, 1886 . . . was much broken in health by long nursing and watching her son.

Married, July 15th, 1886 in Union County, S. C. at the residence of the bride's parents by Rev. R. H. McAulay, Mr. **P. H. Todd** of Woodruff, S. C. and Miss **Addie L. Gauldin**.

- - - July 13th, 1886 at the residence of the bride's father in Iredell County, N. C. by Rev. D. G. Caldwell, Rev. **J. M. Grier** of Mecklenburg County, N. C. and Miss **Columbia Davidson**.

August 5, 1886

Mr. **Henry H. Clamp** died at his home near Little River church [Baptist] of which he had been a member for many years. . . . . he was in the sixty fifth year of his age.

Died, Monday, July 26th, 1886, **William Tully**, son of J. C. and Mrs. Mattie **Haddon** [Due West] . . . . only little more than two years old.

August 12, 1886

Mrs. **U. J. R. Black** departed this life July 28th___, aged 46 years. . . . born in bounds of Neely's Creek. . . . a few years ago the family moved to Tirzah in York County, S. C. . . . She left a husband and a large family of children.

August 19, 1886

Died in Newton County, Ga., July 12th, 1886, **Augustus Stewart**, only child of William and Georgie **Bell**, aged 18 months.

- - - Also, July 21st, **Charlie Todd**, infant son of David and Dollie **Stewart**, aged 13 months.

- - - Also, July 25th, an **infant** son of George and Mattie **Summus**, age nearly 4 months.

Died at Doraville, Ga., July 17th, 1886, little **Stella**, daughter of Mr. and Mrs. J. J. **Sullivan**, aged 1 year and 24 days.

Died in the city of Memphis, Tenn., July 2nd, 1886, **Eddie Alexander**, youngest son of A. J. and M. G. **McQuiston** in the 20th year of his age.

Lottie Lovinia, the daughter of J. H. and Mary **Fiddler**, died July 8th, 1886, aged 18 months wanting 3 days.

August 26, 1886

Died in Madison County, Miss. on the 15th of May, 1886, **Thomas Alberta Simpson** in the 37th year of his age. . . . leaves a widow and two children.

Mrs. **Isabella P. Bryson**, the wife of Mr. William Bryson . . . in the 54th year of her age [died] the 11th of July, 1886. . . . member of Bethel for thirty eight years. She was permitted to see all of her children, save one, gathered into the fold for Christ.

Died in New Albany, Miss. at 5:45 o'clock on Sabbath evening, May 23d, 1886, **James Madison Thompson** in the 37th year of his age. . . . son of Abram and Mrs. Jane E. (Coleman) Thompson and was born in Laurens County, S. C., September 30th, 1849. His father removed to Pontotoc (now Union) County, Miss. in 1852, and settled in the neighborhood of Hopewell church and here James was reared. . . . In 1883 he was elected Sheriff of the County of Union and served two years.

The 12th of July witnessed a sad accident on Elk River four miles west of Fayetteville, Tenn., and in a very short distance of the paternal roof. **Knox Thompson**, a nice young man of eighteen years, who had been subject to epilepsy most of his life and was growing worse in spite of all the remedies of the various schools of physicians, had taken the stock to watering in company with a little brother, and while they were drinking fell from his horse into the water and drowned before help could be obtained.

September 2, 1886

Died in Union County, Miss., July 31st, 1886, Mrs. **Isabella Jones**, widow of James M. Jones, deceased. . . . was born in Abbeville County, S. C., February 13th, 1813. . . . In 1833 with her father's family, she moved to Wilcox County, Ala., and there in the same year was united in marriage with James Jones, Rev. J. P. Pressly officiating. . . . [the couple] moved to Mississippi settling in the bounds of Ebenezer church with which they united.

September 9, 1886

Died at her home in Charlotte, N. C. on Friday, August 6th, 1886, Mrs. **Ann M. Sterrett**, aged 66 years. . . born in County Antrim, Ireland; came to this country with her family in 1836, and settled in Fairfield County, S. C. near Winnsboro. . . lived in Charlotte several years before an A. R. P. congregation was organized, but at its organiztion she went in at once, being one of the charter members.

On the 8th of May, 1886, Mr. **A. V. Falls**, a ruling elder in King's Mountain church, died. . . . born on 1st of February, 1819 . . . first connected with Old Pisgah [church] in Gaston County. When more than thirty years ago, Nebo church in Cleveland County, N. C. was organized, he transferred his membership to Nebo, and a few years later was chosen one of the elders. When King's Mountain congregation was organized, Mr. Falls was one of the [charter members and an elder].

Died in Lafayette County, Miss., April 6th, 1886, **William C. Spence**, aged 32 years, 1 month and 3 days. While reared by Christian parents, Mr. Spence had never connected himself with the church. But . . .[his manner of living was such that] it was often remarked, "He ought to be in the church ."

Died in Waite County, Texas, March 14th, 1886, Miss **Josephine Johnson**, aged 42 years and 12 days. "Miss Joe," as she was familiarly called, was born in Tippah (now Union) County, Miss., and lived there until the spring of 1885 when she, together with a mother and brother, moved to Texas. . . hoping a change in climate would improve her health. . . [member of Ebenezer, Miss.].

Edwin Lyle, infant son of Wylie and Alice **Roddy**, age 1 year, 8 months and 22 days, departed this life, July 20th, 1886.

Married, August 19th, 1886, at the residence of the bride's father by Rev. W. H. Millen, Mr. **P. H. Foster** and **Miss M. E. Davis**. Both of Union County, Miss.

September 16, 1886

Martha Ola Carroll, infant daughter of Mr. and Mrs. Thadcus L. Carroll, departed this life August 22nd, 1886, aged 1 year, 5 months and 18 days.

Mrs. **Martha A. Crawford**, wife of James Crawford of Troy, S. C., and daughter of the late Thomas Cresswell, was born November 10th, 1841, joined the church at Long Cane in the 14th year of her age, and died of dropsy, August 20th, 1886.

Died at Statesville, N. C., June 3d, 1886, Mrs. **Margaret A. Walker**, wife of Col. A. M. Walker. . . . born October 18th, 1821. . . . was married to Col. Walker in 1841. . . . [member of A. R. P. church at New Sterling, later Cambridge, and finally New Perth].

Died in Dallas County, Ala., August 15th, 1886, Mr. **W. R. Brice** in the 41st year of his age. . . . son of the late Samuel Brice, having been reared in the New Hope congregation, S. C. . . . [served] in the famous 6th South Carolina Volunteers, and in the battle around Richmond was severely wounded. In 1868 removed to Alabama [and joined] Prosperity church. In

1877 he was elected ruling elder . . . leaves a wife and eight children.

Married September 7th, 1886 at Orrville, Ala., by Rev. J. A. Lowry, Mr. **C. T. Munnerlyn,** formerly of South Carolina, and Miss **Annie Orr.**

- - - September 8th, 1886 in Yorkville, S. C. at the residence of Mr. John Ashe, by Rev. J. C. Galloway, Mr. **R. Newton Whitesides** and Miss **Mattie Jeffries.** All of York County, S. C.

September 23, 1886

Died at his home in Miller's Township, Alexander County, N. C. on the 29th of August, 1886 of typhoid pneumonia, Mr. **John W. Sherril,** aged 48 years . . . elder elect in Elk Shoal congregation. . . [leaves] widow and four children.

Mr. **Alexander Simely** was born in Augusta County, Va., September 2d, 1814 and died January 23d, 1886 . . . . [member] at Old Providence . . . leaves two sons and several grandchildren.

Married, September 6th, 1886 at Raphine, Va. by Rev. S. W. Haddon, Mr. **N. S. McCormick** and Miss **Louisa Allen.** Both of Rockbridge County, Va.

September 30, 1886

Died on the evening of Thursday, September 23d, 1886 at his home in Due West, S. C., Capt. **R. C. Sharp.** . . . born March __, 1814, in this community. His life, with the exception of a very few years, was spent here.   He was identified with the town and with its most important enterprises from its earliest history. . . last of the elders who constituted the session of this church under the pastorate of Dr. Ebenezer E. Pressly.

On the morning of the 23d of September a few friends gathered in the parlor of Mr. J. L. Presly to witness the marriage of Miss **J. V. LeGal** to Prof. **J. M. Perry** of Greenville. . . . they were married by Dr. W. L. Pressly.

Married, September 15th, 1886 in Old Providence church by Rev. S. W. Haddon, Rev. **C. D. Waller** of McKinley, Ala. to Miss **Marie Dell Callison** of Rockbridge County, Va.

October 7, 1886

Died in Tipton County, Tenn., August 16th, 1886, **Maggie Letitia,** daughter of R. T. and M. A. **Wilson,** aged 10 years.

Died in Gastonia, N. C., September 12th, 1886, Mrs. **Martha**

Frances Blackwood, wife of Samuel Blackwood and daughter of Dorcas Neill and Arthur Neill, deceased. The deceased was born October 10th, 1849, and married December 20th, 1871. . . . [member at Pisgah] . . . leaves five children and sorrowing husband.

Departed this life, June 13th, 1886, in her 73d year, **Margaret Boyce**, sister of Dr. James Boyce and Dr. E. E. Boyce. . . member of Sardis community in Mecklenburg County, N. C.

Capt. **John Smith** departed this life July 2d, 1886. Aged 83 years, 6 months and 17 days. . . . born in Chester County, S. C. . . . early member of Union congregation. . . was married at 19 to Miss Mary Wylie. . . . fruit was twelve children, all of whom except two lived to be grown. In 1846, perhaps, the deceased was married the second time to Mrs. Montgomery, a scion from the McDill stock.

October 14, 1886

Mrs. **Bettie A. Johnston**, daughter of Mrs. M. E. Davidson, died at her mother's residence near Eureka, Navarro County, Texas, July 12th, 1886. The deceased was born August 5th, 1860.

Departed this life in Brighton, Tipton County, Tenn., on the 3d of September, 1886, **Mary Ruth Wilson**. She was born the 10th of September, 1883. . . the daughter of Mr. W. B. and Mrs. Mollie E. Wilson.

October 21, 1886

Died, Thursday, the 14th of October, 1886, **Samuel Bonner**, the youngest child of R. C. and F. F. **Brownlee**. . . just sixteen months [old].

Married, October 13th, 1886 at the residence of the bride's father, Mr. **W. B. Knight** of Monroe, N. C. and Miss **Mollie Hoke** of York, S. C.

- - - October 6th, 1886 at the residence of the bride's parents by Rev. W. Y. Love, Mr. **A. E. Love** of York County, S. C. and Miss **Claudia L. Irwin** of Mecklenburg County, N. C.

- - - October 13th, 1886 by Rev. C. B. Betts, Mr. **A. J. McAteer** of Lancaster County, S. C. and Miss **Carrie Simpson** of Chester County, S. C.

October 28, 1886

An **infant** child of Mr. and Mrs. George **Cornwell** died at King's Mountain, N. C., October 17th, 1886, aged 6 days.

Died in Tipton County, Tenn., August 5th, 1886, **Mary Ella**, infant daughter of W. A. and M. P. **Spencer**. Aged 9 months and 11 days.

A. I. McAteer was born June 11, 1860 and died July 11, 1886.

Died at her home in Newberry County, S. C., June 27th, 1886, Mrs. **Sophia Neel** in the 84th year of her age. . . . loved Cannon Creek church.

Bettie Ida, little daughter of F. M. and A. C. **McAteer** was born January 1st, 1885 and died July 4th, 1886.

The **infant** child of Walter and Ida **Blakely** died September 5th, 1886.

Miss **Jane Bell** (known as Aunt Jennie) was born April 20th, 1799 and died September 5th, 1886. . . . . in Mecklenburg County, N. C. at the same place where she died. . . early member of Gilead A. R. P. church.

Died at the home of her only daughter, Mrs. Caston, in Chester, S. C. on Monday morning, October 4th, 1886, Mrs. **Jane Wilson Hemphill** in the 68th year of her life. . . . maiden name was Brice. . . . She was married to David Hemphill, son of Rev. John Hemphill. . . . She was widowed at the early age of twenty three. . . . two sons Robert and John, were taken from her by the rude hand of war, one dying upon the field of battle in Virginia and the other falling in Georgia.

Married, October 21st, 1886 at the residence of the bride's father, Mr. W. H. Austin, by Rev. W. L. Pressly, Mr. **R. P. Pruit** and Miss **Minnie L. Austin**. All of Abbeville County, S. C.

- - - October 14th, 1886 by Rev. S. A. Agnew, Mr. **F. M. McGill** and Miss **Mary E. Hardy**. All of Union County, Miss.

November 4, 1886

Died, October 8th, 1886, **James Thomas Robinson**, aged 2 months and 13 days. . . son of A. T. and F. A. Robinson.

Departed this life, September 8th, 1886, of cholera infantum, **John Berry**, infant son of John R. and Cleopatra **Walker** of Anderson County, Ky. . . . . one year, one month and one day old.

Mrs. **Jane Gillespie** departed this life, July 30th, 1886. Aged 67 years, 2 months and 27 days. . . . born in Chester County, S. C., here her whole life was spent. . . . . connected with the A. R. Presbyterian church in her 19th year. She was first married to Mr. Joshua Lynn, when she transferred her membership to the A. R. Presbyterian church, Union congrgation, her husband being a member. . . Four children were the fruits of the first marriage; two of whom survive her. The deceased was married the second time to Mr. Thomas Gillespie and this union she survived about eleven years.

Married, October 27th, 1886 in the A. R. P. church at Troy, S. C. by

Rev. R. F. Bradley, Mr. **A. J. Davis** and Miss **Janie McCaslan**. The bride is the eldest child of Mr. G. B. McCaslan.

November 18, 1886

Died of membraneous croup, Friday the 12th inst., **Ruth Maginnis**, youngest child of Rev. J. M. **Todd** . . . . of little more than two years [of age], left an orphan while yet an infant of days.

Died near Generostee A. R. P. church, Anderson County, S. C., October 11th, 1886, Mr. **William Hamilton** in the 54th year of his age . . . not far from the place of his birth, May 26th, 1833. The greater part of his life was spent in the county. He was a successful school teacher, and he had been actively engaged in teaching for near thirty years. . . . He was a sufferer more or less all of his life. He was afflicted with a number of diseases [tributes printed from the Generostee Session and an organization of his former students, Mr. M. Baxter Clinkscales, Treasurer].

Married, November 10th, 1886, at the parsonage by Rev. C. B. Betts, Mr. **John K. Millen** of Mecklenburg Co., N. C. and Mrs. **Mattie McCammon** of Chester County, S. C.

- - - November 9th, 1886, at the U. P. church, Centreview, Mo. by Rev. J. S. Moffatt, assisted by Rev. W. T. Gill of Miami, Mo., Rev. **Jas. T. Curry**, pastor of the Foster Street M. E. church, Nashville, Tenn., and Miss **Mary E. Moffatt**, daughter of Rev. W. S. Moffatt of Centreview, Mo.

November 25, 1886

James, an infant son of Mr. and Mrs. **R. S. Sherrard**, died October 24th, 1886, aged 22 months.

Died at Stirling, Iredell County, N. C., November 12th, 1886, **Laura Agnes**, infant daughter of Rev. W. M. and M. M. **Hunter**. . . one week old.

Died Wednesday, Nov. 4th, 1886, **Dollie**, infant daughter and only child of E. W. and M. E. **Nance** . . . only eleven months old.

Died nar Elk Shoal church, Alexander County, N. C., September 27th, 1886, Miss **Isabella Jane Morrison**, aged 59 years, 5 months and 23 days. . . . member of New Sterling.

Died at her home in Gerrard County, Ky., August 20th, 1886, of consumption, Mrs. **Margaret W. Parkes**, wife of Mr. John B. Parkes. . . . born December 27th, 1847 of pious parents, Salem and Eliza Wallace. Her father was for many years a faithful elder of New Hope church . . . . With this church, Mrs. P. united in May, 1867 and two years later was [married] . . . to Mr. Parkes [survived by husband and two daughters].

Drayton Nance McCaughrin, son of Mr. L. L. McCaughrin, died in Newberry, S. C., October 21st, 1886, aged 12 years, 10 months and 29 days.

Col. **J. M. Thompson** of Birmingham, Ala., was married to Miss **Della Keys** of Anderson, S. C., last Thursday, November 18th, 1886. Col. Thompson will be remembered as a staunch friend of Erskine, having received his education there.

Married, November 17th, 1886. at the residence of the bride's father J. J. McLure, Esq., Chester, S. C. by Rev. George Summey, **Paul Hemphill,** Esq. and Miss **Bessie McLure.**

- - - November 16th, 1886 in Statesville, N. C. by Rev. D. G. Caldwell, assisted by Rev. W. A. Ward, D. D., Mr. **R. R. Clark** and Miss **Nolie E. Rosemon.** All of Statesville, N. C.

- - - September 28th, 1886, in Lafayette County, Miss. by Rev. W. H. Millen, Mr. **E. W. Barclay** of Union County and **Miss E. G. Craig** of Lafayette County.

- - - November 11th, 1886, in Union County, Miss, by Rev. W. H. Millen, Mr. **Virgil H. Craig** and Miss **M. L. Wiseman.**

December 2, 1886

Died at Blackstocks, S. C., September 18th, 1886, little **Sarah,** daughter of A. D. and Mattie **Boyd.** Age just 14 months.

Died September 8th, 1886, at the residence of his son, Mr. James Sanders, Dr. **William Sanders,** age about 76 years. . . . born in Abbeville County and was raised up in the Cedar Springs congregation. . . . joined under the ministry of Dr. John T. Pressly. There he lived until the year 1846 when he moved into the bounds of the Due West congregation. . . . In 1853 he moved with his family to Tippah County, Miss., settling within the bounds of Ebenezer church. For some cause, however, he did not connect himself with this church until several years afterward. . . . Dr. Sanders was twice married. His first wife was Miss Araminta McQuerns who died December 7th, 1865. His second wife was Miss Mary Morton, who also preceded him to the grave by some two years.

Died near Bethel church, York County, S. C., Monday morning, November 8th, 1886 of typhoid fever, Mr. **Joseph Adams,** aged 34 years . . . . married on December 20th, 1876 to Miss Laura Hunter of North Carolina who in ten short years he leaves a widow with four small children.

Died of congestion in Drew County, Ark., September 30th, 1886,

Maggie Lula Shanks. Aged 5 years and 3 months. Youngest child of late John B. and Mrs. Sallie Shanks.

Died in Dallas County, Ala., September 26th, 1886, **Augustus Luther**, youngest child of the late Robert **Brice**, aged 15 months.

Died June 1st, 1886 at her residence in Pawnee City, Neb., **Mrs. S. M. Anderson**, in the 64th year of her age. . . . daughter of the late Salem and Elizabeth Wallace . . . . was born in Madison County, Ky., January 27th, 1822 and was united in marriage to Mr. Irwin W. Anderson, October 26th, 1843. In the year 1850, she with her husband and family moved to Clayton, Ill. where they remained till 1881, when they removed to Pawnee City. All of her children . . . [became] members of the United Presbyterian church; two of her sons (her husband also) ruling elders.

Married, November 11th, 1886, by Rev. S. A. Agnew, Mr. **Samuel P. Caldwell** and Miss **Susie L. Galloway**. All of Union County, Miss.

- - - November 3d, 1886, at Hickory Springs church, Bradley County, Ark., by Rev. J. L. Young, assisted by Revs. F. J. Orr and J. P. Erwin, Mr. **S. A. Boyce** and Miss **Maggie J. Leslie**; Mr. **C. W. Boyd** and Miss **Lou McFadden**; Mr. **J. Z. Drummonds** and Miss **Hattie McFadden**.

- - - November 21st, 1886 at the Baptist church in Siloam, Miss. on Sabbath morning by Rev. H. J. Valandingham, Mr. **J. B. Cooper** and Miss **Nannie A. Hardy**. All of Clay County.

December 9, 1886

On the morning of the 5th inst., **Armathine Lindsay**, youngest child of J. B. and J. H. **Bonner**, was taken from us. . . . of less than four summers.

Died of flux at his home near Monticello, Ark., July 31st, 1886, Mr. **John H. McQuiston**, in the 32d year of his age. . . . born at Bloomington, Tenn., where he spent the earlier part of his life. . . . He afterwards moved to Monticello, Ark. with his father's family where he was happily united in marriage with Miss Addie Moore, March 7th, 1879.

Died at the residence of her brother, Maj. J. G. Smith in Troy, Tenn., November 21st, 1886, Miss **Jane Wallace Smith** . . . was born within the bounds of Hopewell congregation, Chester County, S. C. The family moved to Tipton County, Tenn. when she was quite young and there her life was spent in connection with the Salem congrgation. After the death of her parents, she came to Troy and has since resided with her brother.

Martha Mary, infant daughter of T. H. and Jennie **Moffatt**, departed this life October 14th, 1886. Aged 3 months and 1 day.

Departed this life, October 19th, 1886, infant son of Dr. T. D. and Ella **Marion**. . . nameless babe . . . . [lived] only six hours.

Died in Oak Hill, Wilcox County, Ala., September 9th, 1886, Miss **Mary Elizabeth McBryde**, who was born April 22th, 1848 . . . daughter of Mr. T. C. and Mrs. Eliza McBryde and was baptized in old Lebanon on Prairie Creek, Wilcox County, Ala., by the late Rev. John Miller, D. D. in 1848 and by him received into the church sometime during the war at Bethel or Oak Hill.

Married, November 16th, 1886, at the house of the bride's father, by Rev. C. B. Betts, Mr. **J. W. Simpson** of Chester County, S. C. and Miss **M. E. Lesslie** of York County, S. C.

- - - December 2d, 1886 at the residence of the bride's father, Mr. John Gaulden, by Rev. W. P. Meadors, Mr. **S. M. Davis** and Miss **Ida Kemper Gaulden**. All of Ninety Six, S. C.

- - - November 24th, 1886 by Rev. J. S. Mills at the residence of the bride's father, Mr. Ellison Johnson of Jefferson County, Ga., Mr. **Albert R. Berry** and Miss **Dora Lee Johnson**.

December 16, 1886

Died, **Caro Chalmers**, infant daughter of Milton and Carrie **Bell**. Its mother is related to the Chalmers' of Newberry, S. C. . . . [less than nine months old] when died, October 4th, 1886.

Died in Mecklenburg County, N. C. on October 20th, 1886, Mrs. **Ellen McMillan Sturgis**, in the 82d year of her age. . . . .[joined] Associate church at Neely's Creek in her eighteenth year, but on account of her peculiar situation she did not enjoy communion in any church after the union of the Presbytery of the Carolinas with the A. R. P. Synod of the South until in her old age she became a member in the family of her daughter in the Back Creek congregation. She was a twin sister of Dr. McMillan of California who remembered our Seminary so munificently in his will. . . .she leaves an only daughter.

Lucy Williams, daughter of Mr. W. Y. **Fair** of Newberry, S. C., was born February 7th, 1874 and died November 3d, 1886. . . . [lost her mother] more than a year ago . . . [and] as the eldest child [had] the care of three brothers and a sister.

Married, November 30th, 1886 at the residence of the bride's father, Mr. J. N. Dodgen, by Rev. C. E. Todd, Mr. **T. T. Twitty** and Miss **Lenna Dodgen**. All of DeKalb County, Ga.

December 23, 1886

Died in Prentiss County, Miss., November 20th, 1886, **James Calvin Weston Waters**, eldest child of Mr. W. Wesley and Mrs. E. A. (Bryson) Waters, aged 4 years, 4 months and 3 days. . . . born in Union County, Miss, July 17th, 1882.

Married, December 8th, 1886, by Rev. David Pressly at the late residence of the bride's father, Mr. **James A. McQuiston** and Miss **Mary L. Hart**. All of Tipton County, Tenn.

- - - at the residence of Miss "Matt" Thompson, Atoka, Tenn. by Rev. David Pressly, Mr. **Henry C. Moffatt** and **Miss C. L. Blanchard**, all of Tipton County, Tenn.

- - - November 2d, 1886, at the residence of the bride's mother, Mrs. Jane Moore, by Rev. H. Rabb of Shelby County, Mr. **W. E. Norris** and Miss **Lou Ella Moore** of Tipton County, Tenn.

- - - November 18th, 1886 at the residence of the bride's father, Mr. Neil McNair, by Rev. H. Rabb, Mr. **John A. Hall** and Miss **Mary E. McNair**. All of Shelby County, Tenn.

- - - November 23d, 1886 at Richland church by Rev. H. Rabb, Mr. **B. F. Myers** and Miss **Fannie Canipe**. All of Shelby County, Tenn.

- - - December 9th, 1886 at the residence of the bride's father, Mr. R. W. Bryant, Rev. H. Rabb, Mr. **J. F. Osborn** and Miss **Mary E. Bryant**. All of Shelby County, Tenn.

- - - December 15th, 1886 at the residence of the bride's father, Mr. T. P. Eddins of Tipton, Tenn, by Rev. H. Rabb, Mr. **W. C. Boyce**, son of Rev. J. K. Boyce, deceased, and Miss **Victoria Eddins** of Tipton County, Tenn.

- - - December 16th, 1886, at the house of the bride's father, by Rev. C. B. Betts, Mr. **Tommie Boyd** and Miss **Mattie Hays**. All of York County, S. C.

- - - November 25th, 1886 by the same at the house of the bride's father, Mr. T. C. Harris, Mr. **J. C. Ramsay** and Miss **Mary J. Harris**. All of Chester County, S. C.

- - - December 8th, 1886, by the same at the parsonage, Mr. **C. Allen** and Miss **Mary Fudge**. All of Chester County, S. C.

- - - December 9th, 1886, by Rev. C. E. Todd, Mr. **R. N. Harmon** and Miss **Erie Pittman**. All of Doraville, DeKalb County, Ga.

139

January 6, 1887

Died in Union County, Miss., October 25th, 1886, **Atlas Pinckney Gentry**, aged 28 years, 10 months and 1 day. . . . son of Esq. Levi F. and Mrs. Elizabeth J. (Hunter) Gentry, and was born in Pontotoc County, Miss., December 24th, 1857. He married Miss M. Jenkins Bryson, December 26th, 1879. Died of typhoid pneumonia. . . . leaves a wife and four little children, three boys and a girl.

- - - **Jonathan Beaty Williams** departed this life on the 27th of November, 1886. . . died of Bright's disease. He was in his 42d year.. . . . the son of Geo W. Williams, late of this place [Yorkville]. Mr. Williams entered the army in 1862, and coming home after the surrender completed his course of law and was licensed to practice. In 1872, he removed to Arkansas, but remained only a brief while. When he returned to Yorkville in 1883 he was appointed Probate Judge and continued in this office until his death. In 1869, he was married to Miss Jane Barron, daughter of Dr. A. I. Barron. . . . [she] and four children survive her.

Married, November 23d, 1886, at the residence of the bride's father, Rev. W. M. Grier, D. D. by Rev. W. L. Pressly, D. D., assisted by Rev. J. Boyce, D. D., Rev. **J. S. Moffatt** of Charlotte, N. C. and Miss **Jennie M. Grier** of Due West, S. C.

- - - December 22d, 1886 by Rev. S. A. Agnew, Mr. **F. W. McCarley** and Miss **Lula A. Guyton**. All of Union County, **Miss.**

- - - December 14th, 1886, by Rev. C. E. McDonald, Mr. **J. H. Russ** and Miss **Cora L. Smith**. All of Pineville, N. C.

- - - December 22d, 1886, by Rev. C. E. McDonald, Mr. **C. B. Campbell** and Miss **Mattie Gallant.**All of Mecklenburg County, N. C.

- - - December 22d, 1886, by Rev. C. E. McDonald, Mr. **J. D. Williamson** and Miss **Laura M. Wingate**. All of Mecklenburg County, N. C.

- - - November 25th, 1886 at the residence of the bride's father, Mr. John M. Wiseman by Rev. W. H. Millen, Mr. **J. H. Stewart** of Tippah County, Miss. and Miss **Jennie Wiseman** of Union County, Miss.

- - - November 3d, 1886, at the residence of the bride's father, by Rev. G. R. White, Mr. **Isaac E. Weaner** and Miss **Nora Taylor**. All of Mecklenburg County, N. C.

- - - December 22d, 1886 at the residence of the bride's parents by Rev. G. R. White, Mr. **J. B. Clanton** and Miss **Julia F. Abbernathy**. All of Mecklenburg County, N. C.

- - - December 23d, 1886 at the residence of the bride's father, Mr. R. H. Harris, by Rev. G. R. White, Rev. **C. E. McDonald** of Mecklenburg County, N. C. and Miss **Maggie E. Harris** of York County, S. C.

- - - December 23d, 1886 at the residence of Mr. J. W. Smith by Rev. G. R. White, Mr. **T. H. Merritt** and Miss **Minnie J. Smith**. All of Mecklenburg County, N. C.

- - - December 30th, 1886, by Rev. S. W. Haddon, Mr. **Jno. W. Hemp** and Miss **Lula McCutcheon**. All of Augusta County, Va.

January 13, 1887

Died at his home in Chester County, S. C., December 1st, 1886, Mr. **E. B. McCaw** in the 35th year of his age. . . from effects of measles . . . [leaves] an aged mother, the widow, and the little ones.

Died in Lincoln, Ark., November 14, 1886, **Robt. R. Boyd**, son of Robt. Boyd, Jr. and E. A. Boyd, aged 35 years. And also dead, **Robert Banks Boyd**, infant son . . . on the 13th of November. Age about 10 months. Mr. Boyd was born in Chester County, S. C. and reared under the Christian influence of the Pleasant Grove church. Though he had never joined any church and came to Arkansas in 1871, I [Rev. J. P. Erwin] learned from his intimate acquaintances he never forgot some moral precepts learned in his youth and the fond mother who had taught him. His word was his bond and he was honored and esteemed as a citizen. In the lingering disease [flux] that killed him and his child, he longed to see his mother.

Died November 29th, 1886, Mrs. **Malinda (Fife) Witt**, aged 57 years, 4 months and 2 days. . . . born in Abbeville County, S. C. in Cedar Springs congregation; a good place for one's nativity, not only materially, but spiritually. In early life she came to Wilcox County, Ala. with her father. She did not remain there long, however, for in the year ---, she removed to Mississippi with Mr. James McBryde, Sr. and with him lived until her marriage.

Died, **James Henderson Newton**, son of John and Martha Newton.

Married, December 29th, 1886 by Rev. S. A. Agnew, Mr. **R. B. Outlaw** of Lee and Miss **Sallie E. Phillips** of Union County, Miss.

- - - December 22d, 1886 by Rev. H. T. Sloan, D. D., Mr. **John Wardlaw**, son of D. J. Wardlaw, and **Miss Ida Morrah**, daughter of David Morrah. All of Long Cane.

- - - December 28th, 1886 at the parsonage by Rev. C. B. Betts, Mr. **H. C. Orr** and Miss **Mary E. Varnadore**, all of Chester County, S. C.

- - - January 4th, 1887 at the residence of the bride's father, Mr. David McQuiston, by Rev. David Pressly, Mr. **J. H. Faulkner** and **Miss M. L. McQuiston**. All of Tipton County, Tenn.

- - - January 6th, 1887 in Bloomington church by Rev. David Pressly, Dr. **Thomas E. Nelson** and Miss **Alice Murphy**. All of Tipton County, Tenn.

January 20, 1887

Died in Iredell County, N. C., near New Sterling, Mrs. **Maggie A.**, wife of Mr. Sidney **Patterson**, aged 27 years, 2 months and 11 days. . . . leaves a husband and four small children. . . . with her husband, were members of New Sterling.

Janie Leroy, daughter of J. Walker and L. I. **Griffith**, born September 2d, 1886, died of whooping cough, October 21st, 1886.

Martha Louisa, daughter of J. M. and M. J. **Wilson**, born October 7th, 1885 and died of whooping cough, October 22d, 1886. These little children were cousins, lived within sight of each other.

Died at her home in Fairfield County, S. C., December 5th, 1886, Mrs. **Jane Blain**, wife of Mr. Andrew Blain, in the 84th year of her age. . . . Had she lived sixteen days longer, her married life would have covered a period of sixty years. The husband with whom she lived so long still survives and a number of children, all of whom are married, except one.

Died in Winnsboro, S. C., November 12th, 1886, **infant son** of Mr. Robert M. and Mrs. Maggie (Shaw) **Huey**, aged 5 weeks.

Married, December 22d, 1886, near Troy, Tenn. by Rev. T. P. Pressly, Mr. **John L. Ratterree** and Miss **Katie McRee**.

- - - December 28th, 1886 by Rev. John T. Chalmers at the home of the bride's parents, Mr. **E. A. Lewis** of Charlotte, N. C. and Miss **Mattie Boyd** of Fairfield County, S. C.

- - -December 29th, 1886 in the A. R. Presbyterian church, Winnsboro, S. C., 8 o'clock p. m. by Rev. John T. Chalmers, Mr. **James L. Bryson** and Miss **Emma J. Lauderdale**, all of Winnsboro, S. C.

- - -January 12th, 1887 at the residence of the bride's mother, Mrs. R. Y. Owens, Winnsboro, S. C. by Rev. John T. Chalmers, Mr. **George R. Lauderdale** and Miss **Sallie E. Coleman**, all of Winnsboro, S. C.

- - - December 29th, 1886 by Rev. D. G. Caldwell at the residence of the bride's father near Statesville, N. C., Mr. **Pink Barkley** and Miss **Belle Kimball**.

January 27, 1887

Died in Lee County, Miss. on Wednesday, January 5th, 1887, **an infant daughter** of John W. and Maggie E. (Young) **Bryson**, aged 4 days.

Died January 22d, 1887, **Isaac Pressly**, infant son of John C. and Hattie **Haddon** . . . it is only a few months since they were called to follow one of their children to the grave.

Died January 23d, 1887, **Rebecca V. Nance**, daughter of F. W. R. and Mrs. M. J. Nance. . . . victim of pulmonary consumption. . . . In April, 1886, while yet in the morning of life, she made a public profession of faith in Christ.

Died at his home near Catawba, Catawba County, N. C. on January 12, 1887, Mr. **Jas. McCarnie Lewis**, aged 72 years, 8 months and 17 days. About two years ago his daughter accidentally caught fire from which she subsequently died. In attempting to save her, Mr. Lewis had his hands badly burned. This broke down his usual health and for two years he has been declining. He was a ruling elder in the New Sterling church.

February 3, 1887

Died near East Troy, Tenn., January 19th, 1887, **Sydney**, eldest son of James C. and Mrs. Laura **Hamilton** in the 18th year of his age. . . . was born August 20th, 1869.

Married, December 23d, 1886 of Rev. W. L. Patterson in Freestone County, Texas at the residence of the bride's cousin, Mr. Geo. Bradley, Mr. **Wade H. Butler** and Miss **M. Lula Bradley**.

February 10, 1887

Died, January 18th, 1887, near Crowder's Mt., N. C., Mrs. **Mary Ann Weir**, relic of Alexander Weir and daughter of Enoch McNair. She was born November 15th, 1812 and married October 10th, 1839. In 1854, during one month from September 22d to October 24th, five children were carried away by a malignant flux. Her husband died August 21st, 1862. Mrs. Weir found a warm home with her son-in-law, Wm. Pearson, for many years and died in good standing with her church, Pisgah.

Died in Pope County, Ark., October 31st, 1886, of malarial hematuria, Mr. **E. D. Shaw**, in the 54th year of his age. . . . had been living only about a year in the bounds of the writer's [Rev. Monroe Oates] charge. He was united in marriage to Miss Mattie Shaw, a niece of Rev. John Wilson. They bore testimonials of church membership in Salem church, Tipton County, Tenn., although they had united with the C. P.

church. They were received by certificate as members of the A. R. P. church at Bethany or Pott's Station.

Died at his residence in Mecklenburg County, N. C., January 4th, 1887, **John Pressly Millen**, in the 60th year of his age. . . . born in Chester County, S. C., but for many years had resided in North Carolina and was a member of the Steel Creek congregation. . . . twice married: first to Miss Winnie A. Youngblood, who lived only a short while leaving one son. In 1869, he was married to Miss Margaret L. Knox with whom he lived in peace and harmony for thirty eight years. He raised a large family of children.

[John H. Simpson's "Nongenarians of New Lebanon, W. Va." concerned the next three notices of deaths in his church].

On the 26th of last October, Mrs. **Jennie Finton** died in the 91st year of her age. She was a constant and careful reader of the Bible.

On the 22d of July, 1886, Mrs. **Ingabo Alexander** died in the 92nd year of her age, sitting in an old arm chair without a half hour of pain. . . . Her Bible was first and the *Associate Reformed Presbyterian* was next in her reading. She had no children.

On the 25th of August, 1885, **Tristram Patton** died in the 93rd year of his age. For sixty years he was a believer in Christ, and a liberal and a devoted member of the church. On his death-bed, I asked him if he would like to live his long life over again and he said, "Well, no; I would rather go on than to go back." I also asked him how he managed to live so long and he replied, "O, God was very good to me; I did not live fast; I slept a great deal; ate plain food, took but little medicine, and was never drunk in my life."

Married, February 6th, 1887, by Trial Justice C. V. Martin, Mr. **Samuel B. Bluford** of Troy, S. C. and Miss **Sarah Jane Stewart** of Donnaldsville, S. C.

- - - October 14th, 1886, in Pope County, Ark. by Rev. M. Oates, Mr. **W. H. Cousar** and Mrs. **M. I. Ferguson**.

- - -December 9th, 1886 by Rev. M. Oates, Mr. **S. F. Oates** and Miss **M. F. Wells**.

- - -December 22d, 1886 by Rev. M. Oates, Mr. **W. R. McArthur** and Miss **Irene Henry**.

- - - December 23d, 1886 by Rev. M. Oates, Mr. **A. M. Oates** and Miss **M. A. Gaston**.

- - -January 17th, 1887 by Rev. M. Oates, Mr. **S. R. Wells** and Miss **M. E. Oates**.

- - - January 12th, 1887 at the residence of the bride's mother, Mrs. M.

J. Patton, by Rev. C. B. Betts, Mr. **George A. Cowan** and Miss **Daisy R. Patton**. All of York County, S. C.

<u>February 17, 1887</u>

Mrs. **Mary Ella(Boyd) Ethridge**, wife of Mr. Rose Ethridge, died December 26th, 1886, aged 31 years. . . . joined the church at Cedar Spring when she was only fifteen years old. She was married to Mr. Ethridge, August 15th, 1878, who is now left with his motherless children.

Died, January 30th, 1887, Miss **Janie Bertha Creswell**, aged 15 years, 2 months and 25 days. . . . was a daughter of R. P. and Mary F. Creswell and the second child that these parents have lost in little more than two years.

Samuel Anderson departed this life, January 18th, 1887, aged 34 years, 8 months, and 29 days. . . . In August last connected with M. E. church [died of measles which also took the life of his daughter] **Flora Jennett Anderson**, 9 years, 11 months and 9 days old.

Married February 10th, 1887, by Rev. S. A. Agnew, Mr. **Joseph L. Agnew** and **Miss M. E. Bryson**, daughter of Mr. Porter Bryson. All of Union County, Miss.

<u>February 24, 1887</u>

Departed this life near Clinton, Laurens County, S. C., Mr. **R. T. Blakely**, son of David and Isabella Blakely, who was born May, 1857 and died January 23d, 1887. . . . measles [brought death which] leaves his aged parents and bereaved brothers and sisters.

Sarah T., an infant daughter of Joseph and Sarah **Todd**, died January 26th, 1887, agd 20 months.

Miss **Susan Jane Harris** was born in Rockbridge County, Va., July 17th, 1823 and died in Augusta County, September 12th, 1886. At one time she was a member of Old Providence church, Va.; but at her own request obtained a letter of dismissal. However, we [Rev. S. W. Haddon & Session] think that she never united with any other church.

J. D. Walkup was born September 16th, 1861 and died November 11th, 1886.

R. B. Walkup was born May 25th, 1859, and died November 12th, 1886. . . . brothers. . . . were members of Unity A. R. P. church. . . . The former left a wife betrothed to pine under disappointed hopes. The latter left a wife and one child [brothers were buried in same tomb].

Mr. **W. C. Sherard** of Anderson was married last Wednesday evening to Miss **Tabbie Nance**, the eldest daughter of Mrs. R. D. Nance. Rev. W. F. Pearson, assisted by Rev. Dr. Pressly, married them.

- - - February 3d, 1887 in Jefferson County, Ga. at the residence of Mr. Charles Burke by Rev. J. S. Mills, Mr. **John A. Attaway** and Miss **Lizzie J. Burke**.

- - - February 10th, 1887 by Rev. C. E. Todd, Mr. **W. G. Mayfield** and Miss **Florence Brown**.

- - - February 10th, 1887 by Rev. C. E. Todd, Mr. **D. P. Weldon** and Miss **Belle Sullivan**. All of Milton County, Ga.

March 3, 1887

Died near Huntersville, N. C. on February 11th, 1887, **Paul Wylie**, infant son of Mr. and Mrs. R. M. **Ranson**. Aged 8 months and 11 days.

Died at his residence in Iredell County, N. C. on December 12th, 1886, Dr. **T. C. Halyburton**, aged 54 years, 3 months and 3 days. . . . member of Amity church and for some years an elder.

Died near Broad Creek church, Rockbridge County, Va. of diabetes on January 25th, 1887, little **Eddie**, son of Jas. F. and Mattie S. **Ham**. Aged 10 years, 4 months and 27 days.

Elizabeth W. Dixon was born on Kerr's Creek, Rockbridge County, Va., August 5th, 1805 and died at the home of her son, John C. Dixon, on Timber Ridge, January 6th, 1887. The parents, Andrew and Nancy Walkup, emigrated from Ireland in company with her brother Arthur and others, who were all rigid Presbyterians, and settled in the vicinity of Kerr's Creek, Rockbridge, Va. She had six sisters and one brother, who married in North Carolina and settled in Mississippi. Her sisters, who have, all except one, preceded her to the grave, settled in Rockbridge County. . . . In early life she connected with the G. A. P. church at Old Monmouth, Va. but after her marriage to James Dixon she transferred her membership to the A. R. P. church at Ebenezer, her husband being a member of that church. But they, having moved to Cedar Grove, worshipped at Timber Ridge church, which was under the pastoral care of the late Horatio Thompson, D. D. . . . mother of nine children, three of whom died quite young. . . three children survive her. . . . together with an orphan boy whom she raised.

Mrs. **Sarah A. Kirby** was born September 8th, 1862 and died November 28th, 1886. She was the daughter of Thomas S. and Eliza A. Robertson. She joined the church (New Providence, G. A. P.) in the fifteen year of her age. In her seventeenth year she was married to William A. Kirby. She leaves one child four years sold. She in 1884, in company with her husband and some relatives, moved to Indiana where she resided until her death. . . . She lies buried in the church yard at Old Providence.

Died in Newton County, Ga., January 6th, 1887, **Thelma Ethleen**, daughter of Melvin and Julia **Davis**, and grand daughter of Rev. S. P. Davis, aged 14 years and 4 months. . . . died of spinal meningetis.

Died in Newton County, Ga., January 13th, 1887, **Claudie Belle**, daughter of J. J. and Elizabeth **Thompson**, in the 11th year of her age. Also, January 22d, 1887, **Sarah Lou Zorah**, daughter of Turner and Sarah **Stewart**, aged 13 years and 4 months. These little cousins were playmates in life and in death were not long divided. They both had congestion of the brain.

Also, on January 22d, 1887, Mr. **Clark Stewart**. . . passed away in his 86th year. . . . born in Chester County, S. C. and moved to Newton County, Ga. about sixty years ago. He was one of the first members of Hopewell, and I [Rev. J. E. Martin] believe is the last of that number having lived in connection with it about sixty years. He leaves a widow, his second wife, and step-daughter and two sons, Thomas and Turner, and one daughter, Elizabeth Thompson.

Mr. James Cork, Sr. who lived near Donnalds died last Saturday . . . . originally from Fairfield County, but for several years has been living in this section. He is the father of Prof. J. C. Cork of Prosperity.

Married, February 23d, 1887 at the residence of the bride's father by Rev. W. O. Cochran, assisted by Rev. C. E. McDonald, Mr. **W. S. McLelland** and Miss **Mary L. Brown**. All of Mecklenburg County, N. C.

- - - February 17th, 1887 at the parsonage by Rev. C. B. Betts, Mr. **J. P. Carpenter** of Mecklenburg County, N. C. and Miss **Carrie H. Simpson** of Chester County, S. C.

- - - February 23d, 1887 at the home of the bride's father, Mr. W. B. Simpson by Rev. C. B. Betts, Mr. **John S. Neely** and Miss **Mattie Simpson**. All of Chester County, S. C.

March 10, 1887

Died at the residence of Mr. T. J. Hawthorne in Wilcox County, Ala., November 25th, 1886, **S. Oliver Jones**, M. D., who was born the 16th of September, 1859. . . . The third son of Mr. S. L. and Mrs. E. B. (McReynolds) Jones . . . [attended University of Alabama] graduated in the Mobile Medical College with honor . . . . married to Miss Kate McConico of Wilcox County on the 27th of January, 1855 . . . [member of] Bethel.

Married, January 20th, 1887 in Macon, Ga. at the residence of Capt. R. H. Barron, by Rev. J. S. Mills, Mr. **R. P. Little** and Miss **Ellen Griswold**.

- - - February 23d, 1887, at the residence of the bride's father, Mr. **A. J. Boyd**, by Rev. J. P. Erwin, Mr. **Jno. F. Hunter**, Cleveland County and Miss **Irene Boyd** of Lincoln County, Ark.

March 17, 1887

Died in Tipton County, Tenn., January 28th, 1887, Mrs. **Mary McQuiston**, the beloved wife of Robt. McQuiston, in the 61st year of her age. . . . born in Chester County, S. C. In early life . . . united with Smyrna congregation. In 1850, she trnsferred her membership to Salem, . . . She was twice married. First, to Hugh McHenry. The fruit of this marriage was two lovely daughters, one of whom survives. . . . Having lost the husband of her youth by death she united again by marriage with Robt. McQuiston. . . . for a period of thirty five years.

Died in Tipton County, Tenn. September 1st, 1886, **Katy Irene**, infant daughter of T. L. and Mary **Faulkner**.

Died in Wilcox County, Ala., May 27th, 1886, Mrs. **Elizabeth Norris McBryde** who was born in Abbeville County, July 25th, 1794. daughter of William Norris and was married twice: the first time to William Stewart, the second to Mr. Thomas McBryde. Both of her husbands preceded her to the grave. The fruit of these marriages were seven children, only one of whom survives. . . . Since 1851 she was a widow the second time. From her eighteenth year to 1837 when she came to Wilcox County, Ala. , she was a member of the Associate Reformed Prsbyterian church at Cedar Springs. A short time after her settlement in Wilcox County, she joined Lebanon on Prairie Creek. . . [later] Lebanon situated five miles east of Camden [Ala.]

Married, March 10th, 1887 by Rev. R. M. Kirkpatrick, assisted by Rev. R. M. Stevenson, Mr. **James M. Stroupe** and Miss **Hattie Wallace**, daughter of Mr. Randolph Wallace, Clover, York County, S. C.

- - - February 10th., 1887 at Clover, York County, S. C. by Rev. R. M. Stevenson, Mr. **Cornelius Best** and Miss **Maggie Johnson**.

March 24, 1887

Mrs. **Vashti Burress**. . . . departed this life Monday afternoon, February 21st, 1887 at her home in the city of Anderson, S. C. . . . daughter of Robt. C. Sharp, Sr. and was born January 12th, 1828 near Due West, Abbeville County. In 1850, she was married to Dr. E. G. Gaines of Pickens County who died in 1855, when she returned to make her home with her father. In 1859 she was married to the late Milford Burress of Anderson County who died December 25th, 1869. She was the mother of two children, one son and one daughter. The son was by her first marriage and died in infancy; the daughter was by her last marriage and survives. . . . [early a member of the A. R. P. church in Due West] Later in life, after her second marriage, her religious views . . . underwent a change and she united with the Anderson Baptist church. . . . by her last marriage she became a step-mother of a family of five daughters, four of whom survive.

Married, February 22d, 1887 by Rev. C. E. Todd, Mr. **A. M. Wylie** and Miss **Ophelia Orr**. All of DeKalb County.

- - - December 18th, 1886 at the residence of the bride's father by Rev. E. E. Patterson, Mr. **A. J. Blackman** and Miss **Eula McCaw**. All of Lamar County, Texas.

- - - December 23d, 1886 at the residence of the bride's father by Rev. E. E. Patterson, Mr. **Wm. Black**, formerly of York County, S. C. and Miss **Anella White**. All of Lamar County, Texas.

- - - December 28th, 1886 at the residence of the bride's father by Rev. E. E. Patterson, Mr. **B. Herndon** and Miss **Lavinia Pressly**. All of Lamar County, Texas.

March 31, 1887

Died in Iredell County, N. C. of pneumonia, January 29th, 1887, Miss **Margaret Ann Allison**, aged 22 years, 8 months and 27 days. . . . joined the A. R. church at New Perth at an early age.

Married, March 24th, 1887 at the residence of the bride's fathr, Mr. Wm. Blakely, by Rev. L. K. Glasgow, Mr. **A. Perry Torrence** and Miss **Julia R. Blakely**. All of Mecklenburg County, N. C.

April 7, 1887

Died on the 6th of March, 1887 near Head Spring, Laurens County, S. C., **Walter C.**, son of Mr. Leman and Nancy **Jones**.

Died near White Oak, Fairfield County, S. C., March 2d, 1887, **Nattie Mitchell**, daughter of Mr. and Mrs. W. H. Mitchell, aged about 11 years.

C. B. DeMasters was born in Nelson County, Va., December 19th, 1811 and died in Augusta County, September 11th, 1885. The deceased was twice married. His first wife was Miss Elvira Fitzpatrick by whom he had five children, one of whom still lives. Mr. DeMasters was a cooper by trade. . . . His first wife was a member of Old Providence, Va.; but while the deceased frequently attended church, he never joined.

Died near Wallerville, Union County, Miss., on Sabbath, January 30th, 1887, Mrs. **Elizabeth Bailey** in the 76th year of her age. . . . a daughter of Mr. William Nugent and was born in Laurens County, S. C., March 22d, 1811. . . . [joined] Providence in April, 1844. She married Henry Bailey, October 16th, 1854, and came to Pontotoc, now known as Union County,

Miss. . . .[there she joined Hopewell church]. Her husband died February 2d, 1882 . . .[and she] remained at the family homestead until the time of her death. . . She had no children of her own but leaves step children.

Miss **Sarah Swett** departed this life March 16th, 1887, aged 61 years, 4 months and 7 days. . . . born in York County, S. C.; spent her whole life and died in the same neighborhood . . . connected with Neely's Creek congregation about nine years ago.

Married, February 23d, 1887 by Rev. A. G. Harmon, Mr. **J. B. Harmon** and Miss **Clara A. Robinson**. All of McCormick, S. C.

- - - March 24th, 1887 in Fairfield County, S. C. by the Rev. J. A. White, Mr. **John W. Bankhead** and Mrs. **M. M. Ford**.

April 14, 1887

Rev. **Wilson Ashley** died at his home in this county [Abbeville, S. C.] last week. He was buried last Sabbath at Little River.

Died at her home in Chester County, S. C., March 23d, 1887, Mrs. **Sarah Wylie**, widow of the late Jas. B. Wylie, aged about 75 years.

James Cresswell of Long Cane departed this life, March 25th, 1887, aged about 60 years. . . . A few days before he had gone to spend a week with a married son, but he was smitten with paralysis in the night and the family found him speechless in the morning.

Mrs. **Maggie W. Lynn** died in Tipton County, Tenn., January 23d, 1887 in the 36th year of her age. . . wife of James Lynn and daughter of James and Letitia Caskey. . . . was born in Chester County, S. C., but for twenty one years has been a resident of Tipton County, Tenn. . . a member of the A. R. P. church at Bloomington . . . leaves a husband and three children.

On the 24th of January, 1887, only three days after [?], **John Caskey**, brother of the above, breathed his last on earth. He was in the 50th year of his age. He was a man peculiarly quiet and retiring in disposition.

Married, February 9th, 1887 at the home of the bride's brother, by Rev. J. G. Miller, Mr. **W. H. Wilson** and Miss **Lizzie E. Caskey**. Both of Tipton County, Tenn.

- - - March 23d, 1887 at Mt. Paran church by Rev. J. G. Miller, Mr. **S. T. McLerkin** and Miss **Fannie Adkinson**. Both of Tipton County, Tenn.

- - - March 31st, 1887 at Monticello, Ark. by Rev. J. L. Young, Mr. **L. T. Allen** and Miss **Nannie L. Moore**.

- - - April 3d, 1887 at the residence of the bride's mother, Mrs. M. C. Snell, by Rev. John D. Hartgraves, Mr. **G. L. Emerson** and Miss **Ida Snell**. All of Houston County, Texas.

April 28, 1887

Died at Starkville, Miss., December 4th, 1886, **Nannie R. McKell** in the 14th year of her age. Disease, heredisary [?] consumption.

Died at his home near Elk Shoal church, Alexander County, N.C., March 11th, 1887, Mr. **Andrew C. Morrison**, aged 87 years, 3 months and 27 days. . . . member of New Sterling church.

Mrs. **Mary E. Moore** was born in Augusta County, Va., October 2d, 1813 and died at her home in the same county, January 16th, 1887. . . . [was] the only child of James and Jane Poague. She was married December 5th, 1833 to Archer Moore. The fruits of this union were nine children, six sons and three daughters, all of whom are living except one son who was accidentally killed when first coming into manhood. . . .[joined] Old Providence, Va. in May, 1870. . . lost her husband, February 20th, 1870.

Clark Powell Wright, infant son of Dr. J. D. and Mrs. Lula Wright, died in Louisville, Ga . March 18th, 1887 . . . only 3 months old.

Mrs. M. C. Alexander died January 27th, 1887 at her home in Jefferson County, Ga. . . . born December 2d, 1816. She was the widow of the late John C. Alexander.

Mrs. Thomas Pennington died last January 4th, 1887. . . consistent member of Bethel church (Burke County, Ga.). . . leaves [husband and] two little children.

May 6, 1887

Mrs. M. McAdams, wife of 'Squire Bennett McAdams, died at the home of her son-in-law, Mr. J. O. McClain, on Little River last Tuesday night. She was about 85 years old. . . . long a member of the A. R. P. church . . . . buried in Lindsay graveyard. She leaves several children and one brother, Mr. Joseph Ellis.

Died near Huntersville, N. C. of typhoid fever, March 20th, 1887, Miss **N. Violet Knox**, aged 16 years, 10 months and 5 days.

On Friday, the 30th of April, **Lizzie**, more familiarly known as "Bunnie,"daughter of W. P. and Mrs. Margaret **Kennedy**, died, and on Tuesday, the 3d of May, **Annie Alice**, daughter of W. C. and Mrs. Annie **Brock**, died. . . . the first of seven summers, the second of less than three years. [Both were from Due West and died as a result of measles].

Died in Union County, Miss., February 17th, 1887, with typhoid pneumonia, Miss **Letha A. Johnson**, daughter of George W. and Mary (Miller) Johnson and was the fifth child in a family of nine, all of whom lived to be grown and become members of the church of their father and mother, except the three youngest. Two of these are in Texas and the youngest at home. [Father died "about two months ago."]

Died in Union County, Miss., February 17th, 1887 after a few days of dreadful suffering, Mr. **Robert A. Hanks**, aged 33 years, 9 months and 12 days. . . . born in Wilcox County, Ala.; moved to this State [Mississippi], married and settled within the bounds of Ebenezer church [died of hydrophobia].

Died in Tipton County, Tenn., September 12th, 1886, **Mamie Alexander**, little daughter of J. A. and M. J. **Moore**, in her 6th year.

On the 15th of April, 1887, the same fond parents were called to mourn the death of another beloved daughter, **Cora Erskine Moore**, aged 23 years and 1 day. . . . granddaughter of the late John M. McLerkin, who was a pillar in the congregation of Salem.

Miss **Gertrude Brownlee** of Belton was married last Tuesday, the 16th. ult., 4 o'clock, p. m. to Mr. **Hammond Webb** of Anderson, S. C.

Mr. **S. B. Lathan** of Washington, D. C., son of Rev. R. Lathan, D. D. was married last Wednesday, the 27th ult., to Miss **Jossie Fisher** of Louisville, Ky.

May 19, 1887

J. Calvin Halfacre died at his home in Newberry, S. C., November 30th, 1886. Aged 41 years, 7 months and 23 days. . . .[although] deaf and dumb for life. . . . [nevertheless] he attained a very good education. . . . four years ago he was happily married to Miss Emma Wilson.

Married at the residence of Mr. J. B. McWhorter, Mrs. **Carrie Clinkscales** of Level Land, S. C. to Mr. **C. A. Armstrong** of Lewisburg, Tenn.

May 23, 1887

Died January 34 [sic]th, 1887, **Wm. J. Jennings**, aged 54 years, 2 months and 21 days. . . . born in South Carolina in 1832; moved to Tippah County, Miss. when small and connected himself with the A. R. P. congregation of Ebenezer. . . and remained a member until 1881 when he moved to Yell County, Ark.

Miss **Mollie J. Clinkscales**, a graduate of Due West Female College of the Class of 1865, died near Lowndesville where she had been teaching for several years past. She was buried on Friday at Midway [Baptist church].

Last Monday, **Johnnie O. Hawthorn** of Donalds died at his home in Donnalds, a grandson of the late Col. D. O. Hawthorn. For about four months he has been employed in the *Associate Reformed Presbyterian* office.

On Wednesday aftrnoon of last week at 2 o'clock (May 18) the spirit of **David Kerr** fled from the the earthly tabernacle . . . [of dysentry effects] member of the freshman class of Erskine College . . . youngest son of Rev. David Kerr of Arkansas. Since his father's death, and for the last thirteen years, he has been under the care and guardianship of his uncle, Dr. H. T. Sloan, with whom he lived.

Married, April 20th, 1887, near Statesville, N. C. by Rev. D. G. Caldwell at the residence of the bride's father, Mr. **J. Pressly McLean** and Miss **Julia Walker**.

- - - May 11th, 1887, by Rev. W. A. M. Plaxco, Mr. **R. N. Plaxco** of York County and Miss **Sallie E. Cousar** of Lancaster County, S. C.

June 2, 1887

Mrs. **John Eli Ellis** died at her home about three miles from this place [Due West] last Monday night. She was a good woman and leaves a large family to mourn her death. She was buried at the "Lindsay graveyard."

We announce another death among our friends from the prevailing disease, dysentery. Mrs. **M. A. Payne** at the home of her widowed mother, Mrs. M. D. Drennan, near Mt. Carmel in this county [Abbeville] on Monday evening, May 23d. Recently, we, with our friend and relative, Rev. H. D. Lindsay, the grandson of Mrs. Drennan, visited the family.

Little **Bruce Clifton**, son of J. C. and E. M. **Davis**, was taken March 24th, 1887. . . 10 months and 27 days [old].

Little **Martha**, daughter of Chalmers and Julia **Fleming**, died of brain fever at their home in Ebenezer, Ga., May 16th, 1887. . . about six years old and the third child these parents have lost by this same disease.

Paul Grier, son of N. H. and Sallie (Russell) **Young** was born on the 22d of October, 1885 and died May 16th, 1887.

Died in Union County, Miss. on Sabbath evening, April 17th, 1887, Mrs. **Isabella Caldwell**, wife of David A. Caldwell, aged 31 years, 2 months and 10 days. . . . daughter of Barton and Mrs. Jane B. (Reid) Griffin and was born in Calhoun County, Ala., February 7th, 1856. Her parents removed to Mississippi in 1869. She was married to David A.

Caldwell, November 3d, 1875. She joined the Baptist church while living in Alabama . . . [survived by] a kind husband, two little children and an aged mother.

Mrs. **Elizabeth J. Strain** departed this life, April 26th, 1887. Death resulted from paralysis six days after the stroke. She was born on August 3d, 1821. . . .early united with Allison Creek congregation, an O. S. Presbyterian church. After marriage to Mr. Wm. Forbes, she united with the church of her husband at Tirzah (A. R.P.). Aftr the death of Mr. Forbes, she was united in marriage to Mr. Alexander Strain and survived him several years. At the time of her death she was living with her son-in-law, Mr. Geo. Wallace.

Died, April 26th, 1887 of hemiplegia, **Sarah Leena**, daughter of G. D. and Nannie **Brown**, aged 1 year, 10 months and 5 days.

Departed this life in Tipton County, Tenn. on the 18th of February, 1887, Mrs. **Margaret Eudora Jamison**, the second daughter of Mr. William Hart and the wife of Mr. A. Jamison. She was born on the 8th of July, 1858. . . died of dropsy . . . member of the A. R. church of Bloomington. . . . [survived by] a fond husband and three little children.

Died in Union County, Miss., December 31st, 1886, Mr. **George W. Johnson**, aged 70 years, 2 months and 6 days. . . . born in Abbeville County, S. C., near Due West, in the year 1816. . . . the son of John Henry and Sarah (Wilson) Johnson. Soon after Mr. Johnson had attained to years of majority, or even before then, he, together with an elder brother, emigrated to this State [Mississippi] stopping the first night in Tippah County at or near the place where the present Cotton Plant now stands. Subsequently he settled and lived all his life within one mile of that town. . . It was his pride to say that he had seen and met the Indian Chief Tishemingo. . . If not one of the charter members of this congregation [Ebenezer] he joined it in May, 1843.

Died, March 3d, 1887, Miss **Carrie Price**, aged 22 years. She was the daughter of Mr. Thomas Price of Newberry County, S. C. [member of King's Creek church].

June 9, 1887

Died June 2d, 1887, **Francis Omer**, infant son of Francis and Mrs. C. E. **Drake**.

Died at his home in Fairfield County, S. C., May 15th, 1887, **James Bankhead, Sr.** in the 73rd year of his age. . . . [baptized and first joined Presbyterian church]. But Providence having cast his lot near Ebenezer. . . [he joined A. R. P. church there and later at White Oak A. R. P.].

Died in Mecklenburg County, N. C., March 27th, 1887, **J. N. Wallace**, aged 41 years. . . . graduated at Erskine College in 1869. In 1872 was elected elder in Sardis church and immediately made the clerk of Session . . . survived by a sister, wife, and six children.

Died at her home in Donnaldsville, S. C. on June 1st, 1887 and in the 26th year of her age, Mrs. **Corrie Ophelia Donnald**, wife of W. J. Donnald; and on the 5th of June (five days later) **Erin [Donnald]**, a little girl of 18 months. These were mother and daughter, her first-born and only child.

On the 16th of October, 1886, at her home near Antreville, Abbeville County, S. C., Mrs. **Jane H. Haddon**, wife of Mr. John T. Haddon . . . was born in Ireland. . . moved to this county in infancy and her parents settled in Abbeville County near Greenwood. . . in early life connected with the Rock church. . . . [later] member of Little Mountain.

June 16, 1887

Mrs. **Cynthia Ann Wakefield** died at the home of Mr. John Eli Ellis last Thursday at the advanced age of 88 years. . . [buried at First Creek Baptist church].

Mrs. Lulah Power died last Saturday at the home of her husband, Mr. Henry J. Power, ten miles west of this place [Due West]... member of Little Mountain.

Miss **Mittie Haddon** of Tampa, Fla., a member of the Junior Class in the Female College died last Saturday. . . long a victim of consumption. her remains were interred here [Due West] temporarily.

[another notice in same issue] Entered into rest June 11th, 1887, Miss **Mittie J. Haddon**, aged a little more than 19 years. . . . She came from her Florida home to the Female College seeking health as well as mental culture. . . has been in residence more than a year.

Died on the 16th of May, 1887, in Dallas County, Ala. in the 20th year of her age, Mrs. **Ella LaPelle**, wife of Mr. S. H. **White**. Three years ago our community greeted Mrs. White as a modest, youthful bride from the hills of Tennessee. . . joined Prosperity church where her husband belonged, but stricken with consumption. . . . leaves a young, disconsolate husband and a little babe.

Died of dysentery in the city of Memphis, Tenn., May 12th, 1887, Mr. **James Leonidas Wyatt**, aged 24 years, 4 months and 1 day. . . . son of James B. and May (Wilson) Wyatt and was born in Lincoln County, Tenn. When only an infant his parents moved to Marion County, Ill. where they remained about twelve years, coming thence to Shelby County, Tenn. Here the subject of this notice passed the remainder of his days with the exception of a few months spent in Lincoln immediately after his marriage to Miss Mary Agnes McCown of that county.

Died in Henry County, Ga. on the 2d of May, 1887, **Nettie**, oldest child of Prof. and Mrs. H. A. B. **Weldon** in her 17th year. . . . [joined] the Methodist church at Snapping Shoals, Newton County, Ga. some eight months before her death. . . for several years connected with the Sabbath School of Hopewell (A. R. P.).

Died, May 31st, 1887 at her home near Due West, S. C., Mrs. **Isabella E. Ellis**, wife of John E. Ellis. In early life Mrs. Ellis made a profession of religion in commection with the Baptist church at First Creek, Anderson County. In May, 1874, her membership was transferred to the A. R. P. church at Due West. She left an aged mother, a husband, a number of children.

At the same place on the 9th of June, 1887 (nine days later) and of the same disease (dysentery), **Mrs. C. A. Wakefield** died. Mrs. Wakefield was the relict of the late Hezekiah Wakefield, a prominent member of the First Creek Baptist church and the mother of Mrs. Ellis mentioned above. Her maiden name was Gantt. She was born and baptized and reared in the Associate Reformed church, and always retained a fondness for the sacred songs, but identified herself with the Baptist church at First Creek with her husband. . . she was well advanced in her 86th year.

Mrs. **Nancy Ware**, widow of John Ware and daughter of Wm. Thompson, died in Newton County, Ga., April 4th, 1887. . . was born in Fairfield County, S. C. in 1816 and came to Georgia in 1827. She was full of energy, and though left at her husband's death with four small children, only one of them, a boy who died young, she provided for her family.

Also, Mrs. **Margaret Aiken**, familiarly called "Aunt Peggy," quietly and peacefully passed away on April 18th, 1887 in her 82d year. . . was born in Fairfield County, S. C., February 1st, 1806 and moved with her father's family to Georgia in 1836. She lived with her kindred near Hopewell.

Also, May 7th, 1887, **Lizzie Pearl**, infant daughter of Edward and Jennie **Dabney**, died of cholera infantum.

Died in Madison County, Miss., March 25th, 1887, Mrs. **Drucilla B. Simpson**, aged 72 years and 11 months. . . . born in York County, S. C. . . . . Her maiden name was Miller, and she was a cousin of the late Rev. John Miller, D. D. She married Thomas Simpson, January 23d, 1834. . . . in early life united with Tirzah. Husband and wife moved to Mississippi in 1845. . . After the death of her husband, Mrs. Simpson came to Tipton County, Tenn. where she had three daughters residing. . . Last fall she went in what was intended to be a short visit to her sons in Mississippi [where she became fatally ill].. . .mother of ten children, four of whom preceded her to the grave. Three daughters and three sons [survive].

Mrs. **Jane Finley** died at her home near Auburn, Mo. on Friday evening, March 4th, 1887. . . born in Shelby County, Ky., July 13th, 1809. On the second day of October, 1828, she was married to Mr. James Finley and the next year in the fall of 1829, she removed, with her husband, to Lincoln County, Mo. She had been born and reared in the A. R. church; her husband being a ruling elder in the church at Shelbyville, Ky. At the time of their removal to Missouri, there was no church organization of their order in the State. . . on the first day of August, 1834, Rev. Andrew Bower organized the first A. R. church west of the Mississippi river, in Lincoln County, Mo. Mrs. Finley at this time was received as a member of the church.

June 23, 1887

Mr. **Branch Haddon** died at the home of his father, Mr. Zacheriah Haddon on Saturday morning last and was buried in the A. R. P. cemetery at this place [Due West] last Sabbath. On Monday, Mrs. Haddon, the mother of the deceased and the wife of Mr. Z. Haddon, died.

Departed this life on the 9th of June, 1887 in York County, S. C., **Thomas Spurgeon**, son of J. A. and Lizzie Boyce **McGill**, aged 26 months.

Nanie Louisa, infant daughter of Mr. and Mrs. S. W. **Craig**, was born June 17th, 1886 and died May 28th, 1887 of dysentery.

Died in Statesville, N. C., April 8th, 1887, **Annie Bee**, infant of Rev. and Mrs. D. G. **Caldwell**.

In the same place, June 2d, 1887, **Tossie Lleno**, age about 15 months, child of Mr. and Mrs. N. T. **Milholland**.

Died, May 4th, 1887, Mrs. **Margaret McAdams**, relict of the late Bennett McAdams. Born August 2d, 1802, Mrs. McAdams was in her 85th year and the oldest member of the A. R. church at Due West.

June 20th, 1887, Mrs. **Mary Haddon**, wife of Mr. Zachariah Haddon . . . at the time of her death in her 66th year.

June 16th, 1887, **Janie Bell**, infant daughter of W. A. and Mrs. Mary **Todd**, only 5 months [old]. . . and the only child of her parents.

Mrs. **Alice G. Devlin**, the lovely wife of Mr. R. H. Devlin, departed this life after a lingering illness on the 5th of June, 1887 in the 27th year of her age. . . leaves a devoted husband and three little boys. . . . connected herself with the A. R. church at Due West some five or six years ago. . . buried in the church yard at Cedar Spring.

Died in Pope County, Ark., June 3d, 1887, Mrs. **Sallie Belle**, consort of Mr. F. M. **Oates** and daughter of Mr. George W. and Mary McLure of Augusta County, Va. . . 22 years old the day of her death. . . . came to Arkansas a happy bride about eighteen months past . . . her parents were members of the Presbyterian church at New Providence, Va. . . . . after her marriage . . .[she joined] at Bethany (1886).

John L. Carson, a member of the A. R. church at Pisgah, died in Dallas, N. C., April 2d, 1887, aged 43 years, 4 months and 24 days. . . leaves a widow.

Died in Dallas, N. C., April 21st, 1887, **Annie May**, daughter of John L. and Melissa (Hanna) **Carson**, aged 2 years, 4 months and 24 days.

June 30, 1887

On the evening of Sabbath, June 26th, 1887 in the presence of her husband and children, Mrs. **Harriet D. Sitton**, wife of Mr. Jas. Y. Sitton of Due West, quietly and peacefully passed away. . . . early in life joined the Presbyterian church of her fathers. . . A few years ago this membership was transferred to the A. R. church of Due West where she lived.

Robert A. Hamilton died at his home (four miles west of Fayetteville, Tenn.) on the 1st of June, 1887 and in the 73d year of his age from pneumonia. . . a native of Fairfield County, S. C. of the Old Brick church congregation and came with his father, Peter Hamilton, to this country more than fifty years ago a young man. He subsequently married the eldest daughter of the late P. G. McMullen and raised a family, some of whom, with his beloved wife, have long since passed away. Two daughters and two sons survive. He had long been a consistent member of the A. R. church at Bethel.

Died of consumption at Allenton, Wilcox County, Ala. on the 4th of June, 1887, Miss **Martha Hayes Chestnut**, aged 34 years, 5 months and 24 days . . . . one of the daughters of John and Elizabeth (Craig) Chestnut and was born and reared in the A. R. P. church at Prosperity, Dallas County, Ala. . . [later] moved to Bethel church.

July 7, 1887

Mrs. Arther Sheffield died of cancer on the 27th of May, 1887 in the 43d year of her age. . . for many years a consistent member of the Prosperity A. R. church (Tenn.) and has left a husband and several children. . . . has been a widow and a step-mother. She had not long survived the death of a beloved sister, Mrs. Martha McAlla.

On the 4th of June, 1886. . . [a son was born to Rev. C. E. Todd and wife]; on June 15th, 1887 . . . [the son] **James Bruce Todd** [died].

July 14, 1887

Dietz Cornwall, infant son of Mr. and Mrs. J. R. **Peay**, died June 4th, 1887, aged about 15 months.

Died at her home in Chester County, S. C., June 1st, 1887, Mrs. **Mary McKeown**, aged about 80 years. . . early life her husband and upon her devolved the care and responsibility of rearing and training her family. . . . for many years a consistent and devoted member of Hopewell church.

Died at Doraville, Ga., June 11th, 1887, **Neille McCurry**, son of Mrs. T. T. **Stewart**, aged 2 years and 4 months.

Died near Steel Creek, N. C., June 4th, 1887, with dropsy of the stomach, Miss **Mary Price**, aged 48 years, 2 months and 8 days. . . . daughter of John and Jane (Boyd) Price and born in Newberry County in 1839. When quite young her father moved from South Carolina with his family, settling first in Lauderdale County, Tenn. and subsequently in Mississippi.

Born July 30th, 1886 and died March 15th, 1887, **infant** child of Mr. and Mrs. **Jonathan Montgomery**.

Born in Union County, Miss., October 28th, 1865, and died May 8th, 1887 with typhoid pneumonia, **Charles H. Purnell** son of Jas. M. and Martha (Liddell) Purnell.

July 21, 1887

Mr. **N. W. Wigham** died in Louisville, Ga., April 22d, 1887. . . deacon in Louisville church.

Virginia Betha Lotts was born August 15th, 1886 and died June 16th, 1887.

Ernest C. Robinson was born August 24th, 1880 and died May 14th, 1887.

Mrs. Sinquefield died in Louisville, Ga., April 10th, 1887. In her early youth she became a member of Ebenezer church. At the organization of the Louisville church, she moved her membership there.

Miss **Margaret McMurry** died June 18th, 1887 from dysentery. Aged 65 years. . . . was a native of Lancaster County, S. C. . . .[earlier member] at Tirzah (then A. R. P. church) where she was a consistent member until the disruption in connection with Rev. D. P. Robinson, when in 1875 she became one of the organic members of Unity A. R. P.

Miss **Mittie Patterson** died in Louisville, Ky., June 15th, 1887 . . . . daughter of Mr. A. L. Patterson.

Died in Mecklenburg County, N. C., June 15th, 1887, **Silvanus Grier**, little son of Mr. and Mrs. R. W. **Erwin**, from cholera infantum. Aged 3 months.

Died June 17th of same disease, **Richard Brown**, son of Mr. and Mrs. R. B. **Hunter**, aged 3 months.

Died June 20th of the same disease, **Samuel Boston**, son of Mr. and Mrs. Wilson **Miller**.

Died July 16th, 1887, **Nancy Kennedy**. "Aunt Nancy," as she was familiarly called, was an old colored woman, being, at the time of her death, above fourscore years of age. She was one of the few persons of her race who did not leave their former owners after their emancipation, having never once changed her home; and she was one of the few persons of her race who did not change her church connection. . . but lived and died a member of the Associate Reformed church, first at Cedar Springs and afterwards at Due West. . . . In her death the A. R. church at Due West has lost its only colored member.

Died in Statesville, N. C., June 13th, 1887, **Stella Blanche**, aged 15 months. . . . child of Mr. and Mrs. J. W. Shite.

Died June 15th, 1887 of cholera infantum, **Frances Lucele**, daughter of Alonzo and Fannie **Cannon**, aged 8 months and 17 days. When about two months old, her mother and father were both taken from her by death on the same day, and she, with her little brother and sister, were left to her grandmother Chalmers.

Died at his home in Woodford County, Ky., May 7th, 1887; Mr. **William Guyn**. . . born September 25th, 1809 . . . in 1835, he was married to Miss E. J. Long who with one son survives.

John Robert, infant son of Mr. C. B. and Mrs. M. **Robards** of Harralsburg, Ky. was born September 30th, 1886 and died on June 11th, 1887.

July 28, 1887

Moffatt Grier, the son of Rev. W. W. and Lula Orr, died of typhoid fever at his home in Huntersville, N. C., July 12th, 1887. . . born August-- , 1882.

Died in Lee County, Miss. on Friday, June 17th, 1887, **John Brown Galloway**, aged 44 years and 2 months. . . son of Alexander M. and Nancy M. (Wiley) Galloway, and was born in Lincoln County, Tenn., April

17th, 1843. His father removed to Mississippi and settled in Pontotoc (now Lee) County in 1855, when John was twelve years old and here he grew to manhood, married, lived and died. In his 19th year he became a Confederate soldier, serving faithfully in the 32nd Mississippi Regiment until he was captured in northern Georgia. . . while at Dalton, Ga. [during a revival among the troops, he made a public profession of religion in April, 1864 and in October became a member of Bethany.] . . . elected elder, August 2nd, 1869 and served nearly eighteen years. . .[song leader and superintendent and teacher in Sabbath school]. Justice of the Peace in Lee County in 1875 and served two years. . . . married October 9th, 1867 to Miss Mary T. D. McGee. . . father of five children, two of whom are dead.

Married, July 21st, 1887 in Pope County, Ark. by Rev. M. Oates, Mr. **J. Q. Oates** and Miss **F. B. Whitesides**.

August 4, 1887

Died of dysentery in Shelby County, Tenn., June 19th, 1887, **Oron Oscar**, son of J. G. and E. (Hutchison) **Townsend** . . . aged 9 months and 27 days.

Belle, daughter of Frank N. and Christine **Sibley**, died in Louisville, Ky., June 16th, 1887 of cholera infantum, aged 2 months and 25 days.

Died in Yorkville, S. C., July 28th, 1887, **Anna Rowan Barron**, infant daughter of Walter and Mary Barron.

Died in Huntersville, N. C., July 2d, 1887, little **Herbert Ross**, the only son of Mr. and Mrs. N. L. **Hunter**, aged about 10 months.

Died June 22d, 1887 at the residence of his step-father, Sion Snipes, near Ellistown, Union County, Miss., **Walter Houston Osborn**, aged 11 years, 4 months and 29 days. . . son of Rev. A. H. Osborn and Mrs. Nancy (Peterson) Osborn and was born in Lee County, Miss., June 23rd, 1876. His father died October 4th, 1877 and he was left to the care of his mother. She contracted a second marriage to Mr. Sion Snipes in 1880.

Mary Ann Wylie died on the 8th of July, 1887. . . . born in Chester County, S. C. on the 13th of June, 1842. . . . the daughter of John G. and Sarah Wylie who resided in the bounds of Hopewell. A good many years ago her father and family removed to western York into the bounds of Smyrna congregation of which he is now a worthy ruling elder, though now unable to go to church by reason of paralysis.

August 11, 1887

On Saturday morning, July 23d, 1887, Mrs. **Josephine Galloway**, wife of Rev. J. C. Galloway of Yorkville, S. C. departed this life . . . was born in Chester County, S. C. . . . the daughter of Mrs. Anna Brice and the late Rev. R. W. Brice. She graduated from the Due West Female College about the year 1874. On January 23d, 1879, she was joined in marriage to Rev. J. C. Galloway. . . lasted eight years and a half . . .[produced three daughters].

Married, July 28th, 1887 in Statesville, N. C. by Rev. D. G. Caldwell, Mr. **J. F. Kerr** and Miss **S. Jane Haithcock**. Both of Iredell County, N. C.

August 18, 1887

Died at Ebenezer, York County, S. C. on 31st of July, 1887 of dysentery, **Belle Douglas Miller**, infant daughter of Mr. J. W. B. and Mrs. F. E. Miller, aged 1 year, 6 months and 27 days.

Died August 7th, 1887 at Highlands, N. C., **John Caldwell**, infant son of R. S. and Mrs. Mary **Galloway**. . . lacked a few days of being 1 year old.

Ernest Young, infant son of Dr. E. Y. and Hattie L. **Murphy**, departed this life, June 29th, 1887, aged 3 months and 5 days.

August 25, 1887

An **infant** of Mr. and Mrs. Joseph **Cresswell** was buried on Friday, the 12th inst.

Gen. **P. H. Bradley** died on Sabbath night, August 14th, 1887 from the second stroke of paralysis.

Mrs. **Ida Caroline Wardlaw**, the young and accomplished wife of Mr. John Wardlaw, departed this life August 8th, 1887, in great peace, aged 20 years.

September 1, 1887

Robert Russell Davis was born January 17th, 1873 and died July 18th, 1887. . .[mother died when one year old and taken into the family of Drayton Russell].

On Saturday night, August 20th, 1887, Dr. **A. I. Barron** died, on the 4th of July he had completed fourscore years. . . descendant of James Barron who together with Edward Houp, accompanied John Knox as lay commissioners for the first General Assembly of the Church of Scotland which met in the city of Edinburgh on the 20th of December, 1560. . . From Scotland [his family] emigrated to Ireland, settling in the neighborhood of Carrickfergus about the year 1665. From Ireland, they emigrated to America, settling first in Pennsylvania and afterward, about 1750 or a few years earlier, they came south and settled in York County,

S. C. [first in Ebenezer congregation, but when it became disorganized, connected with Tirzah where Dr. Barron would become an elder.]

Ursula Craig McFadden departed this life, July 31st, 1887, aged 16 years, 10 months and 2 days. [member of Union congregation. C. B. B.]

Married, August 11, 1887 at the parsonage by Rev. C. B. Betts, Mr. **L. J. Hyatt** of Lancaster County, S. C. and Miss **Mattie McFadden** of York County, S. C.

September 15, 1887

Micajah Berry Latimer was born in Abbeville County, S. C., August 4, 1860, and died at Johnston, S. C., July 18, 1887. . . . was a consistent member of the Presbyterian church at Johnston. . . In 1884, he married Miss Lucia Carwile of Johnston, who, with a dear little boy, Edward, he leaves behind.

September 22, 1887

Mrs. **Laura Tisdale** died in Freestone County, Texas, November 20th, 1886, aged 37 years, 2 months and 2 days. . . . daughter of H. B. and R. A. Baldree. . . for many years a consistent member of A. R. P. church.

Janie Belle Bonner, infant daughter of J. L. and Lizzie Bonner, died August 27th, 1887.

Died in Union County, Miss., July 18th, 1887, Mrs. **Jane Brown (Reid) Griffin**, aged 72 years, 3 months and 13 days.. . . . native of Abbeville, S. C. where she was born April 5th, 1815. . . She was married to Barton Griffin, October 7th, 1832, and in 1837 they removed to what is now Calhoun County, Ala. In 1869, they came to Mississippi. Mr. Griffin died in 1880. Her surviving children are all grown and have families. She joined the Baptist church in South Carolina and continued in that denomination.

Death has claimed the infant son of Rev. W. W. and Lula **Orr** of Huntersville, N. C. **John Dales** died the 9th of September, aged about four months. . . . the third child [they have lost, two within two months].

Sarah Tisdale, daughter of Dr. J. R. and Mrs. Harriet **McMaster** of Winnsboro, S. C. . . . . was born September 7th, 1867. . . and died the 9th of August, 1887.

Also, on the same day, Miss **Betsy Stevenson** at the home of her niece in Jefferson County, Ga., aged something over threescore and ten years- perhaps over fourscore. "The writer [D. G. Phillips] has known her as a member of Ebenezer for forty years, and she was always the same consistent, affectionate, humble Christian--Aunt Betsy. Possessed of but small means, she was never known to pass a year that she did not contribute her small stipend for the support of the gospel.

Bessie Blackwood was born May 27th, 1884, died May 23d, 1887. Her parents, John and Isabella Blackwood live near Pisgah, Gaston, N. C.

[Died] August 7th, 1887, Mrs. **Nettie I.**, wife of W. A. **Griffith** of chronic diarrhea in the 30th year of her age. . . . She lived the greater part of her life in the communion of the Associate Reformed church, but at her death was a member of Steele Creek Presbyterian church. . . she leaves a husband and four small children.

September 29, 1887

Married, August 23d, 1887 near Tirzah church, York County, S. C. by Rev. J. C. Galloway, Mr. **Q. B. Bruner** of Matthew's Station, N. C. and **Mrs. M. O. Miller** of Tirzah, S. C.

- - - August 31st at the residence of the bride's father by Rev. W. M. Harden of the South Carolina Conference, Mr. **John A. McDermott** and Miss **M. Malvina Bryant**. All of Horry County, S. C.

October 6, 1887

Died at the home of her son-in-law, Mr. S. M. McDill, August 9th, 1887, Mrs. **Jennett McDaniel**, wife of the late Col. James McDaniel, aged 79 years and 11 months. . . . born and reared in bounds of Union congregation. . . after her marriage, she came into the bounds of Hopewell.

October 13, 1887

Jean McRitchie Young, infant daughter of A. H. and Jean McRitchie Young, was born May 31st, 1886 and died July 24th, 1887.

Lucy Ann Young, infant daughter of J. W. and Beulah Young, was born November 19th, 1886 and died August 23d, 1887.

Miss **Hattie O'Virgil Young**, daughter of Dr. L. S. and Julia Young, was born February 20th, 1871, and died September 7th, 1887.

Died at his home near Doraville, Ga., August 6th, 1887, Mr. **Robert McBryde Wilson**. . . was born in Lancaster District, S. C., July 29th, 1802, and was 85 years and 7 days old. . . . [He] spent his youth and early manhood in Chester District in the bounds of Hopewell church. . . In 1829, he moved to

Newton County, Ga., where he married Miss Sarah Chesnut. Here he lived in the bounds of Hopewell, named for his mother church, till 1852, when he moved to DeKalb County where he spent the remainder of his life.

Thomas Spencer departed this life July 11th, 1887, aged 79 years, 1 month and 1 day. . . was born in York County, S. C. Spent his whole life and now sleeps only a few miles from the place of his birth. . . Connected with Neely's Creek congregation for over a half century. . . . was married in 1843 to Miss Nancy Keenan. Eight children were the fruits of this union. The wife and three children preceded him [in death].

Married, October 12th at 10 o'clock by Rev. G. H. Carter at the residence of the bride's uncle, Mr. L. T. Haddon, near Due West, Miss **Annie M. Emerson** and Mr. **H. M. Greer** of Belton, S. C.

October 20, 1887

Mrs. **Rachel Chisolm** departed this life on Monday the 26th of September at the residence of her daughter, Mrs. Elizabeth Strong near Hopewell, Chester County, S. C. . . . actually attained to her one hundred years and 8 days. . . . born and raised in the town of Larne, Ireland and came to America in 1821 after a voyage of six weeks. The first effective point, after landing at Charleston, was Rocky Creek in Chester County, where she married and remained a year. After that they located within the bounds of New Hope congregation, Fairfield County, where they remained the greater part of their lives. . . five children constituted the family, three daughters and two sons. . . . their youngest child was James Boyce Chisolm [who] was a student at the Seminary [when] he sickened and died the 18th of June, 1855 in the house of Dr. J. I. Bonner. . . . about 1856, she lost her husband and two daughters moved to Tipton, Tenn. About 1870, she followed her children, two daughters and a son, to Tennessee, but after a stay of less than two years, she returned to South Carolina.. . [about] 1876, she repeated her visit to the West against the wishes of her friends --she [was 90 years old]. . . of small size, scarcely attaining to the average in stature or weight. . . she was a weaver in the better parts of her life, and followed it so closely that she sometimes wove into the late hours of night. . . . self taught lover of poetry.

October 27, 1887

Died September 8th, 1887 near Blanche in Lincoln County, Tenn., Mrs. **Thersia Ann Lock**. Aged 25 years, 10 months and 14 days. . . . consistent member of the church.

Married, September 15th, 1887, by Rev. J. L. Young in Drew County,

Ark., Mr. **J. D. P. Craig** and Miss **M. J. Watts**.

- - - October 5th, 1887 at the residence of the bride's father in White Oak, S. C., assisted by Rev. J. S. Moffatt, Mr. **J. H. Moffatt** of Richburg, S. C. and Miss **Macie A. Brice** of White Oak, S. C.

- - - August 18th, 1887 by Rev. S. A. Agnew, Mr. **D. A. Caldwell** and Miss **L. V. Griffin**. All of Union County, Miss.

- - - September 8th, 1887 by Rev. S. A. Agnew, Mr. **W. E. Roberts** and Miss **N. M. Snipes**. All of Union County, Miss.

- - - September 13th, 1887 by Rev. S. A. Agnew, Mr. **W. O. McDonald** of Prentiss and Miss **Alma Bryson**, daughter of Mr. R. Drayton Bryson of Lee County, Miss.

- - - September 22d, 1887 by Rev. S. A. Agnew, Mr. **J. W. Roberts** and Miss **M. A. Snipes**, daughter of Mr. J. M. Snipes. All of Union County, Miss.

November 3, 1887

Died in Dallas County, Ala., September 12th, 1887 in his 8th month, **William Marion**, youngest child of Mrs. Alice **Brice**.

Mrs. **Nannie Pauline Purdy**, wife of Thomas P. Purdy and daughter of Dr. Klugh, died of congestion after a short illness Sabbath morning, September 4th, 1887, aged about 24 years. . . early member of M. E. church. . . . after her marriage she was transferred to the A. R. P. church at Cedar Spring.

Married on Thursday morning the 27th of October by Dr. W. L. Pressly, Miss **Annie Lathan** and Rev. **T. B. Stewart**.

November 17, 1887

Mr. **Lewis Drennan** who lived near Abbeville, dropped suddenly dead while attending to a gin in his place last Friday afternoon. He is the father-in-law of our townsman, Mr. A. D. Kennedy. . . was an elder in the church of Long Cane and Cedar Springs.

Mrs. **Davenport** was born September 14th, 1827 and died October 7th, 1887. . . in her girlhood was a member of the Presbyterian church, but after marriage united with the Methodist. . . . She leaves a husband and several children. She lies buried in Old Providence churchyard in Virginia whence she will be removed to Ashland, Ky.

Died at his home near New Stirling church, Iredell County, N. C., on the 11th day of September, 1887, in the 68th year of his age, Mr. **Thomas Morrison**. . . . member of New Stirling. . . leaves a widow and six children.

Died in Dallas County, Ala., September 22d, 1887, in the 38th year of her age, **Mrs. S. M. Chisolm**, wife of Thomas Chisolm, a ruling elder of Prosperity church.

Died in Huntersville, N. C. on the 17th of July, 1887, Miss **Nona Barker**, aged about 22 years . . . connected with the A. R. P. church of this place.

Died in Huntersville, N. C. on the 21st of July, 1887, Mrs. **Mollie Steele**. . . the only daughter of a widowed mother. . . leaves a husband and little girl. . . early connected with Back Creek (A. R. P.) and after her marriage she cast her lot with the people of God here [Huntersville].

Died near Huntersville, N. C. on the 29th of August, 1887, Mr. **John Lee McAulay**, son of J. C. McAulay.

Married, November 9th, 1887 at the residence of the bride's father, J. D. Neil, M. D. by Rev. H. T. Sloan, D. D., **Laurens N. Kennedy, M. D.** and Miss **L. Emma Neil**.

- - - October 20th, 1887 in Fairfield County, S. C. by Rev. H. B. Garriss, Mr. **Charles E. Cathcart** of Winnsboro, S. C. and Miss **Mary E. Clowney** of Buckhead.

- - - November 1st, 1887 near Spottswood, Va. by Rev. S. W. Haddon, Mr. **William H. Lucas** and Miss **Fannie M. Lotts**. The former of Rockbridge, the latter of Augusta County, Va.

November 24, 1887

Born and died, November 11th, 1887, **infant daughter** of S. A. and Maggie **Boyce**.

Mrs. **Minnie A. L. Oates** was born July 8th, 1866 and died September 9th, 1887. March 6th, 1883, she married Mr. F. T. Oates . . . she leaves a husband and two little children.

Mr. **John A. Causey** died August 8th, 1887. He was born February 14th

1861. . . member of Bethel church, Burke County, Ga. . . . He leaves a wife and one child.

Died September 1st, little **Annie**, the youngest child of M. C. and C. E. **Austin**, aged 2 years, 4 months and 9 days.

Died in Union County, Miss., September 29th, 1887, **Claude Holland**, son of J. K. and Bettie (Billingsley) Holland, aged 10 months and 16 days.

Died in Union County, Miss., October 6th, 1887, **Hiram Gentry** in the 69th year of his age. . . native of Anderson, S. C., son of Bartley and Elizabeth (Willbanks) Gentry and was born January 19, 1819. . . married Miss Jane Caldwell on February 15th, 1844 and in the same year joined the A. R. church at Shiloh. In 1850 he removed to Pontotoc (now Union) County, Miss., and when Hopewell church was organized on May 24th, 1851, he was one of the charter members]. . . . leaves an aged wife, a widowed daughter, and a little grand child, also two sons, one of whom is in Texas.

Died in Union County, Miss, October 16th, 1887, **Gideon Hester Haynie** in the 75th year of his age. . . son of Charles and Susan (Hanks) Haynie and was born in Anderson County, S. C., February 19, 1813. He married Miss Margaret Caldwell, January 17th, 1843. . . [moved to] Mississippi in 1845 . . . first connected with a Baptist church at Fishing Creek. . . several years ago he joined the A. R. church at Hopewell. In Mississippi he has lived in various neighborhoods in Marshall and Union Counties. . . father of six children. Four of these--three sons and a daughter-- together with an aged mother [survive].

[Died] at her home in Louisville, Ky, October 9th, 1887, **Mrs. S. J. McBride**, would have been 42 years old on October 20th. . . daughter of Mr. A. R. Guyn . . . early joined New Hope A. R. church, Madison County, Ky.

Died in Pontotoc County, Miss., November 13th, 1886, **Elijah Buchanan** in the 78th year of his age. . . born April 10th, 1809. His parents Samuel and Jane (Edwards) Buchanan moved early in the present century from Pendleton District, S. C. to Bedford County, Tenn. and we are not sure whether the subject was a native of South Carolina or Tennessee. He was reared in Bedford County and was one of those ministered to by Rev. Henry Bryson in his first labors in Middle Tennessee. At an early date the Buchanans moved to Tuscaloosa, Ala. where they connected with an Associate church which once existed in that city. About forty years ago they moved to the neighborhood of Fredonia in Pontotoc County. About thirty years ago, he connected himself with Hopewell church, but living remotely from the church, he rarely attended services there. There was, however, in 1860, preaching to the little group of A. R. Presbyterians who lived near Fredonia. On March 15th, 1875, a terrific tornado passed through North Mississippi and Mr. Buchanan's home was in its track and was blown down. Some logs fell on him and his head received a severe hurt. . . He was twice married: first to a Miss Gillespie of Tuscaloosa and the second time to a Miss Shettles who [along with "several children"] survive.

Died in Gastonia, N. C., **Lawson Jenkins**, October 21st, 1887, aged 76 years and 17 days. . . . reared in York County, S. C., Bethany congregation. In early life settled in the bounds of Sharon, and became a member, afterwards an elder. .. last year of life was spent in Gastonia wher his youngest son moved.

Prince Edgar, the infant son of O. H. and M. J. **Butler** [was] born August 28, 1886 and died September 17th, 1887.

John H. Lyle was born at Edge Hill, December 1st, 1837 and died October 16rgm 1886 of Bright's disease at Brownsburg, Va. . . . at the opening of the late war he joined the army and entered Gen. Hood's command, but when he came home on a furlough, he was transferred to Gen. Lee's command. . . .his father was an elder in the Presbyterian church on Timber Ridge. . . he leaves a widow, several children, one sister and several brothers.

Married, October 11th, 1887 by Rev. S. A. Agnew, Mr. **S. P. Tapp** and **Miss S. E. Stevenson**, all of Prentiss County, Miss.

- - - November 10th, 1887 by Rev. T. P. Pressly at the residence of the brides's father near Troy, Tenn., Prof. **J. D. Woodburn** and Miss **Mollie King**. All of Obion County, Tenn.

December 1, 1887

Departed this life September 3d, 1887, **Luther McAdams**, only son of S. H. McAdams of Belfast, Tenn... born October 16th, 1867. . . his father for many years has been an elder in Head Springs church [as was his grandfather].

Died at the home of his father in Lamar County, Texas, November 18th, 1887, **R. Lee Gill** in his 12th year. . . oldest child and only son of J. J. L. and Mrs. Rebecca Gill, formerly of Dr. E. E. Boyce's charge.

Landly J. Wiley died on the 31st of October, 1887 after fourteen months of suffering from injuries received from the upsetting of his carriage caused by the running away of his team. . . consistent member of the church at New Hope for nearly thirty years. . . left a wife and five children.

Died in Tipton County, Tenn., November 4th, 1887, **Alexander Shannon**, little son of John G. and Mattie **McCain**.

Miss **Rose E. Sheffield** died of consumption on the 3d of November, 1887 and in the 19th year of her age. . . member of Prosperity some two years.

Died in Somersville, Tenn., September 17, 1887, Mrs. **Ellen E. McKinstry** in the 71st year of her age. . . born in Mecklenburg County, N. C. near Charlotte. Her father, H. J. McCain, Esq., removed from that place to Tipton County, Tenn. in 1833. Ellen [was] his oldest daughter. . . [he headed] a large and interesting family of sons and daughters who took a prominent part in organization of the A. R. P. congregation of Salem. One of his sons at that date was chosen an elder and two others soon afterwards became officers. In 1838, [Ellen] married Wm. P. McKinstry . . . [they had] five children. . . two daughters and one son sickened and died in a short space of time. Soon after marriage, Mr. McKinstry settled in Fayette County, Tenn. . . and [they] became identified with the A. R. P. church of Sardis. . . while that organization lasted. . . . [when it disbanded] Mrs. McKinstry, now a widow, connected herself with the Presbyterian church of Macon.

Died at his home in Wilcox County, Ala., September 28th, 1887, Mr. **Isaac Newberry** in the 83d year of his age. . . married and father of two daughters and a son. His wife, a daughter and the son preceded him to the grave. The last years of his life were spent with his daughter, Mrs. Julia N. Bonner.

Miss **Sara Jane Johnston** died August 15th, 1887 in the 43d year of her age. . . Nominally a new member of the church at Huntersville, but she connected herself first with the church at Sardis.

Sallie, a daughter of Robert N and Octavia B. **Blanks**, departed this life September 15th, 1887, aged 15 years and 18 days.

Died on October 14th, 1887, **Samuel Martin**, little son of Mr. D. W. **Lathan**. . . [before his second birthday]. Killed by falling from a horse, **Freddie**, son of Mr. H. M. **Pyles**, eight years and almost eight months old. . . . In a short time the flock at Troy, Tenn. has been twice visited by death.

Died of congestion of th lungs in Camden, Wilcox County, Ala., October 17th, 1887, Mr. **Junius C. Jones**, aged 33 years, 11 months and 7 days. . . son of J. Clark and Julia McR. Jones, and the only one that did not avail himself of a collegiate education. He chose farming. . . was engaged to be married and was on the way to visit his betrothed when he was suddenly smitten with a great pain in his chest, caused perhaps by a fall gotten a few days before as he was crossing on horseback an old rail bridge in one of his fields. . . member of church at Bethel.

Robert Organ McCormick was born January 20th, 1852 and died August 28th, 1887 . . . oldest child of Dr. McCormick and E. Virginia

McCormick. Losing his father in the late war when he was only about ten years old, he assumed many responsible duties. . . married December 20th, 1883 to Miss Leonora Davénport of Asland, Ky. . . in March last connected with Old Providence church. . . leaves a widow, a widowed mother, a sister, and four brothers.

December 8, 1887

Died in Shiloh Township, Iredell County, N. C. on November 1st, 1887, **Robert Ira**, infant son of Mr. H. B. and Jane **Reice**, aged 7 weeks.

Born December 16th, 1886 and died September 17th, 1887, **Jesse Lavinia**, daughter of G. M. and Lou **Hanks**.

Died of dropsy, June--, 1887, in Union County, Miss, Mrs. **Mary Caroline (Miller) Johnson**, wife of G. W. Johnson. . . was born October 20th, 1821 in Abbeville County, S. C. When quite young she came to this State [Mississippi] where she has resided ever since.. . . member of Ebenezer.

Joseph Fred, son of R. P. and Carrie **Clinkscales**, died September 30, 1887, aged 2 years, 5 months and 25 days.

Died of malarial fever, September 13th, 1887, Mr. **John I. Mitchell** of Anderson County, S. C. Aged 29 years. . . son of the late Mr. Marshall Mitchell of this county. . .early in communion of the Baptist church [but has since been] a consistent member of Concord A. R. P. church for a period of twelve years.

Died in Pope County, Ark. of typhoid fever, October 4th, 1887, Mr. **Jimmie Morrow** in the 36th year of his age. . . early united with A. R. P. church of Pisgah, N. C. [but]connected himself with the Presbyterian church of Mt. Zion after coming to Arkansas, as he lived at that time in a Presbyterian family. He became careless and neglected his privileges and duties as a church member. He was married three times. All of his wives were members of the A. R. P. church.

Mr. **J. Lewis Drennan** of Cedar Spring and Long Cane, S. C., died suddenly of some heart trouble between 2 and 3 o'clock, p. m. on Friday, November 11th in the 56th year of his age. He had only complained of his heart for a few weeks. During court week, while acting as a juror, he made it known to his wife. . . son of Elder James Drennan who held that office under three pastorates for about forty six years. On the death of the father the son was elected and has filled that office with honor for fourteen years. . . has left a widow and four children.

171

Married, November 3d, 1887 at the residence of the bride's mother in Iredell County, N. C. by Rev. W. M. Hunter, Mr. **J. T. Morrison** and Miss **Tirzah Halyburton**, daughter of the late Dr. Halyburton.

- - - November 17th, 1887, at the residence of the bride's father by Rev. W. M. Hunter, Mr. **A. M. Johnson** and Miss **Sallie B. Gant**. All of Shiloh Township, Iredell County, N. C.

- - - September 10th, 1887 in Drew County, Ark. by Rev. J. L. Young, Mr. **Robert F. Harper** and Miss **Mattie Davis**.

December 15, 1887

Died in Pope County, Ark., October 12th, 1887 of typhoid fever, Mr. **F. P. Oates**, aged 30 years.

Died, October 7th, 1887, **Alexander H. Smith** in the 53d year of his age. . . . born in September, 1835 within the bounds of Hopewell congregation, Chester County, S. C. A few years after the family moved to Tipton County, Tenn. In 1858, he entered Erskine College; being ambitious to excel, he applied himself closely to his studies, and in a few months his mind became impaired. He came home in February, 1859 and repaired to the asylum for the insane located at Nashville, Tenn. in the month following. Under medical treatment there was rapid improvement; after a few months he was relieved and released, so that in the fall he returned to college, graduating with the class of 1860. He taught school for a short time; enlisted in the army in '61 in the 51st Tenn. Infantry under Col. Chester; served throughout the war and was unhurt, excepting being struck by a spent ball at the battle of Stone River or Murfreesboro In 1870, his health failed; in 1872 he returned to the asylum and there remained. . . [buried by] his brother, . . .[he had been] the only surviving member of his family. . . he was a man of more than ordinary intellect and ability . . . and a man of decided and devout religious convictions.

Luther McAdams died September 6th, 1887 of fever and lacked ten days of being 20 years of age. . . one of the twelve the writer [J. A. M.] took into the church of Head Springs, Marshall County, Tenn. at a protracted meeting two years ago.

Mary Ann Melissa Walthall, wife of L. H. Walthall, Esq. was born November 17th, 1842 and died September 15th, 1887. For six or seven years she has been on the decline with serious mental derangement. In the midst of the most distressing providences, however, the religion of Christ seems not to have forsaken her, for she is said to have refused positively to take part in the dancing and other diversions which the authorities of the asylum arranged for their patients.

Died in Tippah County, Miss., August 14th, 1887, Mr. **John H. Wright**, aged 51 years, 6 months and 8 days. . . son of good, pious Christian Methodist parents and was born in Conecuh County, Ala., February 6th, 1836, and there resided until some fifteen years ago when he, with his family and other friends, moved to this State, settling first in Union and afterwards in Tippah County. . . [joined] Ebenezer congregation.

Mrs. **Mary Waters** departed this life, August 31st, 1887. Aged 88 years, 2 months and 12 days. . . born and spent the whole of her life in Chester County, S. C. . . member for seventy years of Union congregation . . . married her 22d year. . . six children were the fruits. . . three [are dead]. Her descendants all told number 102; grandchildren - 35; great-grandchildren - 61.

Jacob H. Thompson died on the 20th of October, 1887 at his home in Lincoln County, Tenn. Aged 43 years . . . native of congregation of Cannon's Creek, S. C. and emigrated to this county in 1866. . . member and elder of New Hope. . leaves wife and two children.

Mr. **Jonathan Davis** died October 26th, 1887 in Bradley County, Ark. Aged 88 years, 11 months and 8 days. . . born November 18th, 1799 in York County, S. C. . . . early member of Neely's Creek congregation [and] afterwards served as an elder in that congregation for about thirty years. . . [married] Miss Ellenor Kenmore . Eight children were born to them, five survive. He moved with his children and a number of relatives and friends in 1857 to Bradley County [where he took part in the] organization of the A. R. P. church at Hickory Springs.

Died in Guntown, Miss., October 19th, 1887, Mrs. **Margaret Ellen Houston** in the 47th year of her age. . . daughter of Samuel and Jane (Milam) Bryson and was born in Laaurens County, S. C., March 8th, 1841. In 1851, her father removed to Mississippi. . . [she] was reared in the bounds of Bethany. On January 17th, 1861, she was married to Thomas E. Watt [recently installed as elder at Bethany]. . . . her husband died July 23d, 1862 of fever in the Confederate army, leaving his wife with a little child, now Mrs. Jennie Tyner of Corinth, Miss. On December 11th, 1867 she was married to Thomas W. Houston. . . Since 1869, she has been a resident of Guntown where her husband was engaged in mercantile business. By her last husband, she had five children, one of whom is dead.

Married, December 7th, 1887 in Monterey, Butler County, Ala. at the home of the bride's father, Dr. James G. Donald, Mr. **Thomas E. Moore** and Miss **Mamie Donald**.

December 22, 1887

Died of congestion, October 10th, 1887, **Archibald Boggs**, infant son of W. H. and F. J. **Kennedy**. . . eight months [old].

Died, November 22d, 1887, Miss **Sarah Jane Clark** in her 28th year.

Died in Lafayette County, Miss., September 2d, 1887, Mrs. **Martha Jane (Boyd) Spence**, wife of John N. P. Spence. Aged 64 years, 8 months and 1 day. . . daughter of Thomas and Elizabeth Boyd and was born in Newberry County, S. C., January 1st, 1823. In 1846 on the 28th of October, she was married to Mr. Spence.

Mrs. **Sarah Jane Moorhead** died Friday, October 14th, 1887 of typhoid malaria. . . born November 27th, 1839. Her entire life was spent in the community [Anderson, S. C.] in which she died. . . . married to Mr. John M. Moorhead in November, 1861 . . . three children. . . member of Concord Associate Reformed church.

Married, December 8th, 1887 at the residence of the bride by Rev. C. B. Betts, Mr. **Israel Allen** and Miss **M. J. Patton**, all of York County, S. C.

- - - December 18th, 1887 by Rev. C. B. Betts at the parsonage, Mr. **J. W. Franklin** and Miss **M. J. Simpson**. All of Chester County, S. C.

- - - December 14th, 1887 at the residence of the bride's father, Mr. G. G. McKnight, by Rev. T. B. Stewart, Mr. **E. C. Deaton** of Charlotte, N. C. and Miss **Jennie McKnight** of Mooresville, N. C.

January 5, 1888

Mr. **David Crawford** died at his residence near this place [Due West] last Monday morning. He has been suffering since August last . . .[he] is widely known throughout the county, having held the office of school commissioner for one term. . . He was buried at Little Mountain church.

Married, December 7th, 1887 at the residence of Mr. J. M. Galloway, White Oak, S. C., by Rev. J. C. Galloway, assisted by Rev. J. A. White, Mr. **Gray Boulware** and Miss **Maggie Robinson**, all of Fairfield County, S. C.

- - - December 21st, 1887, in Drew County, Ark., at the residence of her step-father, Mr. Trotter, by Rev. J. P. Erwin, Mr. **Robert S. McQuiston** and **Miss Eddie Ford**.

Married, December 22d, 1887 in Bradley County, Ark., at the residence of the bride's father, Mr. **J. W. Pierce** by Rev. J. S. A. Hunter, assisted Rev. N. C. Denson, Mr. **S. D. Wardlaw** and Miss **Mary Pierce**.

- - - December 22d, 1887 by Rev. O. Y. Bonner, at the residence of the bride's mother Mr. **W. D. Watson** and Miss **Ada B. Dandridge**. All of Molino, Lincoln County, Tenn.

- - - November 1st, 1887 by Rev. W. F. Pearson, Mr. **Clarence E. Sharp** and Miss **Anna Lizzie Donnald**. Both of Donnalds, S. C.

- - - December 21st, 1887 by Rev. W. F. Pearson, Mr. **Charley H. Dodson** and Miss **Bertie E. Seawright**. Both of Donnalds, S. C.

- - - December 27, 1887 by Rev. W. F. Pearson, Mr. **Patrick Noble Bell** and Miss **P. Hassie Pratt**. Both of Level Land, S. C.

- - - December 27th, 1887 by Rev. W. F. Pearson, Mr. **Alfred Agnew** and Miss **Mamie E. Cochran**. Both of Due West, S. C.

January 12, 1888

Died in Union County, Miss., December 6th, 1887, **Jessie Robinson Magill**, only child of H. M. and Mary E. (Hardy) Magill, aged nine days.

Died in Steele Creek, N. C., December 28th, 1887, Mr. **Martin Millen** in the 36th year of her age. . . On the evening preceding his death he went out hunting with his brother, and while standing on a fence, his gun was accidentally discharged, the whole load entering his head . . . He leaves a wife and five children.

Lizzie Robison died November 6th, 1887, 32 years old. Born on the Sabbath and died at the same hour Sabbath. Spent ten years in wedded life. Her husband, Samuel Robison, died just one month before. Both had typhoid fever. Left four little sons; one, Meek McElwen, a helpless babe six months old. . .Mr. Robison was an honored elder in the Presbyterian church, Olney. Mrs. Robison was reared in the A. R. church at Pisgah, Gaston County, N. C. . . . She was the daughter of William and Jane Crawford.

Died at the home of Mrs. F. L. Adams, November 4th, 1887, Mrs. **Martha Frances Best**. . .*nee* Miss Fitzpatrick was born in Madison County, Ky., January 27th, 1818. In early youth she connected with Paint Lick (G. A. P.) church. In the spring of 1848, she married Mr. Tyre Best. After his death she made her home with her daughter, Mrs. Adams, and moved her membership to New Hope.

Robert Lee Gill, son of J. J. L. and Rebecca Gill, was born in York County, S. C. on th 11th of May, 1876, died in Lamar County, Texas, November 18th, 1887, aged 11 years, 6 months and 7 days of hematuria.

Mrs. **Jane (McCormick) Wiley** died of typhoid pneumonia on the 8th of December, 1887 in the 79th year of her age. . . . born in Abbeville County, S. C. near the present site of Verdery; obtaining her education at the Asbury church; was married to James Wiley, and with him came to Tennessee about 1826. For a while they lived in Maury County on Big Bigby in the bounds of old Union A. R. congregation, and then settled on the bank of the beautiful Elk River. . . member of church for more than threescore years and survived her husband about twenty-five years. They raised six children; four sons, two of whom "fell in battle"; and one died a month before her decease, and a married daughter who died twenty years ago, leaving one son and a widowed daughter surviving.

James McKnight Hanna of Gaston County, N. C. departed this life in the 85th year of his age, on the 7th of November, 1887.

Mrs. **Rebecca Hanna** in the 84th year of her age, died December 6th, 1887. Sixty years in harmonious wedded life. . .[both were buried in] Pisgah graveyard. Mr. Hanna's early life was spent on the Catawba, and they crossed the river to worship at Steel Creek. In the year 1825, Miss Rebecca Blackwood of near Crowther's Mountain, became his wife, and he was from that time a member of Pisgah and soon became an elder.

Born April 10th, 1886 and died September 22d, 1887, **infant son** of R. T. and E. J. **Davis**.

Mrs. **M. J. Moffatt**, wife of Mr. T. H. Moffatt, departed this life, September 16th, 1887, aged 28 years, 3 months and 26 days. . . was raised by her grandmother, Mrs. Hagins, having lost her mother in infancy. . . connected with the M. E. church, South. She was married November 16th, 1881, when she transferred her membership to A. R. church, Union congregation, the church of her husband.

On November 4th, 1887, Mr. **John C. Flenniken** passed from earth. He was born in Chester County, S. C., March 16th, 1842. . . the son of Rev. Warren and Mrs. Jane H. Flenniken. . . grandson on his mother's side of Dr. Samuel Pressly . . . entered Erskine College when quite a boy. From college he was called into the war. . . connected with Hopewell A. R. P. church. Moving near the Pleasant Grove Presbyterian church, which then used the Psalms, he connected with it and was made a deacon. About three years ago he came into the Chester A. R. P. church. . . He was married to Miss Lottie Bradley [and she and five children survive].

January 19, 1888

Nancy Elizabeth, daughter of W. S. and M. **Lesslie**, departed this life, January 2d, 1888, aged 2 years, 9 months and 17 days.

David P. Waters departed this life, November 26th, 1887, aged 63 years and 21 days. . . . was born in Chester County, S. C. and spent his whole life in the immediate neighborhood in which he was born. . . connected with the A. R. church, Union congregation in the spring of '62. . . When he had been but four years a church member, he was made an elder. . . Mr. Waters was twice married. The last wife preceded him to the grave some two years; also three children were sent before. Six children survive.

Married, December 14th, 1887 in the parsonage at Auburn, Mo. by Rev. D. P. Pressly, Mr. **Charles Gladney** and Miss **Lettie Admire**. Both of Lincoln, Mo.

- - -December 27th, 1887 at the parsonage by Rev. C. B. Betts, Mr. **Joseph Proctor** and Miss **Mary Orr**. All of Chester County, S. C.

- - - December 20th, 1887 by Rev. E. E. Pressly, Mr. **J. E. P. Ross**, editor of Fulton County (Ark.) *Banner* and Miss **Dora Pressly** of Scott's X Roads, Iredell County, N. C.

- - - December 29th, 1887 at the residence of the bride's mother, Mrs. Nannie Hunter, by Rev. W. M. Hunter, Mr. **John Harris** and Miss **Sallie Gamble**. All of Alexander County, N. C.

- - - January 4th, 1888 in Rehoboth, Ala. by Rev. J. A. Lowry, Dr. **J. J. Hall** and Miss **L. T. Chalmers**.

- - - January 11th, 1888 by Rev. H. B. Blakely, Mr. **J. C. Wilson** and Miss **M. M. Johnson**. All of Fairfield County, S. C.

- - - January 3d, 1888 at the parsonage by Rev. C. B. Betts, Mr. **J. F. Garrison** of York County and Miss **Lizzie J. McFadden** of Chester County, S. C.

The nuptials of Mr. **J. A. Nance** and Miss **Beulah Clinkscales** were solemnized on the 11th inst. by Rev. D. W. Hiott at the residence of the bride's grandmother, Mrs. Margaret Clinkscales who lives near here [Due West].

Died near Providence church, Laurens County, S. C., January 1st, 1888, Mr. **James M. Blakely** in the 29th year of his age. . . leaves an aged father and numerous relatives.

Mrs. **Jane Cathcart Madden** died in Winnsboro, S. C., October 20th, 1887, aged 86 years. . . was a daughter of James and Nancy Cathcart. In 1822, she was married to Rev. Campbell Madden, a minister of the Reformed Presbyterian church. Rev. Madden was a native of Ireland and came to America in 1820. He accepted a call from a Reformed Presbyterian (Covenanter) church in Chester District, S. C., where he was ordained and installed in 1822. He died in 1828. Mrs. Madden was thus early left a widow to car for three fatherless children. One, Mary, died in 1854, and two, Thomas B. Madden, M. D., and Mrs. Nancy Cathcart survive.

Mrs. **Sarah A. Reid**, widow of the late David Reid, died at her home in Auburn, Mo., August 24th, 1887, in the 66th year of her age. . . born andreared in Shelby County, Ky; removed with her husband to Missouri about 1840, and settled in the bounds of Mt. Zion congregation.

Departed this life near Brighton, Tipton County, Tenn. on the 15th of September, 1887, **Charles Hill**, a son of Mr. Wallace and Mattie Hill. Aged 3 years, 10 months and 8 days.

Also, removed by death on the 26th of November, 1887, Mr. **Wm. D. Strain**, aged 65 years, 11 months and 19 days. . . had disposed of a wagon load of cotton seed and was in the act of delivering them at the railroad station in Covington, Tipton County, Tenn. The arrival of a train gave the alarm to the team. While making an attempt to jump from the wagon, Mr. Strain was tripped up by the lines. . .[lived for three weeks]. . . was born in York County, S. C., the 7th of January, 1822; moved to Tipton County in 1845. He was three times married: first, to Miss Jennett McQuiston, December 22d, 1847, second to Miss Elizabeth A. Faulkner, April 10th, 1851, third to Miss Susan J. Blain, September --, 1873. . . . ruling elder in Bloomington church from its sorganization. Three sons (children of his second wife) and an adopted daughter [survive].

Miss **Rachel A. Anderson** was removed by death on the 10th of January, 1888. She was born January 4th, 1827. Aged 61 years and 4 days. . . member of Beulah church, Shelby County. . . [survived by] two brothers (Messrs. E. A. and John Anderson and two sisters.

Married, January 15th, 1888 at the residence of Dr. D. R. Anderson by

Rev. T. B. Craig, assisted by Rev. M. C. Britt, Mr. **A. Selden Kennedy** of Due West, S. C. and Miss **Jennie R. Anderson** of Fairview, S. C.

- - - at the residence of Willie Carrol in York County, S. C. by Rev. J. B. Traywick, Mr. **Robt. S. McElroy** and Miss **Maggie Dorsey**. Both of Chester County, S. C.

- - - January 5th, 1888 by Rev. David Pressly at the residence of the bride's father, Mr. **Robert B. Dewese** and Miss **Betta Moore**. All of Tipton County, Tenn.

- - - January 11th, 1888 in Bloomington church by Rev. David Pressly, Dr. **W. A. L. McLister** and Miss **Effie Dewese**. Both of Brighton, Tipton County, Tenn.

Wednesday evening, January 25th, Miss **Carrie L. Todd** of this place [Due West] was married to Mr. **J. O. C. Fleming** of Laurens in the A. R. P. church by Rev. W. L. Pressly, D. D.

February 2, 1888

Maggie Louise, daughter of Mr. George and Mrs. Margaret **Smith,** died of pneumonia, November 15th, 1887. Aged 14 months and 15 days.

James G. Hyndman died at his residence, Tipton County, Tenn, January 1st, 1888 of heart disease in the 61st year of his age. . . was born in South Carolina, but the greater part of his life was spent in Tennessee. . . was for more than forty years a consistent member of Salem congregation. . . he left a wife and four children.

Died near Millersburg, Ky., January 18th, 1888. Mr. **James T. Marshall**. . . about 25 years of age. . died of consumption. . . connected with the Presbyterian church of Millersburg. His father, Mr. John T. Marshall, is an elder in the Hinkston congregation.

Died in Union County, Miss., October 24th, 1887, Mrs. **Mary Irene (Wright) Spencer,** aged 21 years and 2 days. . . eldest daughter of John H. and Rebecca Wright and was born in Wilcox County, Ala., October 22d, 1866. With her father, when quite small, she came to this State, and has since then made this her home. . . connected with the Ebenezer congregation. . . On the 25th of December, 1866, she was married to Mr. Richard Spencer.

Died near New Albany, Union County, Miss., October 19th, 1887, Mr. **Robert R. McBride,** aged 69 years and 2 months. . . the eldest son of Maj.

179

Robt. McBride by his second wife and was born in Abbeville County, S. C. in the bounds of Cedar Spring congregation. . . When a lad he left South Carolina with his father and settled and lived for a while in Wilcox County, Ala., but subsequently came to this State, settled in Tippah County where the present Cotton Plant is located.

Died near Dunwoody, DeKalb County, Ga., October 20th, 1887, Mr. **William Weldon** aged 65 years, 6 months and 7 days. . . born in Fairfield County, S. C. He was left an orphan when quite a child, but . . . [found] a home with Mr. John Simonton. The greater part of his life was spent in Newton and DeKalb Counties, Ga. He leaves a wife, ten children and many grandchildren. . . for more than forty years a member of the church.

Died with croup in Union County, Miss., December 8th, 1887, **Emma Elizabeth Ellis**, daughter of J. L. and Addie Ellis, aged 6 years, 8 months and 11 days.

Married, January 18th, 1888 at the home of the bride's father, Mr. Robert McElroy, by Rev. J. S. Moffatt, Mr. **James H. Walker** and Miss **Carrie A. McElroy**. Both of Chester, S. C.

- - - January 17th, 1888 in the church in Orrville, Ala. by Rev. J. A. Lowry, Mr. **Rufus Gill** and Miss **Ella Mills**.

- - - January 4th, 1888 in DeKalb County, Ga. at the home of the bride's father, Mr. David Chestnut, by Rev. R. E. Patterson, Mr. **Jno. Monday** and Miss **Mattie Chestnut**.

- - - January 17th, 1888 at the residence of the bride's parents by Rev. J. L. Hemphill, Mr. **John M. Johnson** of Newberry County, S. C. and Miss **Cora Lee Young** of Coweta County, Ga.

February 9, 188

Died at the residence of his brother, Mr. Calvin Neel, in Newberry County, S. C., January 17th, 1888, **J. B. Neel**, who was born November 18th, 1840. . . son of Robert and Sophie Neel. For eleven years he was sorely afflicted with rheumatism. His religious life, according to his own confession, was far from being satisfactory to himself, yet he died in hope.

The news of the death of Miss **Sallie McGee** of Walnut Grove was received. She was a student in the Female College in 1886. . . a devoted member of the Walnut Grove Baptist church. While here [in Due West] her home was with her brother, Mr. M. B. McGee.

Married, January 24th, 1888 by Rev. S. A. Agnew, Mr. **W. H. Gibson** and Miss **Blanche Epting**, daughter of Mr. L. D. Epting. All of Lee County, Miss.

February 16, 1888

Died at his home in Braden, Fayette County, Tenn., January 6th, 1888, Mr. **J. C. Jones** in the sixty fifth year of his age. Huntersville, N. C. papers please copy.

Married, January 19th, 1888, at the residence of Mr. H. C. Mosely by Rev. J. C. Boyd, Dr. **John M. Langford** and Miss **Jennie Johnson**. All of Prosperity, S. C.

- - - February 1st, 1888, at the home of Mr. J. M. Parish by Rev. J. S. Moffatt, Mr. **Branch Long** and Miss **Sallie Proctor**,both of Chester, S. C.

February 23, 1888

Died in Lexington, Va., October 6th, 1887, little **John Simonton**, son of W. R. and Mrs. Bruce **Douglas**, aged 20 months.

John Huxley departed this life February 4th, 1888 at the family residence in Louisville, Ky . . . lacking only five days of being twenty one. . . faithful member of Associate Reformed church.

Mrs. **Dallas Reid** died in Newberry, S. C., February 5th, 1888, in the 46th year of her age. . . born and raised and had spent most of her life in sight of the place at which she died. She was married while young to Mr. Joseph S. Reid and connected herself with the A. R. P. church. Having no children, they adopted a little girl which some family in New Orleans had procured for them.

Married, February 9th, 1888, at the parsonage by Rev. W. A. M. Plaxco, Mr. **D. R. Jennings** of Mecklenburg, N. C. and **Miss M. J. McAteer** of Lancaster, S. C.

- - - January 26th, 1888 at the residence of the bride's mother, Mrs. H. M. McCarley, Winnsboro, S. C. by Rev. Jno. T. Chalmers, Mr. **S. B. Stevenson** of Blackstocks, S. C. and **Miss E. A. McCarley** of Winnsboro, S. C.

- - - February 7th at the Winnsboro Hotel, Winnsboro, S. C. by Rev. Jno. T. Chalmers, assisted by Rev. C. E. McDonald, **J. Killough Henry**, Esq. of Chester and Miss **Ella S. Hamilton** of Marissa, Ill.

March 8, 1888

Died of pneumonia, in Shelby County, Tenn., February 2d, 1888, Miss **Cynthia Jane Hutchison**, aged 37 years, 11 months and 22 days . . . the daughter of Wm. W and Sarah Hutchison.

Died in Shelby County, Tenn., January 15th, 1888, from th combined effects of measles and croup, **Sarah Elizabeth Lyon**, aged 3 years, 3 months and 42 days. . . . the daughter of R. P. and M. J. Lyon, who had but recently come from Lee County, Miss.

Died of inflammation of the brain, in Shelby County, Tenn., January 29th, 1888, **Fannie McCalla**, aged 13 years, 10 months and 28 days . . . a daughter of Thos. G. and M. L. McCalla.

Married, December --, 1887, at the residence of the bride's mother, by Rev. R. G. Miller, **Mr.** **Hooks** of Union County and Miss **Flora Bost** of Mecklenburg County, N. C.

- - - January --, 1888, at the residence of John Spittle by Rev. R. G. Miller, Mr. **Allen Elliott** and Miss **Sallie Robinson**. All of Mecklenburg, N. C.

- - - February 15th, 1888, at the residence of the bride's mother in Charlotte by Rev. R. G. Miller, Mr. **W. R. Grier** of Matthews and Miss **Mattie Duncan** of Charlotte, N. C.

March 15, 1888

Married, December 28th, 1887, by Rev. M. Oates, Mr. **A. H. Boggess** and Miss **M. Nola Oates**. All of Arkansas.

- - - March 1st, 1888, by Rev. O. Y. Bonner, at the residence of the bride's father, Mr. **C. L. Stewart** and Miss **E. E. Towrey**. All of Lincoln County, Tenn.

March 22, 1888

Died, January 14th, 1888, Mrs. **Rhoda Freeze**, wife of William Freeze. . . [She] was about 40 years old. . . member of New Perth . . . leaves six children and husband.

On the 7th of January, 1888, Mr. **J. F. Brown** died of pneumonia . . . in his 22d year.

Miss **Rachel E. Bell** departed this life on February 19th, 1888 at her home in Mecklenburg County, N. C. . . . was born October 20th, 1832. . . member of A. R. church at Gilead.

Died, February 3d, 1888, Mr. **Hugh S. McKeown** in the 34th year of his age. . . leaves a wife and three children.

Departed this life on the 14th of September, 1887, near Brighton, Tipton County, Tenn., **"Demont,"** a son of John and Caroline **McLister.** Aged 3 years and 1 week.

March 29, 1888

Died at his home in Charlotte, N. C., March 5th, 1888, Capt. **D. R. Nesbit** in the 54th year of his age. . . . was reared in the Associate Reformed Presbyterian church, but coming to Charlotte when there was no church of his fathers here, he joined the G. A. P. church. For more than thirty years he was closely identified with the business interests of Charlotte. . . A wife, three children, a brother, two sisters [survive].

Mr. **N. R. McCormick** was born May 22d, 1830 in Chester County, S. C.; came to Tipton County, Tenn. in the fall of 1850; joined the A. R. P. church in 1854, of which he lived an acceptable member until his death, February 15th, 1888, in Covington, Tenn. He was crushed to death by a train. On the 29th of August, 1855, he was happily united in marriage with Miss Julia Hindman. . . He raised nine children, six sons and three daughters. . . buried at Salem graveyard.

April 5, 1888

Died in Statesville, March 5th, 1888, Mrs. **Tirzah McEwen,** aged 86 years.

Robert Claude Leland, son of Mr. and Mrs. R. B. **Mills,** died March 12th, 1888, aged 9 years, 1 month and 19 days.

Mrs. **Jane Boyd,** wife of the late James Boyd, died at the home of her sister in Chester County, in February, 1888, aged about 60 years.

Frances Folsom, infant of Mr. and Mrs. Jones F. **Todd,** died in Newberry, S. C., March 11th, 1888, aged 2 months and 19 days.

Died of pneumonia in Shelby County, Tenn., March 2d, 1888, Mr. **A. O. Erwin,** aged 55 years, 5 months and 18 days. - - - was a nephew of Rev.

Warren Flenniken and brother of Rev. J. P. Erwin. He was the son of Davis and Mary (Flenniken) Erwin, and was born in Mecklenburg County, N. C. in the bounds of Sardis congregation, September 13th, 1832. His parents moved in 1839 to Tipton County, Tenn. where they reared a family of six sons and four daughters--four of whom(two sons and two daughters) survive. . .Member of Richland A. R. P. church

Married, March 15th, 1888 at the residence of the bride's father, by Rev. D. G. Caldwell, Mr. **J. A. King** and Miss **Mamie Neil**. Both of Iredell County, N. C.

- - - March 22d, 1888 aat the residence of the bride's father, Mr. **W. H. Salser** and Miss **M. E. Damron**. All of Lincoln County, Tenn.

- - - February 22d, 1888, by Rev. E. P. McClintock, assisted by Rev. W. C. Schaeffer, Mr. **W. Y. Miller** and Miss **Mary Whaley**. All of Newberry, S. C.

April 19, 1888

Died, December, 1887, **Mrs. A. M. Oates**, consort of Mr. W. R. Oates. . .[in Arkansas]. . . . member of A. R. P. church.

Died in Pope County, Ark., September 26th, 1887 of hemorrhage of the bowels, Mr. **H. H. Patrick** in the 56th year of his age. Mr. Patrick was a cousin and likewise brother-in-law of the late Rev. John Patrick.

Died in Newberry County, S. C., February 14th, 1888, **Robert Neel**, aged 21 years. Robbie was the son of J. Calvin and Elizabeth Neel.

Died suddenly near Cornwell, S. C., February 16th, 1888, Mrs. **Maggie E. Strong**, wife of Mr. T. C. Strong in the 33d year of her age. . . leaves husband and two little children.

Died at the residence of her son-in-law, Mr. J. P. Flanigan in Statesville, Iredell County, N. C., Mrs. **Tirzah (Morrison) McEwen**, March 5th, 1888 in the 86th year of her age. We [J. E. P.] knew her for thirty seven years as a member of the New Perth congregation, and in her own home during her second widowhood, as her first husband was a Witherspoon. . . She raised and trained a family of five children. . . only one is living.

Born in Shelby County, Ala., December 25th, 1827 and died in Union County, Miss., January 7th, 1888, **William Hunter Wiseman**, son of Hugh and Martha Wiseman, the direct cause of the death of this good man was the effects of a wound received in the battle around Atlanta, Ga. in the year 1864.

That would was a severe one, removing a part of the crown of his head. Although Mr. Wiseman lived for quite a number of years after receiving the wound, he was never the same, stout man, either mentally or physically, that he was before he went into service.

Married, April 5th, 1888, by Rev. W. S. Moffatt, at the home of W. L. Chestnut, Esq., Mr. **W. A. Richardson** and Miss **Georgie Ann Chesnut**.

- - - April 12th, 1888, by Rev. S. A. Agnew, Prof. **W. R. Brooks** and **Mrs. M. T. Galloway**. All of Lee County, Miss.

May 3, 1888

Died at his residence in Troy, Tenn., March 18th, 1888, Maj. **A. B. Enloe** in the 61st year of his age. . . born within five miles of the place of his death. . . was licensed to practice law in 1853; was married to Miss Amanda Brice of South Carolina in 1872, having lived a widower for a number of years preceding that date. . . [became member of] Troy A. R. P. church in 1887. . . leaves a wife and three children.

May 17, 1888

Died, April 9th, 1888 . . . of brain fever, **Willie Boyce**, son of William A. **Grier** of Pisgah, Gaston County, N. C. and grandson of Pringle Grier of Steel Creek. . . 6 months and 12 days old.

Died, April 15th, 1888, Mrs. **Elizabeth Benson**, aged 46 years. . . member of Associate Reformed church.

Died, April 2d, 1888, Mrs. **Isabella Simril** in the 61st year of her age. . . daughter of William McGill of York County, S. C. and wife of Thomas J. Simril whom she married in October, 1848. . . early member of Smyrna and afterwards with her husband at Steel Creek.

May 24, 1888

Rachel N. Allison died on the 27th day of March, aged 50 years, 7 months and 3 days. She was the wife of Dr. J. W. Allison to whom she was married about twenty five years ago. She was the daughter of John and Naomi Kennedy. . . [member of] Sharon A. R. P. congregation, York County, S. C. . . . bore eight children. Four of them preceded her to the other world.

Died in Pope County, Ark., of pneumonia, Mr. **Henry S. Elliot**, aged 29 years. . . was not brought up in the A. R. P. church, but connected himself with it, of which his wife was a member.

Bettie, youngest child of Mr. and Mrs. J. C. **Bascom,** was taken from her pleasant home in Louisville, Ky. . . . on the morning of April 13th, 1888, aafter two weeks suffering with tubercular meningetis. . . [had lived] four and aa half years.

Mrs. Jesse Jones died in Newberry, S. C., March 10th, 1888, in the 22d year of her age. . . . a native of the county. In her childhood her father, Col. William Chalmers, removed to Texas. Miss Jesse there enjoyed the excellent school advantages of that State, and in addition to this collegiate training. Some four years aago she returned to this place and made it into her home. during the first year two most important events in her history occurred; she was received on profession of faith into membership in Thompson Street [A. R. P.] church and happily united in marriage to Mr. S. B. Jones.

Married, April 26th, 1888, at Pleasant Hill, Ala., by Rev. J. A. Lowry, **Thomas J. Craig,** Esq. and Miss **Callie McLean.**

June 7, 1888

After a long and painful illness, little **Charlie Stinson,** only son of Rev. C. E. and M. H. **McDonald,** peacefully fell asleep on April 28th, aged 4 months and 16 days.

Infant son of Francis McD. and Hattie **Simpson** departed this life, February 5th, 1888. The life was short, three weeks and one day only.

June 14, 1888

Died at his home in Abbeville County, S. C., Mr. **James McElvey,** aged 86 years. . . an elder in the A. R. P. church.

Died at his home in Freestone County, Texas. April 16th, 1888, Mr. **James Robinson,** about 82 years old. . . was born in Abbeville County, S. C. In early life he united with the church of his fathers. In 1831, in the full vigor of manhood, he came to Alabama. In 1837, he and sister Eliza Ann Bonner [Rev. T. J. Bonner wrote the sketch] were married; in 1853 he moved to Texas. When Richland church was organized, he was one of the first to enroll his name. . . leaves a wife, four sons and four daughters.

Died in Troy, Tenn., March 18th, 1888, **A. B. Enloe.** Born April 6th, 1827 about five miles from Troy. . . He ranked with the leading members of the bar in West Tennessee. . . [leaves a wife] Amanda (daughter of Robert Brice of

Fairfield, S. C.) and three children, two sons and a daughter.

Died on the 26th of March, 1888 in Shelby County, Tenn., **Mrs. E. R. W. Wylie**, wife of Mr. Elmore Wylie. Her maiden name was Miss E. R. W. Sexton . . . was born June 11th, 1851. In May, 1863 she united with Neely's Creek church . . . on the 22d of December, 1870 she married Mr. Franklin Elmore Wylie. In company with him she moved in December, 1875 to Tipton County, Tenn. . . [later] she and her husband located in Shelby County and identified themselves with the A. R. church , Beulah.

Wm. G. Cordier, aged about seventy-seven years, died at his home in Fairfield County, S. C., May 30th, 1888. . .[member of] Hopewell.

Mrs. **Cora Ferguson**, *nee* Morrow, the wife of Mr. Thomas Ferguson, died suddenly, April 24th, 1888 in the 21st year of her age. Four months and ten days before, on her twentieth birthday, she stood at the bridal altar. . . [member of] old Cedar Spring [church].

Departed this life at the residence of her brother, J. W. Strong, the 15th of April, 1888, Mrs. **Elizabeth Wright**, aged 68 years and 4 days. . . born in Chester County, S. C. . . She removed with many of her endeared kindred from Chester. . . to Tipton County, Tenn. . . . [became] member of A. R. church of Salem of which one of her brother, Rev. James H. Strong, has been pastor for more than twenty-seven years. . . [she] was twice married and was the mother of nine children. It is a remarkable circumstance that her husbands and children all preceded her to the grave.

Mrs. **Ann Maria Nickell** died on the 17th of November, 1887 in the 76th year of her age. . . member of New Lebanon church, West Va.

Andy Ballentine Boyd died April 7th, 1888 in the 67th year of her age. . . a member of New Lebanon church, West Va.

Married, May 15th, 1888, by Rev. W. L. Pressly at the residence of the bride, Mr. **George Anderson** of Indiana and Miss **Martha Dickson** of Abbeville County, S. C.

- - - May 17th, 1888, at the residence of the bride's mother by Rev. H. M. Henry, Mr. **E. D. Spiva** of Harrells, Dallas County, Ala., and Miss **Jennie McBryde** of Oak Hill, Wilcox County, Ala.

- - - June 5th, 1888 in the A. R. church at Timber Ridge, Va. by Rev. S. W. Haddon, assisted by Rev. J. H. Simpson, **Rev. John McClintock Todd** and Miss **Ella Belle McClung**, the former of Due West, S. C., the latter of Rockbridge County, Va.

- - - May 28th, 1888 by Rev. J. C. McDonald, Mr. **James A. Stephenson** and Miss **Rosa J. Brooks**. All of Izard County, Ark.

June 21, 1888

James Harvey McCreary, M. D., died peacefully and triumphantly May 5th, 1888 in the 65th year of his age. . . was the last and youngest of the McCreary family of Cedar Springs. His father was an elder, his brother Joseph, a minister of the gospel, of the ill-fated "Lucy Walker" fame. He also had the confidence of his brothers, and was selected to bear rule in the house of God in the year 1873, and was ordained with five others, January 2d, 1874. . . leaves a widow and six children, four daughters and two sons.

Died in DeKalb County, Ga., February 18th, 1888, Mrs. **Mary Weldon**, in the 64th year of her age. . . was the widow of Mr. William Weldon, who preceded her in death only four months. Ten children and many grandchildren "call her blessed."

June 28, 1888

Departed this life on the 6th of March, 1888 in Tipton County, Tenn., Mr. **David H. McQuiston**. Aged 67 years, 9 months and 6 days. . . was born in Fairfield County, S. C. on the 30th of May, 1820 and enjoyed religious advantages in connection with Hopewell congregation in Chester County. . . in company with his father (Mr. Andrew McQuiston) he removed in 1838 to Tipton County, Tenn. . . .became identified with Bloomington congregation at the time of its organization, and for many years . . . [a deacon]. Three times married; first to Miss Margaret Wright in 1843, second to Mrs. Nancy J. Wham in 1853, and third to Miss Mary A. McQuiston in 1870. Two children of the first marriage and five of the second still survive.

Died on June 5th, 1888 in Newton County, Ga., **Livingston Quigg**, only child of Mr. and Mrs. J. J. **Bell**.

Married, May--, 1888 at the residence of the bride's uncle, Mr. T. R. Magill in Charlotte, N. C. by Rev. C. E. Todd, Mr. **S. S. McNinch** of Charlotte and Miss **J. I. Magill** of Richburg, S. C.

- - - June 14, 1888, by Rev. H. T. Sloan, Mr. **E. P. Lipscomb** and Miss **Mamie Hearst**, daughter of T. J. Hearst. All of Abbeville County, S. C.

July 5, 1888

Charles Bernard Rowan was born October 17th, 1887 and died June

4th, 1888.

Died in Pope County, Ark., May--, 1888, **Mrs. M. Henry**, aged 97 years, 6 months and 7 days. . . . native of York District, S. C. . . . [joined] Old School Presbyterian church at Bethel at sixteen. . . widow for forty years and lived with son Alexander. . . leaves two sons and many grandchildren.

Died in Pope County, Ark, April 30th, 1888 of consumption, Mr. **A. A. Cousar** in the 45th year of his age. . . came to Arkansas last winter, rented land and commenced a crop. . . was married twice and had five living children by his first wife and two by his second.

Died at her home in Charlotte, N. C., May 3d, 1888, Mrs. **Elizabeth Wilson** in the eighty-fifth year of her age. . . born and reared in bounds of Sardis A. R. P. church. . . [spent] latter part of her life in connection with our mission in Charlotte. . . wife of John Wilson, deceased, and leaves four children.

Died in Lee County, Miss., May 31st, 1888, Mrs. **Emma Fitzpatrick** aged 32 years, 1 month and 3 days. . . daughter of William and Martha E. (Strong) Brice and was born in Chester County, S. C., April 28, 1856. Her parents moved to Mississippi while she was a child and she grew up in the neighborhood of Bethany. . . leaves two little girls.

Died on the 8th of March, 1888 in the vicinity of Mt. Carmel church in Marshall County, Miss., **Nannie Jane**, the youngest child of Mr. J. W. and Mrs. Nettie **Moffatt**. . . born November 3d, 1886.

Removed also by death on the 11th of March, 1888, Mrs. **Nettie Moffatt**, wife of Mr. J. W. Moffatt and mother [of above]. . . She was born November 1st, 1855 and her age is 32 years, 4 months and 10 days. . . oldest daughter of Mr. and Mrs. J. G. McCalla.

July 12, 1888

Mr. **Samuel Thomas Service** died near Pisgah, Gaston County, N. C., on the 16th of June, 1888, being in the 66th year since April 25th. . . wife and seven children left behind.

Mr. **Lucius Q. C. Brown** died at his home in Jefferson County, Ga., on the 12th of June, 1888, aged about 72 years. . . had been for a number of years a deacon in Ebenezer church.

On June 15th, 1888, Mrs. **Cynthia Stevenson** died at her home in Fairfield County, S. C. She was born January 17th, 1810 and was married to

Mr. Samuel H. Stevenson, January 28, 1828. He still survives . . . with three children and a number of grandchildren.

Died in Tipton County, Tenn., June 6th, 1888, **Robert M. Banks** in the 68th year of his age. . . was born in Fairfield County, S. C., but for forty years or more he has been a leading citizen . . . In 1853 . . . was happily married to Miss Louisa Strong. . . one of the most enterprising and successful farmers. . . member of Presbyterian church. . . leaves a wife and seven children.

July 19, 1888

Died, June 20th, 1888, **Meek McElwen**, son of Sam and Lizzie **Robison**, Gaston County, N. C. This child's parents both died in one month seven months before, leaving him in the care of his grandparents, James and Jane Furgeson. . . was born May 4th, 1887.

July 26, 1888

Miss **Sallie Bradley**, eldest daughter of Mrs. Mary (Drennon) Bradley, died suddenly June 25th, 1888. . . member of church at Long Cane for many years.

Mrs. **Mary (Paul) Devlin**, widow of the late J. J. Devlin of Cedar Spring, departed this life July 5th, 1888. . . aged 75 years. Her ten children survive her.

H. C. McCain was born in Mecklenburg County, N. C., January--, 1829; died in Tipton County, Tenn, July 1st, 1888 in the 60th year of his age.. . the youngest of a large and pious family. . . Two of his brothers are elders in the church, one a deacon and another a minister of the gospel now in Texas. . . .[member for about forty years of] Salem. . .Recently he received a government appointment, connected with the transportation of the mail. . . but as soon as he ascertained that the position obligated him to work one hour on the Lord's Day he promptly resigned and came home. . . left a wife and adopted daughter.

August 2, 1888

Died in Newberry County, S. C., June 25th, 1888, Mr. **Joseph Caldwell** in the 81st year of his age. . . . born and reared in Newberry County, S. C. and served King's Creek A. R. P. church as a ruling elder for forty years.

Mrs. **Rachel Hudson**, wife of Newnan Hudson, departed this life June 10th, 1888, aged 49 years, 11 months and 9 days. . . member of the Women's Missionary Society of Union congregation . . leaves four children, all grown, and a husband. . . five children preceded [her to the grave].

Married, July 12th, 1888, by Rev. W. M. Hunter, Mr. **J. R. McLain** of Iredell County and Miss **Martha E. McLelland** of Alexander County, N. C.

August 9, 1888

Carrie Leona, little daughter of Mr. and Mrs. W. T. **Sherril**, died May 23d, 1888, aged 4 years, 11 months and 6 days.

Died, near Coddle Creek church, Cabarrus County, N. C., on the 9th of May, 1888, Mrs. **Louisa M. Irwin**, wife of E. G. Irwin, Esq., aged 56 years and 3 months. . . for about twenty-five years had been a consistent member of Coddle Creek church.

Mrs. **Elizabeth Waters**, wife of James Waters, departed this life May 31st, 1888, being in her 41st year. . . member of A. R. P. church, Union congregation, Chester County, S. C. . . leaves husband and three children.

August 16, 1888

Died in Union County, Miss. . . July 18th, 1888, **James Calvin Branyon**, youngest child of William M. and Eliza (Vandiver) Branyon, aged 2 years, 10 months and 9 days. . . of dysentery.

[Died] Mrs. **Annie J. Patterson** of bilious congestive fever, June 19th, 1888, in the 29th year of her age. . . daughter of Mr. John G. and Nancy (Stewart) Watt. On the 21st of January, 1884, she married Mr. Augustus C. Patterson. . . leaves a little daughter and a husband.

Mr. **John Watt** of Corner Township, Anderson County, S. C. [died] December 17th, 1887 . . . born May 5th, 1821. . . entire life was spent in the same parental homestead. . member of Baptist church.

Died in Anderson County, S. C., March 26th, 1888, Mrs. **Martha Jane McAlister** in her 62d year. . . Martha Jane Lewis was born in York County, June 6th, 1826. In 1842 she moved to Pickens County. . . to Abbeville where she was married to Mr. Lewis W. McAlister, June 18th, 1850. In youth she joined the M. E. church . . . after her marriage she went with her husband who was a ruling elder in Generostee A. R. P. church.

Mrs. **Mary Malinda Patterson** died June 8th, 1888 of bilious congestive fever in the 36th year of her age. . . daughter of Mr. William Stewart, deceased, and Mrs. Mary Ann Stewart and the wife of John J. Patterson. . .

leaves a husband and five little children.

Mr. **Leroy Purdy**, a consistent member of Cedar Springs congregation, departed this life July 23d, 1888 in the 78th year of his age. . . son-in-law of Col. Devlin. . . [his wife died earlier]. . . leaves three sons and three daughters with their families.

Died March 10th, 1888 of pneumonia after one week of illness, **James F. Harper**, M. D. in the 69th year of his age. . . born in South Carolina, December 24th, 1819. . . moved with his parents to Obion County, Tenn. when he was five years old, was left an orphan while he was quite young, being bereft of both parents in one week. . .April 4th, 1844, he was married to Miss Elizabeth S. Johnston who with his two daughters survive. . .read medicine with an older brother and attended lectures at Memphis in 1848. . . settled in Tipton County where he practiced his profession for 10 years. In 1862, he moved to Clayton, Adams County, Ill. He spent the winters of '69 and '70 in Keokuk, Iowa. . . attending lectures in the medical college. The remaining years of his life with the exception of a short time at LaPrairie, Ill. were spent in Hancock County, Ill. . . . even those who differed with him had no evil thing to say of him.

August 23, 1888

Died, February 15th, 1888, Mrs. **Missouri Frances (Adkinson) McLerkin**, aged 22 years and 7 months, who was the wife of Mr. Samuel T. McLerkin. . . member of Mt. Paran A. R. P. church in Tipton County, Tenn. . . leaves husband and infant daughter.

August 30, 1888

Died in Statesville, N. C., July 23d, 1888, **Maggie Bream**.

Died of congestion in Shelby County, Tenn., July 26th, 1888, Mr. **W. H. Moore**. Aged 47 years, 9 months and 1 day, Mr. Harrison Moore, for so he was known, was the son of William and Rebecca Moore and was born and reared in Lincoln County, Tenn. December 16th, 1868, he was married to Miss Cassenea Moore. Eight children were born to them. . . in January, 1884, he removed to Shelby County.

Married, August 22d, 1888 at the home of the bride's brother, Mr. J. K. Bohn, by Rev. R. H. McAulay, Mr. **J. J. Yarborough** of Spartanburg and Miss **Sallie F. Bohn** of Due West, S. C.

- - - August 9th, 1888, by W. L. Chesnut, J. P., Mr. **W. S. Ussery** and

Miss **Julia Chesnut**. Both of Arkansas.

<u>September 6, 1888</u>

Died in Shelby County, Tenn., July 16th, 1888, **Mattie**, infant daughter of T. G. and M. L. McCalla. Aged 2 years, 6 months and 18 days.

Barron Bruce, second son of Wallace and Lizzie Bruce, was born October 19th, 1886 and died at their home in Newberry, S. C., May 5th, 1888.

On the 28th of August, 1888 near Richmond, Ky., Mrs. **Elizabeth Mitchell** departed this life. . . born July 29th, 1810 and was perhaps the oldest member of New Hope church. Her life was spent in Garrard and Madison Counties within the limits of New Hope congregation.

Mrs. **Elizabeth A. Steeley** was born about the year 1841 in South Carolina; moved to Mississippi while very young; shortly afterwards she joined the A. R. P. church. . . About twelve years ago, she with her husband and two children, moved to Lovelady, Texas. On the 19th of December, 1866, she was married to Mr. B. H. Steeley, to whom she bore three children, two of whom preceded her to the glory world. One (Hutchinson) is left with his father.

Married, June 27th, 1888 at the residence of the bride's mother, Mrs. Jane H. Paden, by Rev. J. C. McDonald, Rev. **W. S. Moffatt** and **Mrs. J. E. Livingston**.

- - - August 23d, 1888, in Tipton County, Tenn. by Rev. J. H. Strong, Mr. **R. E. Robison** and Miss **Lena Douglass** of Plant City, Fla.

- - - August 29th, 1888 in the Presbyterian church, Gastonia, N. C., by Rev. W. E. McIlwain, assisted by Rev. W. M. McElwee, Mr. **Samuel N. Boyce** and Miss **Stella Holland**, daughter of J. Q. Holland, Esq.

<u>September 13, 1888</u>

Married, September 5th, 1888, at the residence of the bride's mother, Mr. **W. E. Bell** of Abbeville and Miss **Claudia Ellis** of Due West, S. C.

<u>September 27, 1888</u>

Mr. **John E. Love** was born August 25th, 1822 and died September 3d, 1888 . . . for many years a member of Bethany church, York County, S. C. . . . leaves a wife and four children.

Eli Madison McAteer was born May 5th, 1812 and died August 3d, 1888. His parents came from County of Antrim, Ireland in 1790 and settled in Lancaster County, S. C;. . . . [did not join the church until] 1845 under Rev. Millen's ministry at Shiloh, Lancaster County, S. C. . . He was very good to visit the sick. Even at his advanced age he would go and sit all night by the bedside of the sick. He went and sat all night by the bedside of one of his neighbors, went home the next morning and was never well anymore. . . He leaves a wife and seven children.

Married, September 18th, 1888 at Brownsburg, Va., by Rev. S. W. Haddon, Mr. **Samuel E. Miley** and Miss **Clemmie H. Terrell**. Both of Rockbridge County, Va.

- - - September 20th, 1888 at the residence of the bride's father, by Rev. W. L. Pressly, Rev. **R. Y. Mills** of Lancaster, S. C. and **Miss M. Lois Martin**, daughter of Rev. I. Martin of Newton County, Ga.

October 4, 1888

Married, September 18th, 1888, by Rev. R. E. Patterson, Mr. **J. D. McCurdy** and Miss **Jane Sellers**. Both of DeKalb County, Ga.

October 25, 1888

Married, October 11th, 1888 at the residence of the bride, by Rev. R. H. McAulay, Mr. **J. N. Anderson** and Miss **Ina Gaulden**, both of Spartanburg County, S. C.

November 1, 1888

Died in New Stirling, Iredell County, N. C. from the effects of a cancer, Mrs. **Martha Johnson**. . . had long been a consistent member of New Stirling. . . a wife and a mother.

Miss **Mary Ellen Beard**, born August 1st, 1849, died of meningetis, February 4th, 1888.
Callie Bell, youngest child of Samuel and Lizzie Bell, died of meningetis on the 22d day of March, 1888, aged 12 years and 2 months.
A. C. Beard, born on the 2d of August, 1858, was drowned May 17th, 1888.
Mr. **Samuel Bell** of Mt. Mourne died after a very short illness on the 17th day of June, 1888, aged aabout 54 years. Thus within the short space of five months the death angel has visited the same family, almost the same household and carried away four of its loved ones.

Died near Eureka, Navarro County, Texas, August 27th, 1888, Mrs. **Jane Wilson**, wife of Hugh Wilson, in the 72d year of her age. . . leaves husband with whom she has lived fifty-four years and five children . . . was born in South Carolina . . . a daughter of Andrew McQuiston. She removed, after the marriage, to Tipton County, Tenn where she and her husband lived seventeen years. Then they made a second move and went to Drew County, Ark. where they remained for thirty years or more. They again in their old age moved to Texas. . . consistent member of A. R. P. church.

Died at Tipton County, Tenn., September 24th of diptheria, **Minnie**, infant daughter of Dr. W. F. and A. E. **Cooper**.

Also, on September 26th, of the same disease, their little son **James Lynn**, aged 2 years, 3 months and 8 days. Thus in less than one week these fond parents were called to mourn the loss of two dear children (their all).

Married, October 3d, 1888, near Steele's Tavern, Va., by Rev. S. W. Haddon, Mr. **Thos. L. Ramsey** and Miss **Annette S. Houser**.

- - - October 25th, 1888 at the residence of the bride's father, Mr. G. W. Martin, by Rev. J. E. Pressly, D. D., Mr. **N. McSims** and Miss **Maggie Martin**.

November 8, 1888

Mrs. **Sallie (Davis) Caughran**, wife of Mr. W. H. Caughran, died suddenly of peritoneal inflammation . . . on the 10th of September, 1888 at their home in New Hope congregation. She was 36 years of age. On her marriage and settlement in this county, she made a profession of religion. . . She never knew a mother's love, but a kind sister trained her. . . A husband and four child (one but three days old) . . . [survive.

Died September 25th, 1888, Miss **Mamie Lora Connaway**, aged 16 years and 4 months. . .[member of] New Hope.

Thomas J. Love was born November 27th, 1864 . . .[and] died July 7th, 1888. In the fall of 1887, he went to the Commercial College at Louisville, Ky. . . . [where] he contracted a cold which settled in his lungs. After a time he went to Texas. . . towards the spring of 1888 he returned to his father's in York County, S. C. . . He was the youngest brother of Rev. W. Y. Love. . .[and] on the 12th of May, 1883 . . . [joined] the church at Sharon.

Died in Sardis congregation, Mecklenburg County, N. C., June 12th, 1888, **Joseph Wilson Johnston** in the fourteenth year of his age. . . . pneumonia.

Louis Wylie, infant son of J. W. and Alice **Roddy**, departed this life

September 24th, 1888, aged 1 year, 7 months and 12 days. Once, twice, thrice and once again, the angel of death has visited this family.

Married, October 31st, 1888, at the residence of the bride, by Rev. W. M. Grier, D. D., Miss **Cora Haddon** of Due West, S. C. and Mr. **Julian Sibley** of Augusta, Ga.

- - - November 1st, 1888, by Rev. W. M. Grier, D. D., at the residence of the bride, Miss **Mary Henry** of Due West, S. C. and Mr. **Wm. Marshall** of Tallapoosa, Ga.

November 15, 1888

Died at Shepherd's Cross Roads, Iredell County, N. C., August 15th, 1888, **J. W. Brawley**, aged 55 years, 10 months and 23 days. . . an affectionate husband, a kind and indulgent father.

Mrs. **Sarah R. (Gault) Brooks** departed this life after a few hours of illness in Izard County, Ark., August 31st, 1888. . . born March 25th, 1838, in Lincoln County, Tenn. and moved to Hempstead County, Ark. with her parents, while young, where she was united in marriage with William Brooks, November 12th, 1858. . . member of A. R. P. church of New Hope, Izard County. . . leaves husband and large family.

Clifford Murphy, an infant son of Mr. W. A. and O. O. **Wylie** was born September 19th, 1888 and died October 20th.

Mr. **R. Alfred Agnew** who lately married Miss Mamie Cochran of this place [Due West], died at Lewiedale, S. C. on the 13th.

Mr. **J. Henry Brooks** of Level Land, S. C. was married to Miss **Lillie Wingo** of Spartanburg, S. C. on the 8th inst.

Mr. **W. Ed Hagan** and Miss **Mattie Crawford** were married by Rev. W. F. Pearson on the evening of the 1st of November.

November 22, 1888

Died at Union County, Miss. on Tuesday, August 28th, 1888, Mrs. **Mary Jane Snipes**, wife of Mr. S. Walker Snipes, aged 23 years, 3 months and 18 days. . . daughter of Alexander M. and Martha E. (Spence) Galloway and was born in Pontotoc (now Lee) County, Miss., May 10th, 1865. . . joined at Bethany [church], August 6th, 1879. . . was married to S. W. Snipes, December 19th, 1883. They moved to neighborhood of Hopewell in the fall of 1884. . .

mother of three children [one died previously]. . . one but six days old when his mother died.

Died in Lee County, Miss. on Wednesday night, September 12th, 1888, Mrs. **Ann Elizabeth Milam**, wife of Mr. Thomas P. Milam, aged forty-four years, two months and eleven days. . . daughter of Eli and Margaret A. (McCullough) Crockett, and was born in Tippah County, Miss., July 1st, 1844. . . married to T. P. Milam of Lawrence County, Ala., December 27th, 1864. . . mother of seven children.

Died in Lee County, Miss. on Tuesday evening, October 30th, 1888, Mr. **William Brice** in the 87th year of his life. . . son of William and Elizabeth (Phillips) Brice and was born in Fairfield, S. C., February 1st, 1802. . . born and reared in A. R. church. When a boy he joined the Presbyterian church near Winnsboro, S. C., but very soon thereafter transferred his connection to the church of his fathers. He married Miss Martha E. Strong, August 15th, 1843 and soon afterward became a member of Hopewell in Chester County. He removed in 1859 to Pontotoc (now Lee) County, Miss. and joined Bethany church. . . In 1860, he, in company with Joseph Agnew, Thomas E. Watt and John Haddon were elected and ordained ruling elders of Bethany . . was father of six children, two of whom are dead.

Jas. R. Kennedy was born the 2d of April, 1862 [and] died on the 2d of October, 1888. . . . the son of F. R. and E. T. Kennedy. . . [who] were members of the A. R. P. church at Sharon, York County, S. C. . . [joined the church] in September, 1880. . . was a merchant. . . [with the firm name of] Parish & Kennedy in Yorkville, S. C.

Mrs. **Mary Wilson** died at the house of her son near Union City, Obion County, Tenn. on the 12th of September, 1888 in the 73d year of her age. Her family, the McMillans, emigrated from Long Cane, S. C. about fifty years ago to Lincoln County, Tenn. Here she married the late Clinton Wilson and raised a family . . . member at Bethel. . . It is believed that she is the last survivor of the McMillan family.

Mr. **John Pratt**, one of the most highly respected citizens of this county [Abbeville, S. C.] died last Sabbath at the residence of Dr. John A. Robinson. Mr. Pratt was upwards of eighty years of age and, though not subscribing to the same views of faith as ourselves, was a subscriber of our church paper for more than thirty years.

December 6, 1888

Died in Pope County, Ark., August 25th, 1888, Mrs. **Nancy**, consort of the late Thomas **Falkner**, aged 85 years past. . . was native of Rutherford

County, N. C., but after her marriage resided in York County, S. C. in the bounds of Smyrna congregation. Mr. Falkner was a member of Smyrna Session for several years previous to his removal to Arkansas.

Died in Pope County, Ark., October 18th, 1888, Mrs. **Margaret**, consort of the late Gregory **Sinclair**, aged 81 years and 17 days. . . daughter of John Blackwood who resided near Crowder's Mountain, N. C. in the bounds of Pisgah church. . . Her piety was humble and unobtrusive.

Departed this life, October 17th, 1888, Mr. **H. A. Query**, aged 77 years. . . for several years a ruling elder in the Pleasant Hills Presbyterian church. . .but at his death was a member of Steel Creek Presbyterian church. . . leaves several sons and daughters, one of whom is Rev. Walter Query.

Died in Lancaster County, S. C., September 10th, 1888, Mrs. **Elizabeth Henry Belk**, consort of John W. Belk, aged 73 years, 8 months and 19 days. In the year 1832, she was married. . . the husband and five children mourn her death. During the same year they both . . .[joined] Tirzah (then A. R. P.) in Lancaster County, S. C. . . [when its pastor] Rev. D. P. Robinson went to the G. A. P. church. . . then she, with her husband, went into the organization of Unity A. R. P. church.

Married, November 6th, 1888 by Rev. J. A. Lowry, Mr. **John E. Young** and Miss **Fannie Fort**, all of Dallas County, Ala.

- - - November 14th, 1888 near Sardis at the home of the bride's father, Mr. **J. D. Jenkins** and Miss **Sarah Hayes**, all of Mecklenburg County, N. C.

- - - November 17th, 1888 at the residence of the officiating minister, Rev. J. E. Pressly, D. D., Mr. **John Rape** of Mecklenburg County and Miss **Eliza E. G. Henry** of Cabarrus County, N. C.

- - - October 25th, 1888 at the residence of Mr. A. B. Ware, the bride's father, by Rev. J. M. Grier, Dr. **Jas. G. Glenn** of Gastonia, N. C. to Miss **Amanda Ware** of Cleveland County, N. C.

- - - November 26th, 1888 at King's Mountain, N. C. by Rev. J. M. Grier, Mr. **Samuel Cornwell** of Rock Hill to Miss **Florence Ware** of King's Mountain, N. C.

December 13, 1888

Mr. **John H. Crawford**, son of Robert Crawford, deceased, of this neighborhood, died recently at his home in Pontotoc, Miss. Mr. Crawford was a brother of the late David Crawford and also of R. W. Crawford, well known to citizens of this place [Due West]. He was for a time a student at Erskine College. . . he occupied several offices of trust in his adopted home in the West, being at the time of his death, editor of the *Pontotoc Democrat.*

Miss **Etta May Fite,** daughter of Mr. F. S. and Mrs. M. R. (Banks) Fite. . . was born August 7th, 1867 and died October 18th, 1888.

Died in Pope County, Ark., September 14th, 1888, Mrs. **Emily M. Ferguson.** Her husband, Warner Ferguson, died in a short time after they came to Arkansas. She was left in charge of three children.

Departed this life near Beulah church, Shelby County, Tenn. on the 19th of July, 1888, **Florence Rebecca Eugenia**, infant daughter of Mr. Franklin Elmore **Wylie**. . . age was 6 months and 11 days.

On the morning of October 2d, **James J. Faulkner** was discovered dead in bed at his home in Tipton County, Tenn. . . born in Lancaster County, S. C. and was in the 68th year of his age. . . . attended by his wife and daughter. . a ruling elder in Salem.

Married, November 1st, 1888 by Rev. S. A. Agnew, Mr. **John M. Tatum** and **Miss S. E. Phillips**, all of Lee County, Miss.

- - - November 24th, 1888 by Rev. S. A. Agnew, Mr. **Charles H. Parker** and **Miss S. M. McLeod**, all of Union County, Miss.

- - - December 5th, 1888 at the residence of the officiating minister, Rev. J. E. Pressly, D. D. Mr. **Watson F. Smith** and **Mrs. Lula M. Bell**, both of Cabarrus County, N. C.

December 20, 1888

Mary Melissa, infant daughter of Thos. and Sallie **McDonald**, was born September 30th, 1887 and died October 12, 1888.

Mr. Robt. E. **Moore** and his wife, Mrs. Emma F. Moore, members of Mt. Paran congregation, were on January 12th, 1888, called to mourn the death of their little daughter, **Willie Edith**, aged 1 year and 12 days.

Died near Ora Station, Laurens County, S. C., November 8th, 1888, Mrs. **Sara Jane Barker** in the 39th year of her age. . . .[member of] Bethel.

The **infant daughter** of W. H. and Lula **Simpson** departed this life November 10th, 1888, aged 2 weeks and 2 hours.

William Cardwell died in York County, S. C. on the 4th of November, 1888 in the 80th year of his age. . . . Some fifty-five or sixty years ago he . . . [joined] Bethany. . . In 1836 he married May, daughter of W. McGill, Esq. who bore him ten children--six sons and four daughters. Of these, five are still living, and all worthy members of the A. R. P. church. He had three sons-- noble and brave fellows--killed in the late war.

Edward McFadden departed this life June 20th, 1888, aged 73 years, 4 months and 10 days. . . born and raised in the A. R. P. church and now sleeps with his fathers in the shadow of Union church. . . A lone sister with whom he had spent his life, and many friends, mourn their loss.

Died of paralysis of the brain in Tipton County, Tenn., October 21st, 1888, Mrs. **Mattie Louisa Brown**, aged 26 years, 3 months and 12 days. . . daughter of S. H. Sloan and wife of Robt. A. Brown, having been. . . [married] December 21st, 1882. . . [joined] Richland church, September 5, 1874.

Mrs. **Mary F. Davis** was born in York County, S. C., October 12th, 1861, and died November 14th, 1888. . . united in marriage to William J. Davis, December 4th, 1883. . . [member of] Bethany church . . . left two children.

Miss **Dorkie W. Henry**, youngest daughter of our townsman, Dr. N. Henry, was married to Dr. **B. L. Strange** of Jessup, Ga. on Wednesday of last week in Augusta, Ga., by Dr. Burrows.

Married, November 29th, 1888, by Rev. James Boyce in the A. R. P. church, Mr. **William A. Black** and Miss **M. Irene Haydon**, all of Woodford County, Ky.

- - - December 13th, 1888, at one o'clock, p. m., Mr. **E. M. Everett** of Augusta, Ga. and **"Miss Bessie,"** daughter of Mr. and Mrs. E. W. **Henderson** of Verdery, S. C., Rev. H. T. Sloan officiating.

- - - November 29th, 1888 by Rev. R. F. Bradley, at the residence of the bride's father, Mr. **George M. Wilson** and Miss **Mattie Bosdell**, all of Abbeville County, S. C.

- - - December 11th, 1888 by Rev. R. F. Bradley at the residence of Mr. Sadrack Burnett, **H. L. Culbertson**, M. D. of Lincoln County, Ga. and Miss **M. Robbie Drennan** of Troy, S. C.

- - - December 12th, 1888 at the residence of Mr. J. E. Bradley, by Rev. R. F. Bradley, assisted by Rev. H. T. Sloan, D. D., **J. C. Klugh**, Esq. and Miss **F. Carrie Bradley**, all of Abbeville County, S. C.

R. M., 148
Kistler, John, 52
 P. F., 37
Kitrer, Millie, 13
Klugh, Dr., 166
 J. C., 200
Knight, H. D., 116
 Nannie D. (Perry), 107
 W. B., 107, 133
Knox, Mrs., 35
 Ann, 70
 Margaret L., 144
 Mary Jane, 22
 N. Violet, 151
 Samuel Boyce, 70
 Wm., 75
Kuhlmann, Dora J., 40

Lackey, Mary Bell, 67
Laird, John B., 1
 William Patton, 31
Langford, John M., 181
Lankester, Kittie, 99
Larimore, R. B., 126
Lathan, Annie, 166
 D. W., 170
 Jane, 108
 M., 107
 Mary Lucinda (Faulkner), 107
 Nancy, 41, 92
 Rev. R., 58, 152
 S. B., 152
 Samuel, 41
 Samuel David, 119
 Samuel Martin, 170
Lathem, Jane, 88
 R. A., 88, 90
Latimer, Edward, 163
 Micajah Berry, 163
 T. D., 69
 Wm. C., 50
Lauderdale, Effie, 57
 Emma J., 142
 George R., 142
Leaptrot, Mrs. Jesse, 60
Leath, D. W., 75

Leavell, Edward M., 124
Ledford, Sallie, 68
Lee, Lou, 64
 W. A., 36
LeGal, Miss J. V., 132
LeGare, John G., 45
Leonard, Mollie C., 47
Leslie, Maggie J., 137
 Mary E., 61
 N. Josie, 59
Lesslie, M., 177
 Miss M. E., 138
 Nancy Elizabeth, 177
 R. B., 122
 T. F., 85
 W. S., 177
Lessly, Margaret, 76
 Robert, 76
 William Jasper, 76
Lewis, E. A., 142
 Franklin G., 11
 Jane, 30
 Jas. McCarnie, 143
 Martha Jane, 191
Liddell, J. S., 54
 Jane, 54
Lindsay, Mrs., 1
 Rev. H. D., 153
 Rev. Henry Drennan, 75
 Rev. J. O., 11, 35
 James, 20
 Jane, 128
 John, Sr., 60
 Mrs. P. A., 20
 Mrs. S. A., 120
 W. P., 120
Link, Robt., 55
Linn, Rosannah, 20
Lipscomb, E. P., 188
Lites, Capt., 67
 Eve Lillian, 31
 Jenny, 1
 Mary Isabella, 119
 Mary J., 31
 R. W., 31, 119
Little, Berta, 101

www.ingramcontent.com/pod-product-compliance
Lightning Source LLC
Chambersburg PA
CBHW071853270326
41929CB00013B/2219